Psychic Dictatorship in the U.S.A.

Psychic Dictatorship in the U.S.A.

by Alex Constantine

Feral House

ISBN 0-922915-28-8

Published by Feral House
P.O. Box 3466
Portland, OR 97208

Illustration by Frank Kozik
Design by Linda Hayashi

10 9 8 7 6 5 4 3

For Mae Brussell

Acknowledgments

Nobody can do everything. But everyone can do something.
If everyone does something, everything will be done.
—Gil Scott-Heron

No thanks to the CIA, which has attempted for six years to subvert my radio broadcasts and magazine articles by assaulting me with "non-lethal" weapons, an untraceable form of torture perfected by the U.S. government, made something of an art form. A delusion? No. The grim history of American electromagnetic torture is contained herein.

Much sane counsel was given by Sandy Munro, who maintains a secret life comprised of chasing down obscure dirt on covert ops, driven by an awesome sense of justice. Will Robinson and Marilyn Colman, hosts of "The Lighthouse Report," aired my political research for five years over KAZU-FM in Monterey, California, rare types who understood my obsession to promote respect for human life in a country that doesn't. Adam Parfrey, Feral House publisher, provided more wise counsel, the title to this volume and much-needed friendship in the bleakest moments. Child therapists Catherine Gould, Vicky Graham-Costain and Nita Vallens brought me up to date on ritual abuse after a long hiatus from this particular nightmare to take on less stressful research on Nazi death squads, George Bush and the like.

Charles Higham, author of *American Swastika*, spent long Sunday mornings over breakfast filling my ears with eloquent tales of political subterfuge too thick with scandal to see the light of day for years. His best, unfortunately neglected advice: "Write about people who are dead—you'll have less trouble that way." The editors of *Hustler* have enthusiastically supported my research, as have Patrick Formey, Martin Cannon and Andy Boehm at Prevailing Winds. Virginia McCullough, a researcher with an incredibly active mind and a memory liuke a steel trap, provided much professional guidance. Ted Gunderson and Jackie MacGauley shared the results of their research freely. Michael Sheppard peeled me off the floor in moments of desperation (pursuing Nazi treacheries can get to one; so can an apartment constantly filled with infra-sound and pulsed microwaves, and the occasional pyromaniac out to stop my wagging tongue once and for all). Dave Armstrong, former editor of *Random Lengths* in Long Beach, was one of the few in the press willing to publish stories on the CIA's domestic excesses. Ron Silver, an actor turned dragon slayer, earned a place in the book. John Lambros, a victim of CIA mind control experiments, contributed a burgeoning file on his tormentors.

The late Mae Brussell's work has proven invaluable, providing the keys to the universe and inspiration to "Brussell Sprouts" in all walks of life, including myself.

lex Constantine

Introduction

The Deep Politics of Psychocivilization

Rent-a-Tent, Rent-a-Tent...

For the past fifty years a pathological science has evolved in the netherworld of the national security elite. Like a buxom siren, the science of mind control beckons the technocrat with Machiavellian ambitions into assuming the position of a petty god.

He dreams of cybernetic control of whole populations.

At one point in their careers, in fact, most of the upper-tier academics employed in federal mind control research have publicly expressed a yearning for a psychocivilized society. Subjects of the experimentation have glimpsed their dream—a daily regimen of dehumanizing harrassment and even torture from a remote source, usually veiled by hypnotic memories of "alien" contact or the like. The number of human guinea pigs is growing. The experiments have encompassed entire cities. Electromagnetic influence over the brain and body—flashy comic book technology—is a recurring theme in these pages, which attempts to cut through the veil thrown up by the media around the skulking of the CIA and other totalitarian branches of government.

The science of mind control has achieved the scale of a criminal subculture, and left a wide path of chaos and confusion that crosses all international boundaries. The carnage takes place under the noses of the public, obscured by cover stories and dead witnesses and the incredible naivete of most news reporters. The cover stories take variegated forms:

◆ Brain Studies—On occasion, with startling candor, federally-funded psychiatrists sometimes blurt out to reporters their deepest desires. Dr. Karl Pribram, director of the Neuropsychology Research Laboratory at Stanford University, once boasted, "I certainly could educate a child by putting an electrode in the lateral hypothalamus." Selective stimulation, he said, meant that "I can grossly change his behavior." In *Psychology Today* for October, 1973 M.I.T. Professor Stephan Chorover observed: "Too many contemporary neuro- and behavioral-scientists seem committed to a narrow, unrealistic view of human social behavior. They focus mainly on the possibility of controlling behavior. If this continues, psychotechnology will increasingly become a favorite tool of social and political repression."

◆ The "Alien" Invasion—a very active cover story for the development of mind control technology. Supposedly (as those weird syndicated UFO television programs keep reminding us) alien scientists have voyaged millions of light years to place CIA implants in the bodies of human subjects. This incredible cover story is widely believed—yet most "skeptics" scoff at the notion that human scientists might want to do the same thing. The aliens have been pounded into the heads of the American consumer by a slue of books penned by military intelligence officers.

◆ Parapsychology, ESP and Remote Viewing Experiments—the type that made history at Stanford University and UCLA. These are usually astonishingly successful and passed off as proof of the paranormal, when in fact they are augmented by telemetric brain technology, and cannot help but succeed if the microwave transmitter is operating and set to the brain frequency of the percipient. Remote viewing, for example, is possible when an image is beamed to the visual pathways.

Psychic Spying?

Four years ago, officers of the Central Intelligence Agency and the National Security Agency participated in a series of unusual experiments run by Stanford Research Institute (SRI) to verify claims that certain people have psychic abilities. The results SRI reported were astonishing.

The SRI investigators, physicists Harold E. Puthoff (a former NSA research engineer) and Russell Targ, set out to demonstrate to their CIA sponsor that their subjects, noted psychic Ingo Swann and a middle-aged businessman named Pat Price, could describe distant locations merely by knowing which geographic coordinates to "look at." Some parapsychologists call this alleged ability "astral projection," or "out of body experience." Puthoff and Targ prefer the term "remote viewing."

Targ and Puthoff—who have disavowed working for the CIA—have in common credentials in advanced laser technology. Puthoff, a high-ranking Scientologist, is the inventor of the tunable laser. Targ once designed a microwave plasma generator. Twilight Zone studies often front for the development of intrusive machines that interact with the cortex. (CIA critic Ken Lawrence sniffed, "it takes considerable mind-bending to suppose the CIA hired men with these skills to try to read the Kremlin's classified zener cards.")

The remote viewing study, code-named "Project Scanate," makes sense when considered a techno-organic test drive conducted under the "rigorous control" of "the sponsor." The *Washington Post* reported that the Agency admitted transmitting "coordinates" from a monitor in Washington, D.C. to Stanford University. After the experiment, Pat Price, a "psychic" test subjects (yet another Scientologist), was asked to mentally revisit the site. She supplied the following details:

Top of desk had papers labeled:
FLYTRAP
MINERVA

File cabinet on north wall labeled:
OPERATION POOL

Folders inside cabinet labeled:
CUEBALL
14 BALL
4 BALL
RACKUP

Name of Site vague, seems like Hayford or Haystack Personnel:
COL. R.J. HAMILTON
MAJ. GEN. GEORGE R. NASH
MAJ. JOHN C. CALHOUN

But Mr. Price wasn't nearly satisfied with merely describing a top-secret satellite interrogation station complete with code words used to eavesdrop of Soviet space vehicles (if, in fact, he saw anything at all.) He volunteered to scan "the other side of the globe for a (Soviet) Bloc equivalent, and found one in the Urals," according to the Stanford report on the experiment. He managed to give the map coordinates of the Soviet installation, described it in minute detail, including heliports, radar arrays, railroad tracks, and the observation of an "unusually high ratio of women to men, at least at night."

♦ Space-Based Defense—As much as half the funding for Star Wars has *disappeared* into classified R&D programs (see "Blue Smoke and Lasers"). All along, Congress was assured by SDI officials that the funds were spent on the programs for which they were intended. Behind the Pentagon's search for the perfect space-based X-ray laser, replete with faked testing and slick public relations, lurked a secret electromagnetic weapons program, and intrigues that proved fatal to 23 British scientists. Otherwise rational Ph.Ds were driven by an inexplicable, overpowering urge to destroy themselves by biting on live wires and driving furiously into brick walls.

Under the increasingly anxious skies of California, SDI development was housed at Lawrence Livermore labs—once the site of "remote viewing" experiments similar to those at Stanford University.

♦ Non-lethal weapons—goop guns, robotic soldier-ants and acoustic bullets serve as a much-publicized Trojan horse for the proliferation and introduction of electromagnetic pulse weapons, infra-sound guns, plasma generators, killer satellites, computer-aided mental projection, cranial surveillance devices, EM brain-blasters, pulsed-microwave thought transference, cyborgian psychic driving techniques, computer-enhanced subliminal transmissions and other military spin-offs of remote mind control technology.

♦ Ritual child abuse—since 1963 the CIA and select branches of military intelligence have been intensely involved in the occult underground. Some of the most menticidal of the Mystery Cults participate in psychoactive drug experimentation, the development of harassment techniques, the testing of brain-intrusive devices on unwary human targets, hypno-programming, and so on.

Dr. Catherine Gould, an Encino, California-based child therapist specializing in ritual abuse, found that "mind control is originally established when the victim is a child under six years old. During this formative stage of development, perpetrating cult members systematically combine dissociation-enhancing drugs, pain, sexual assault, terror, and other forms of psychological abuse in such a way that the child dissociates the intolerable traumatic experience."

Ad nauseum.

Mediaeko, the Swedish investigative group, found that the hidden professional body of the mind control fraternity, "wherever it operated internationally, together with the secret police, was to preserve the secrecy of mind control, since they could systematically certify any person who insisted that he or she had been subjected to such abuse. Now, the conviction of being externally-controlled, of being mind-read or subjected to long-term experimentation with radio-signals was due to the psychoses often referred to as persecution mania, paranoia or schizophrenia." The media have led the public at large to accept that such claims are the ravings of classic persecution mania.

But once the curious political researcher learns his way around the covert mind control universe, it unfolds in media reports like a fine-point Oriental mural on torn rice paper. This volume is an encryption guide for reconstructing the picture from scraps of media disinformation of the type that flows from the False Memory Syndrome Foundation.

Introduction

Section One

Telemetric Mind Control

Section One

Telemetric Mind Control

Chapter One

Hearing "Voices"

The Hidden History of CIA and Pentagon Electromagnetic Mind Control Experiments on Involuntary Human Subjects

Ricardo S. Caputo was a very disturbed man, as the *New York Times* blared:

INNER VOICES DEMAND BLOOD:
CONFESSION DIARY IN THE KILLING OF 4 WOMEN

In dozens of sessions with his attorney and psychiatrist, Caputo spoke of hearing "bizarre voices" and "seeing hallucinations" when driven to murderous fits. He described the three personalities inside him. In his diary, the killer wrote of his violent moods, preceded by "broad lines" crossing his vision whenever his emotional state deteriorated and the voices taunted him into a murderous rage.

Desperate, Caputo turned to his brother Alfredo and hired the attorney. Heeding their advice, he surrendered to the Argentine authorities, but "police and judges simply threw up their hands," the *Times* reported, "claiming that since no charges were pending against him, *he could not be arrested,* no matter how many crimes he confessed to." In his diary Caputo described the four killings, the "broad lines" scoring his vision when his emotions swung out of control and the voices harassed him. The "voices," he said, "did not let me have any peace."[1]

An equally repugnant story was told by Carl Campbell, described by his mother as a troubled man haunted by "voices." On May 5, 1991 Campbell strolled to a bus stop in the Pentagon parking lot and emptied five pistol rounds into the chest and abdomen of Navy Commander Edward J. Higgins, an arms control specialist for the DoD. Campbell was taken into custody by federal police and charged with first-degree murder.

Psychologists submitted a report to U.S. Magistrate W. Curtis Sewell in Alexandria. In it, they wrote that Campbell claimed the CIA had "injected" him with a microchip that controlled his mind.[2] In fact, there is a little known technique used by the CIA for injecting a computer chip into the bloodstream, which delivers it to the brain where it catches and lodges.[3] The question is, how did Campbell, ruled mentally incompetent by the court, a gibbering psychotic, become familiar with an obscure procedure for implanting a biomedical telemetry chip?

Early Giants of Remote Mind Control

The CIA's experiments in radio control of the brain are based on the development of the EEG in the 1920s. In 1934 Drs. Chaffee and Light published a pivotal monograph, "A Method for Remote Control of Electrical Stimulation of the Nervous System." Work along the same lines allowed Dr. Jose Delgado of Cordoba, Spain to climb into bull-ring and, with the push of a button, trigger an electrode in the head of a charging bull and stop the beast in its tracks.

Further groundbreaking advances were made by L.L. Vasiliev, the famed Russian physiologist and doyan of parapsychology, in "Critical Evaluation of the Hypnogenic Method." The article detailed the experiments of Dr. I.F. Tomashevsky in remote radio control of the brain, "at a distance of one or more rooms and under conditions where the participant would not know or suspect that she would be experimented with.... One such experiment was carried out in a park at a distance," Vasiliev

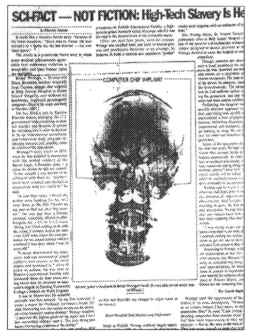

reported, and "a post-hypnotic mental suggestion to go to sleep was complied with within a minute."[4]

By 1956 Curtiss Shafer, an electrical engineer for the Norden-Ketay Corporation, could explore the possibilities at the National Electronics Conference in Chicago. "The ultimate achievement of biocontrol may be man himself," Shafer said. "The controlled subjects would never be permitted to think as individuals. A few months after birth, a surgeon would equip each child with a socket mounted under the scalp and electrodes reaching selected areas of brain tissue." In this psycho-Arcadia, "sensory perceptions and muscular activity could be either modified or completely controlled by bioelectric signals radiating from state-controlled transmitters."[5]

The CIA had already rushed headlong into Shafer's EMR dystopia with the founding of an experimental mind control clinic in Montreal, directed by the notorious D. Ewen Cameron, M.D. on grants from the Rockefeller Foundation and J.D. McConnell of the *Montreal Star.* Another pool of funding was the Gerschickter Foundation, named for Dr. Charles Gerschickter of Georgetown University Hospital, who had tested potent drugs on mental patients and the terminally ill, and bombarded monkeys with radar waves until they passed out at the behest of the CIA.[6]

Allan Memorial was housed in a limestone mansion atop Mount Royal, donated by Sir Hugh Allan and staffed with emigre psychiatrists from war-crushed Europe.

Cameron shared a bloodless, sadistic character with the Nazis he analyzed early in his career. Allan Memorial opened in 1942. Three years later he was invited to Nuremberg to evaluate the mental state of Rudolph Hess. In Germany Cameron could dissect the aberrations of fascist rule. Dr. Harvey Weinstein, a psychiatrist whose father was a guinea pig for Cameron's mind control experiments, writes that Germany was "a laboratory in which the issues of authority, powerlessness, individual motivation and behavior could be examined."[7] And ruthlessly applied in Montreal. Cameron's early revulsion at Nazi violence gave way to a growing elitist sensibility. His scorn for the weak, including his own mentally-crippled patients, qualified him for the carnage to come.

In 1992 retired Colonel L. Fletcher Prouty, formerly a Pentagon liaison to the CIA, told author Dick Russell that Allan Memorial "was pretty well organized." Prouty:

> If you get ahold of a directory for the American Psychiatric Association in around 1956 or 1957, you'll be surprised to find that an enormous percentage of the individuals listed are foreign-born. Mostly they came out of Germany and Eastern Europe in a big wave. They were all called "technical specialists," but really they were psychiatrists. They went into jobs at universities mostly—but many were working on these 'unconventional' mind control programs for U.S. intelligence…. These would go to people like Dr. Cameron in Canada.[8]

Not one of Cameron's patients was ever cured in the Radio Telemetry Laboratory, a makeshift torture chamber assembled in the cellar of his own private Bedlam. The financial underpinnings for the experiments came from Cornell's Society for the Investigation of Human Ecology, a CIA front. Cameron's right-hand man was Leonard Rubenstein, an electrical whiz of Cockney descent who lacked medical bona fides, but passionately exercised a fascination with remote brain control. He foresaw the telemetry lab as the foundation of a sprawling psychopolitical Apparat "that will keep tabs on people without their knowing," as he told a fellow staffer.[9]

Cameron's left hand was Dr. Walter Freeman, who had performed no less than 4,000 frontal lobotomies in 20 years of practice—often on patients suffering only mild depression or paranoia. Dr. Freeman went on to become a respected San Francisco brain specialist.[10]

The psychotronic heart of the laboratory was the Grid Room, with its verticed, Amazing Tales interior. The subject was strapped into a chair involuntarily, by force, his head bristling with electrodes and transducers. Any resistance was met with a paralyzing dose of curare. The subject's brain waves were beamed to a nearby reception room crammed with voice analyzers, a wire recorder and radio receivers cobbled together by Rubenstein.[11] The systematic annihilation, or "depatterning" of a subject's mind and memory, was accomplished with overdoses of LSD, barbiturate sleep for 65 days at a stretch and ECT shocks at 75 times the recommended dosage. Psychic driving, the repetition of a recorded message for 16 hours a day, programmed the empty mind. Fragile patients referred to Allan Memorial for help were thus turned into carbuncular jellyfish.[12]

Yet Cameron, before his death in 1967, was president of the American and Canadian Psychiatric Associations.

His work in brain emissions was balanced elsewhere by experiments in reception. Honeywell, Inc., for instance, launched into "a method to penetrate inside a man's mind and control his brain waves over long distance."[13] The Scientific Engineering Institute in Boston, another CIA cover, was established in 1956 to study radar. In 1962 the SEI set up a "Life Sciences" lab to study the effects of electrodes deep within the brain.[14] At the National Institutes of Health, Dr. Maitland Baldwin beamed radio signals into the brains of lobotomized monkeys. His CIA monitors noted weird excesses: in one experiment, Baldwin decapitated a monkey and transplanted its head to the body of another, then attempted to restore it to life with radar saturation.[15]

At Langley the experiments were presided over by Dr. Stephen Aldrich, a patron of occult research, foreshadowing the use of mind control technology by satanic cults in the 1980s and '90s, according to Julianne McKinney, director of the Electronic Surveillance Project of the Association of National Security Alumni.[16] Dr. Aldrich, a graduate of Amherst and Northwestern, took control of The Firm's Office of Research and Development (ORD) in 1962 upon the departure of Sidney Gottleib. The occasion marked the birth of Operation Often, an investigation of the occult. With Houston sorceress Sybil Leek as their guide,

CIA behaviorists studied the arcana of the occult underground.[17]

The SEI contributed a social laboratory to Often in 1972 at the University of South Carolina in the form of a course in rituals of demonology and voodoo.[18]

Aldrich's interest in the occult (shared by scores of others in the intelligence world.[19]) may explain his penchant for remote brain manipulation, based as it is in "psychic" technology. Under the direction of Aldrich, writes John Marks in *The Search for the Manchurian Candidate*, ORD technocrats "kept probing for ways to control human behavior, and they were doing so with space-age technology that made the days of MKULTRA look like the horse-and buggy era."[20] Particularly useful to CIA scientists were advances in stereotaxic surgery, simplifying the implantation of electrodes in the brain to wipe out a subject's memories in preparation for hypnotic reconstructive surgery.

In 1965 the *New York Times* learned of obscure electronic experiments quietly funded by the government, and went tabloid with the front-page headline:

MIND CONTROL COMING, SCIENTIST WARNS

Dr. David Krech, a psychology professor at the University of California, warned that "our research may carry with it even more serious implications than the awful, in both senses of the word, achievements of the atomic physicists." When leaks to the press exposed the horror stories, he said, "let us not find ourselves in the position of being caught foolishly surprised, naively perplexed and touchingly full of publicly displayed guilt."[21]

On May 6 Dr. Delgado, the Spanish bulltamer and postwar Yale researcher, closed a lecture on the evolution of the brain at the American Museum of Natural History in New York with the announcement that "science has developed a new electrical methodology for the study and control of cerebral function in animals and humans."[22]

Operation Bloodbath

Encouraged by progress in transforming human beings into cordless automatons, the CIA picked up the pace. Two years before Dr. Krech's admonition, a CIA manual was prepared on the electronic wizardry of Radio-Hypnotic Intracerebral Control (RHIC), originally developed by the Pentagon, according to a 1975 issue of *Modern People:*

> When a part of your brain receives a tiny electrical impulse
> from outside sources, such as vision, hearing, etc., an emotion is
> produced—anger at the sight of a gang of boys beating an old

woman, for example. The same emotions of anger can be created by artificial radio signals sent to your brain by a controller. You could instantly feel the same white hot anger without any apparent reason.[23]

The objective of Project ARTICHOKE, the CIA's umbrella remote mind control program in the 1950s (as reported in innumerable men's magazines) was the creation of a "Manchurian" killer-puppet with a revolver and a memory like a steel sieve, both emptied by electrical stimulation.

The technology existed by the early 1960s to support the contention of former FBI agent Lincoln Lawrence (an alias) and researcher Art Ford in the classic investigation of CIA mind control ops, *Were We Controlled?*, that Lee Harvey Oswald was a hypnogenic assassin—with a malfunctioning electrical implant in his head.

That a political assassin could be directed from afar to strike on cue is not so implausible as it may seem to the uninitiated. The authors' reconstruction holds up as well today as it did in 1968, when the book was published. If only persons involved with the book proved as durable. Lawrence's attorney, the late Martin Scheiman, was gunned down inside the Time-Life Building. A condensation of the book by Damon Runyon, Jr. (an adherent to New Orleans D.A. Jim Garrison's recreation of the Kennedy assassination) was preempted by death. In April, 1968 the celebrated writer suffered a mortal fall from a bridge in Washington, D.C.'s Rock Creek Park.[24]

The CIA circle in the Inferno swelled with odd deaths, disappearances and "suicides."

In 1975 Herman Kimsey, a veteran Army counter intelligence operative and a ranking CIA official until his resignation in 1962, surfaced posthumously in Hugh MacDonald's *Appointment in Dallas:* "Oswald was programmed to kill," Kimsey told MacDonald, "like a medium at a seance. Then the mechanism went on the blink and Oswald became a dangerous toy without direction."[25] Three weeks after the interview, Kimsey perished of heart failure.[26]

Likewise, Oswald crony David Ferrie, a CIA pilot and hypnotist, was found dead in his New Orleans apartment, surrounded by fifteen empty medicine bottles, a seeming suicide. But the coroner's final ruling was that the cause of death was a berry aneurysm. Forensic specialists ventured that the blood vessel had hemorrhaged as the result of a karate blow to back of his head. Raiding police carted off Ferrie's effusive notes on hypnosis and a pile of books on post-hypnotic suggestion. His cohorts went into hiding after his death, but one, Jack Martin, surfaced long enough, according to Walter Bowart in *Operation Mind Control,* "to suggest that Oswald had been programmed by Ferrie to go to Dallas and kill the President."[27]

A shadow cabinet of intelligence officials guided the CIA's remote mind control program. The reigning Big Brother was Richard Helms, then plans director, a product of the Eastern cryptocracy (his grandfather was the first director of the International Bank of Settlements, and past president of the Federal Reserve), and a former United Press reporter, in which capacity he interviewed Adolph Hitler in 1937.[28] In the wake of the Bay of Pigs tragedy, Helms was selected by CIA Director John McCone to run the "dirty tricks" department. Appointed to the position of Director of Central Intelligence in 1966, he left the Agency six years later. Before departing, Helms kept the secrets by ordering the destruction of all files relating to MKULTRA.[29]

He was a Machiavelli with a mission. An avid proponent of telemetry as a form of low-intensity warfare, Helms commandeered a vast research network in pursuit of such subtle depth persuasion techniques as the transmission of strategic subliminal messages to the brains of enemy populations. He advocated the use of high-frequencies to affect memory and even the unconscious. Helms ordered up a scientific cabal to study automata theory.[30] In a memo to the Warren Commission, he made mention of "biological radio communication."[31]

The 1964 memo was prophetic. Helms:

> Cybernetics can be used in *molding of a child's character,* the inculcation of knowledge and techniques, the amassing of experience, the establishment of social behavior patterns... all functions which can be summarized as control of the growth processes of the individual.[32]

Cybernetics technology that responds to thought was in the offing. In his memo, Helms diverted attention from CIA-funded research and development by alluding to the Soviets. But then they had no technology the U.S. did not also have, he conceded.

A subsequent CIA directive, summarized in a brochure on the "Cybernetic Technique" distributed by Mankind Research Unlimited (MRU), a research front in the District of Columbia, gleefully discusses the Agency's development of a "means by which information of modest rate can be fed to humans utilizing other senses than sight or hearing." The Cybernetic Technique, "based on Eastern European research," involves beaming information to individual nerve cells. The purpose, the directive states, is the enhancement of mental and physical performance.[33]

The cyborg was born.

Cyborg Nazis and the MASERS of Pandora

In 1965, upon discovering the microwave dousing of the American embassy in Moscow, the DoD's secretive Advanced Research Projects Agency (ARPA) set up a laboratory at the Walter Reed Army Institute of Research in Washington, D.C. ARPA had already developed a prodigious arsenal of electromagnetic weapons. Dr. Jose Delgado (whose work with radio-waves was underwritten by the CIA and Navy) thought these invisible weapons "more dangerous than atomic destruction." With knowledge of the brain, he said, "we may transform, we may shape, direct, robotize man. I think the great danger of the future is... that we will have robotized human beings who are not aware that they have been robotized."[34] Touching, but Delgado's sudden fit of conscience was belated. America's EM arsenal owes its very existence to his brain transponder experiments, which robotized humans.

But the beaming of the American embassy was an unexpected turn in the Invisible Cold War. What were the Ruskies up to?

The Moscow Signal, Paul Brodeur speculates in *The Zapping of America*, may be a perennial stern warning to the DoD to curb any geopolitical ambitions that EM weapons might inspire. He also interprets the Signal as retaliation for "the threat or fact of unwarranted irradiation of their population by powerful electromagnetic devices that now encircle them and look down on them from outer space."[35]

Baffled officials of the intelligence community consulted experts on the biological effects of the radiation. Dr. Milton Zaret, a leading microwave scientist recruited by PANDORA, recalls that the CIA inquired "whether I thought electromagnetic radiation beamed at the brain from a distance could affect the way a person might act," and "could microwaves be used to facilitate brainwashing or to break down prisoners under investigation."[36] The State Department chose to keep the Signal a secret from embassy employees—and studied the side-effects instead. Ambassador Stoessel's office was situated in the beam's center. He fell prey to a blood disease, bleeding eyes, nausea, and eventually lymphoma. Two other State Department employees, Charles Bohlen and Llewellyn Thompson, have been stricken with cancer. The existence of the Soviet beam was only acknowledged by the U.S. in 1976, in response to a Jack Anderson column.

The State Department declared that the microwave saturation of the embassy activated bugging devices in the walls. But Dr. Zaret has conducted his own tests, simulating the Moscow emissions, and reviewed Soviet medical literature. He concluded that the Moscow Signal was psychoactive: "Whatever other reasons the Russians may have had, they believed the beam would modify the behavior of personnel."[37]

In 1965 the Pentagon's investigation of microwaves was "broadened to include ARPA and code-named Project PANDORA, based at the Walter

Reed Army Institute of Research. PANDORA scientists began by zapping monkeys to study the biological effects of highly concentrated microwave frequencies.[38] Similar studies were conducted at the Veterans' Administration Hospital in Kansas City, the University of Rochester, Brooks Air Force Base in Texas, Johns Hopkins, MIT, the Mitre Corporation, the University of Pennsylvania, and scores of other domestic and foreign research laboratories.

CIA researchers, meanwhile, explored other bands on the EM spectrum. The ubiquitous Dr. Delgado blasted the amygdala and hippocampus of four of his patients with radio waves. He reported that they experienced sundry emotions, sensations, and "colored visions."[39] Scientists at the National Institutes of Health duplicated Rubenstein's medieval telemetry lab at Allan Memorial.[40] And at UCLA, Dr. Ross Adey (who worked closely with emigre Nazi technicians after WW II) rigged the brains of lab animals to transmit to a radio receiver, which shot signals back to a device that sparked any behavior desired by the researcher.[41]

Such gadgets have turned up in startling places.

In *The Controllers,* mind control researcher Martin Cannon argues that the brain transmitters and "stimoceivers" of the 1960s were "similar to those now viewed in (UFO) abductee MRI scans." The press ceased coverage of brain telemetry experiments in the mid-seventies. But

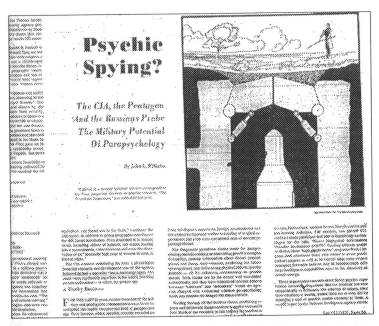

Washington Post story for August 7, 1977 explained how the CIA beamed signals to Stanford University at the very time researchers there conducted remote viewing experiments. Were images beamed to the heads of the percipients?

Cannon's study of abduction accounts led him to conclude that effects of brain stimulation "can now be elicited with microwaves and other forms of electromagnetic radiation, with and without electrodes."[42]

In the scientific underground the development of microwave weapons suffered inevitable eruptions, making the front pages. Retaliation for the Moscow Signal is the probable background of one flat-toned *LA Times* news brief on England's EM "death ray":

> The official Soviet newspaper Izvestia said that high-frequency radio waves used to power British eavesdropping devices may have killed two Soviet citizens in London. In an article headlined "Rays Bring Death," the newspaper said microwave radiation was used to control sophisticated listening devices implanted in the walls of the diplomatic compound in London.... A senior British Foreign Office official denied any government connection with the deaths.[43]

The U.S. conceived its own electromagnetic "death ray" in 1965. The patent, according to officials of McFarlane, an independent R&D firm, was stolen from them by NASA. The theft was reported in hearings before the House Subcommittee on DoD appropriations, chaired by Rep. George Mahon of Texas. The invention, a "Modulated Electron-Gun X-Ray Nuclear Booster," could be adapted to "communications, remote control and guidance systems, electromagnetic radiation telemetering and death ray applications," according to company literature.

McFarlane submitted the prototype to NASA in 1964, along with detailed plans, circuit drawings and technical data. But NASA's Inventions and Contributions Board dismissed the device as "of no significant value in our aeronautical and space program." The Booster was rejected. A year later NASA proposed to Congress the development of MIROS, a point-to-point orbital "communications system" (any offensive military intention went unspoken), based on principles conceived by McFarlane with acknowledged "death ray" applications."[44]

"Why," a company official asked the subcommittee, "does NASA appear before congressional committees to ask for funds for these very same developments, which they have told us are of no value? Why the double standard?"[45]

Electronic warfare was the invisible axis of the Cold War. The McFarlane design anticipated Star Wars by twenty years, but even then the subject of EM killer satellites was never publicly raised.

The militarization of psychotronics branched into every conceivable direction. Systems Consultants, Inc., the federal proprietary, was founded in 1966 with branch offices in Virginia and "a permanent, professional staff of 250 concentrated on problem solving in the areas of intelligence, electronic warfare, sensor technology and applications."[46] The aforementioned Mankind Research Unlimited is a spin-off of Systems Consultants. MRU advertises that "biological effects" can be "modified by action of energies, or biological force fields." More to the point, MRU maintains that the Soviet Union has "more than twenty centers for the study of biocommunications"—or ESP and related technology "with an annual budget estimated to be over 12 million rubles ($13 million) for 1967." The U.S., an MRU spokesman lamented in a company brochure, lagged far behind. "Mankind Research hopes to counter and reverse this trend so that the full fruits and benefits derived from this research are also made available to the United States."[47]

MRU's primary interests (and so the CIA's) were an open book: "Biocybernetics," "Psycho-Technology Research" and "Behavioral Neuropsychiatry," among other mind-dominating military and intelligence systems.

Vietnam burned in the political background. Students marched. The Nixon camp was poised to assume power and strategic political murders assured they would. The mind control netherworld erupted yet again with the assassination of Robert Kennedy in Los Angeles on June 5, 1968.

"I'll never forget his eyes," Western Union operator Mary Grohs said of Sirhan Sirhan, whom she met an hour before the shooting at the Ambassador Hotel. Others also noticed his eyes. "Dark brown and peaceful," said George Plimpton, one of six men required to wrestle Sirhan into submission as Kennedy lay dying.[48] Sirhan, in the opinion of many prominent researchers, was a hypno-patsy.

"Sirhan's trial was, and will be remembered, as the psychiatric blunder of the century," argues Dr. Eduard Simson-Kallas, senior psychologist of the California prison system when he examined Sirhan.[49] In his March 9, 1973 affidavit, Simson-Kallas reported that he was "appalled at the conduct of mental health professionals involved in this case." He agreed to read the transcripts at Sirhan's request, concluding that psychological findings submitted to the court were "strongly in conflict with the trial's main witnesses." At no point in the evidence did he find that Sirhan was a "paranoid schizophrenic" or "psychotic," as several government psychologists testified. One, Dr. Diamond, has diagnosed Sirhan as a sufferer of "dementia praecox." But if this were true, Simson-Kallas wrote, "Sirhan would have to be incurably insane. That is what the label means. Sirhan was not incurably insane,' or even 'insane.'"

"Whatever strange behavior I showed in court," Sirhan told him, "was the result of my outrage over Dr. Diamond's and other doctor's testimony. They were saying many things about me that were grossly untrue, nor did I give them permission to testify in my behalf in court."

Furthermore, Simson-Kallas insists that "Dr. Diamond was wrong in testifying that the evidence for psychosis was obtained when Sirhan was under hypnosis. The fact is, paranoid schizophrenics are almost impossible to hypnotize." Sirhan dropped into a trance easily. "Psychotics in general are among the poorest subjects for hypnosis. They cannot concentrate, they do not follow instructions and basically do not trust." Sirhan had no such aversion to hypnosis. On the contrary, he once made a trance disk and practiced self-hypnosis as a distraction from Death Row malaise. This required "considerable self-control, which no psychotic has," Simson-Kallas says. "That Sirhan was easy to hypnotize... proves he was not a paranoid schizophrenic."[50]

Sirhan wasn't demented; he was controlled. His inability to recall the murder is either the aftermath of post-hypnotic suggestion or a synapse-deadening radio blast ("Electronic Dissolution of Memory," or EDOM, a CIA technique exposed by Lincoln Lawrence). There are other indications of hynotic—possibly radio-hypnotic—control of Sirhan:

♦ Thane Eugene Cesar, a "security guard," is widely considered to be the designated assassin. Like all participants in the murders of John and Robert Kennedy, Cesar was politically hard-right. He told Ted Charach, co-producer of *The Second Gun,* an assassination documentary, that he'd been to "American-Nazi conclaves." Cesar held down a fuzzily-defined job at Lockheed, a company on intimate terms with the CIA, and a PANDORA contractor. Jim Yoder, a retired Lockheed engineer, told former FBI agent William Turner that Cesar worked floating assignments in an "off-limits" area operated by the CIA.[51] (Lockheed was also on cozy terms with Richard Nixon's political circle, particularly William Rogers, former secretary of state, who in 1975 urged Henry Kissinger to purge the names of Lockheed agents from a Justice Department probe of bribery allegations.[52])

Sirhan under hypnosis: "PRACTICE, PRACTICE, PRACTICE..." "Practice what?" asked Dr. Diamond. "MIND CONTROL, MIND CONTROL, MIND CONTROL, MIND CONTROL..."[53] The repetition recalls Dr. Cameron's "psychic driving."

♦ Charles McQuiston, a former Army intelligence officer, applied a technique called Psychological Stress Evaluation to tape recordings of Sirhan. McQuiston concluded that "Sirhan was under some kind of hypnotic influence... kept repeating certain phrases." Again, psychic driving, a pet CIA technique, enters Sirhan's mental profile. "I believe Sirhan was brainwashed under hypnosis by the constant repetition of words like, 'You are nobody, you're nothing, the American dream is gone.'"[54] This is precisely the sort of ego-trashing epistle used in Cameron's classified experiments at Allan Memorial's Telemetry Lab.[55] When Sirhan believed it, McQuiston says, "someone implanted an idea, kill RFK, and under hypnosis the brainwashed Sirhan accepted it." Similar messages have long been radioed to auditory receivers buried in the cochlea or brains of the CIA's experimental subjects.

♦ Assassination researchers accuse William Bryan, a Los Angeles hypnotist, of programming Sirhan. Bryan was a brainwashing specialist for the Air Force in Korea, and thereafter an adviser to the CIA's mind control program. In L.A. he ran the American Institute of Hypnosis, a therapeutic clinic.[56]

♦ Sirhan disappeared for three months in 1967. A neighbor of Sirhan's family told the FBI that his mother was "extremely worried" and "she did not know his whereabouts for some time." When Sirhan returned home, he displayed a fascination with the occult. His co-enthusiast was Walter Thomas Rathke, described by a friend as "far-right politically."[57] Rathke trained Sirhan in self-hypnosis with mirrors and candles. In his self-induced trances, psychic driving messages (according to McQuiston) programmed him to empty his revolver on cue. In all, twelve shots were fired.

The only gap in the mind control picture is this: Sirhan's trances were self-induced. Alone in the dark with his mirrors and candles, it's unlikely he provided the "messages" himself. Their source has yet to be determined. Reports by victims of CIA auditory-frequency experiments date them to the mid-sixties, and may explain Sirhan's agitated, robotic speech patterns.

Breaking the ESP Barrier

The "voices" were conceived in a lightning bolt. In 1956 two geophysicists, Holzer and Deal, noticed that naturally-occurring electromagnetic signals in the auditory range were tossed off by thunderstorms.[58] With little variation, most of the EM bursts were metered at 25 to 130 cycles/sec., with a very low attenuation rate. In other words, lightning discharges could be picked up anywhere in the world as "magnetic noise" on the ELF radio dial.

Two years on, Dr. Allan Frey, a biophysicist at General Electric's Advanced Electronics Center, Cornell University (and a contractor for the Office of Naval Research), published a "technical note" in Aerospace Medicine reporting that the auditory system responds "to electromagnetic energy in at least a portion of the radio frequency (RF) spectrum. Further, this response is instantaneous and occurs at low power densities... well below that necessary for biological damage."[59] Frey's subjects "heard" buzzes and knocks when exposed to low frequency radio emissions. In one experiment a radio beam swept over a subject, and with each sweep he "heard the radio frequency (RF) sound for a few seconds and reported it." When Frey modulated power densities, he discovered that even clinically deaf subjects perceived RF sounds. He played with transmitter settings, and was shocked to find that radio beams "can induce the perception of severe buffeting of the head," or prick the skin like needles.[60]

It seems that the brain is a powerful receiver. Frey: "The human auditory system and a table radio may be one order of magnitude apart in sensitivity to RF energy."[61] The area of the brain most sensitive to radio energy was just above the temporal lobe. The vocabulary of RF noises was expanded by modulating the pulse (with "no information placed in the signal"), perceived by the subject as originating from within or slightly behind the head.

Among practical applications of auditory stimulation, Frey proposed "stimulating the nervous system without the damage caused by electrodes."[62]

It was a significant discovery—but met with a wall of yawns from the status-quo scientific community. To his horror, he became the butt of jokes in letters to peer review journals. But PANDORA's technocrats supported his experiments and took the obvious military applications very seriously. Frey's work with microwaves had obvious uses in covert operations. In one experiment, for instance, he synchronized pulsed microwaves with the myocardia rhythm of a frog. Its heart stopped. He microwaved cats and found that stimulation of the hypothalamus had a powerful effect on emotions.[63]

Frey was reluctant to experiment on humans for ethical reasons. But PANDORA was manned by a full complement of Nazi Paperclip imports, and they did not balk at irradiating human subjects.

One of the German scientists employed by the government was Dr. Dietrich Beischer, who exposed some 7,000 Naval crewmen to dangerous levels of microwave energy at the Naval Aerospace Research Laboratory in Pensacola, Florida. Data on exposure limits, he declared at a symposium in Dahlgren, Virginia in 1973, could be "obtained in no other way," given the "exquisitely complex and dynamic nature of the human organism."[64]

Alas, Dr. Beischer, like scores of other scientists engaged in the experiments, died or disappeared in 1977. Among his last personal contacts was Nobel laureate, ESP researcher and fellow PANDORAN Robert O. Becker:

> Just before the meeting, I got a call from him. With no preamble or explanation, he blurted out: "I'm at a pay phone. I can't talk long. They are watching me. I can't come to the meeting or ever communicate with you again. I'm sorry. You've been a good friend. Goodbye." Soon afterward I called his office at Pensacola

and was told, "I'm sorry, there is no one here by that name," just as in the movies. A guy who had done important research there for decades just disappeared.[65]

The Promethean architects of Psychocivilization guarded the emerging technology jealously. "They" were more likely to be the CIA than the KGB.

An "official" halt to PANDORA's excesses was called in 1970, but the research had turned a historic corner and classified RF mind control testing quickly became a military armed drugs, ECT, torture, brain surgery or most other forms of behavior modification. The CIA and Pentagon concentrated their efforts on electromagnetism. Why the fuss?

A computerized form of telepathy.

"Biocommunication," the dream of Richard Helms, was tested on humans within a few years of his memo to the Warren Commission. The CIA had achieved direct communication between brain and computer by the late sixties, and had demonstrated in the laboratory that computer-assisted automatic learning was possible by pin-pointing neuron clusters in the brain with radio signals.[66] Microwaves easily penetrated the head's protective shielding of bone and membrane. Miniaturization of the receiver linked the mind to a remote computer. Brain waves were unscrambled and deciphered, recorded, beamed to another person—two-way mental communication.[67]

In *Technospies* (1978), author Ford Rowan foresaw the possibilities:

> Computers that can communicate with the brain may help people in all sorts of intellectual tasks. A tiny terminal implanted in a person's brain would give him access to giant computer banks, for instance, and with the miniaturization of computers, an actual computer could be implanted in the brain. From the individual's viewpoint it would become a part of his brain, extending his knowledge and memory immensely.[68]

The mind-reading venture was the culmination of a goal fixed as early as 1951 to Project ARTICHOKE, the CIA's development of behavior control techniques employing drugs, hypnosis, electroshock and extrasensory perception.[69]

Robert Naeslund, by his own account a subject of the experiments, claims to have been implanted unaware while undergoing surgery in 1967. He describes the "brain transmitter" in his head (with X-ray verification) as a device that floods the brain with radio energy, "picks up the sensory functions of the brain... Vision, thoughts, images, hearing, etc. are completely obvious to the person who has the receiver connected to his head." A Stockholm physician consulted by Naeslund told him: "young children were also used for these experiments in order to evaluate thought activity and reactions in children."[70]

The development of remote mind-reading machines in secret academic enclaves picked up with ARPA backing in the early 1970s. Scientists mapped the brain, gigahertzed the nervous system and gauged biohazards at MIT, NYU and UCLA. NASA launched its program. A story on the ARPA brain control effort appeared, not in the corporate press, but the *National Enquirer* for June 22, 1976. The Pentagon did not exactly deny the story. Robert L. Gilliat, an assistant general counsel for the Department of Defense, replied meekly: "The so-called 'brain-wave' machine... is not capable of reading brain waves of *anyone other than a willing participant* in the laboratory efforts to develop that particular device."[71] Presumably, the brain of an unwilling subject was impenetrable to microwaves.

In 1972 an ARPA report to Congress announced, after Helms, that "the long-sought goal (is) direct and intimate coupling between man and the computer." Four years later ARPA reported that thought-wave research had gone beyond communication to enhance memory by downloading information into the brain. Based on these capabilities, the post-PANDORA team set out to upgrade the interpretation of neural signals, and broaden the program to invent realistic tasks of "military significance."[72]

This side of the electronic battlefield, the experiments contributed to medicine the "transmitter-reinforcer," a device that transmits data on a patient's health. Ford:

> The transmitter-reinforcer utilizes space age technology to send accurate readings on the patient's condition to a computer, which digests the data. The computer can monitor many patients simultaneously. If a patient needs a dose of aversion treatment, the computer acts as controller, delivering a tone signal or shock.

The original, clandestine purpose of the "reinforcer" was not lost on authoritarian types in the psychiatric wings. Rowan:

> One study suggested that radio transmitter receivers should be implanted into the brains of patients to broadcast information to a computer which would monitor and control the patients' behavior.[73]

Other "constructive" uses of CIA/PANDORA telemetric brain implants were championed by criminologists. In 1972, Drs. Barton Ingraham and Gerald Smith advocated the implantation of brain transmitters to monitor and manipulate the minds of probationers. "The technique of telemetric control of human beings offers the possibility of regulating behavior with precision on a subconscious level," the authors enthused in a 1972 *Issues in Criminology* article.[74]

Surveillance expert Joseph Meyer of the DoD carried the idea a step further, proposing that electromagnetic mind control devices "surround the criminal with a kind of externalized conscience, an electronic substitute for social conditioning, group pressure and inner motivation." The ideal subject for testing the implants was "the poor and uneducated urban dweller (who) is fundamentally unnecessary to the economy," Meyer said.

Military doctors with hard-right political views were naturally drawn to electronic mind control as the final solution to the "useless eaters" quandary. One Air Force doctor went so far as to recommend, in the *New England Journal of Medicine,* that if a criminal's brain waves did not test "normal" after five years, he should be put to death.[75]

Dr. Louis Jolyon West, formerly a CIA brainwashing specialist and LSD experimenter, proposed establishing a computerized system employing space technology to monitor and control the violence-prone.[76] At UCLA's Neuropsychiatric Institute, under West's direction, a biofeedback device was developed to control sexual deviants that fits the penis. Sexual arousal set off an audible signal that became louder as the device expanded. At the same time, heart beat rate and muscular tension were monitored by telemetric computer.[77] This sort of Orwellian thinking led opponents of West to fear the prospect that computer data on young children could be used as justification for implanting them for state control.[78]

The nagging ethical considerations prompted a report on future applications and possible abuses. Scientists at Lockheed and Stanford Research Institute prepared the report, which postulated the rise of "a technocratic elite" with dominion over intelligence and identification systems to monitor whole countries. Wars would be waged by robots.

Technological advances anticipated by the authors included computer-operated artificial organs, biocybernetic devices to provide "social conversation, entertainment, companionship and even physical gratification," and a "machine-animal symbiant," an animal or human monitor that transmits its perceptions to a central authority. Partially funded by the National Science Foundation, the report recommended the formation of an oversight panel of artificial intelligence specialists to uphold ethical standards.[79]

"Voices" in the Attic

The moral squalor of the government's RF mind control program cried out for oversight, as one case history from the *Los Angeles Herald Examiner* (for March 21, 1979) makes clear:

A SUIT OVER BRAIN SURGERY—
MAN HALLUCINATES, SAY MICROWAVES ARE MURDERING HIM

The subject was Leonard Kille, a talented electronics engineer. Kille was the holder of patents for inventions willed to MIT when his brain was disabled by CIA psychiatrists Vernon Mark of Boston City Hospital and UCLA's Frank Ervin.

Kille was a co-inventor of the Land camera, named for Edwin Land of the Polaroid Corporation, an old boy of the CIA's mind control program. It was Land, in fact, who founded the Scientific Engineering Institute on behalf of the CIA.[81] (The SEI appeared earlier in this account hosting a course on demonology and witchcraft at the University of South Carolina, and planting electrodes in the brains of human subjects.) Land's CIA clique of "behaviorists" apparently drew their moral inspiration from the Death's Head Order of the Waffen SS. At South Vietnam's Bien Hoa Hospital, for example, an SEI team team buried electrodes in the skulls of Vietcong POWs and attempted to spur them into violence by remote control. Upon completion of the experiments, the POWs were shot and cremated by a company of "America's best," the Green Berets.[82]

Kille's story is no less lurid. In 1966 he suspected that his wife was having an affair. She denied it. He didn't believe her and flew into rages. A psychiatrist interpreted his anger as a "personality pattern distur-bance," and referred him to Mark and Ervin for neurological tests. They diagnosed him a mild psychomotor epileptic, and his jealousy was obvi-ously "paranoia." (As it happens, his wife *was* carrying on an affair with a boarder.) His psychiatrists described Kille as "uncontrolled," "danger-ous." (In fact, Kille's most violent outburst consisted of throwing tin cans at his wife—he missed her.) Kille was hospitalized and pressured into brain surgery. He refused at first, but his wife threatened divorce if he didn't submit to his psychiatrists. The cruel irony was that she divorced him after the surgery anyway to marry her paramour.

In the operating room, four electrical strands running the length of his brain were implanted. Each strand was studded with 20 or so electrodes. It was only *after* surgery that Kille was asked to sign his consent with the strands in place, already zinging his brain.[83]

Internal EEG activity was recorded. The voltage of the stimoceivers was boosted as part of Kille's "treatment."[84]

Dr. Peter Breggin of the Center to Study Psychiatry, a rare ombuds-man of psychiatric abuses, investigated the case and found despite the glowing reports of Mark and Ervin that the patient was "totally disabled, chronically hospitalized, and subject to nightmarish terrors that he will be caught and operated on again at the Massachusetts General Hospital."[85]

In 1971 an attendant found him with a wastebasket on his head to "stop the microwaves." A sympathetic doctor at Boston's VA hospital, where he was transferred, ordered for him "a large sheet of aluminum foil so he may fashion a protective helmet for himself. Good luck." The VA doctors were not informed that Kille had been fitted with the electrode strands, and wrote him off as a delusional paranoiac.

"The Mass General and labs... (are) killing all the useful cells in my brain," he confided in a note to a VA doctor when the electrodes burned lesions into his amygdala, another "treatment." It left him permanently paralyzed from the waist down.

Sweet and Ervin controlled his moods with electronic stimulation. They turned him up and turned him down, he said. The "haunting fear" left by Kille's ordeal, a psychiatrist wrote in the *New England Journal of Medicine,* is that "men may be become slaves, perhaps, to an authoritarian state."[86]

A significant step in this direction was taken at Walter Reed Army Hospital of Research in 1973 by Dr. Joseph Sharp. Inside an isolation chamber, Sharp heard words beamed at him in a pulsed-microwave audiogram. (An audiogram is a computerized analog of the spoken voice.) ARPA's Robert O. Becker foresaw in the experiment "obvious applications in covert operations." He imagined a barrage of "voices" driving an enemy insane, and post-hypnotic suggestions radioed to a programmed assassin.

Sure enough, hybrid EMR-hypnosis beams bearing "voices" were tested a year later by Dr. J.F. Shapitz, who proposed: "In this investigation it will be shown that the spoken word of the hypnotist may also be conveyed by modulated electromagnetic energy directly into the subconscious parts of the human brain"—another dream of Richard Helms was about to pass. The "voices," Schapitz wrote, would program the subconscious mind "without employing any technical devices for receiving or transcoding the messages and without the person exposed to such influence having a chance to control the information input."[87]

The Soviets were experimenting along the same lines. Russia's EM mind control state-of-the-art surfaced at the Conference on Psychotronic Research in 1973. Topics on the agenda of the meeting, held in Prague, included:

- Erasure of the Subconscious Mind
- Development of Extrasensory Perception
- The Induction of Paranormal Effects in Dreams
- The Mechanical Equivalent of Neuropsychic Energy
- The Psi Gene

And so on.[88]

The American mind control initiative was every bit as exotic. In Los Altos Hills, California, scientists drawing from the CIA's "black" budget cash cow applied acoustical telemetry in the development of transmitters that create scallops of infra-sound waves in the head, wiping clean all information stored by the brain cells.[89] Brain researcher Wilder Penfield demonstrated that electrical stimulation kicked up lost memories with perfect recall.[90]

True to the traditional interests of The Firm, drugs were sought to make experimental subjects more susceptible to hypno-programming. The guinea-pig was drugged, bathed with pulsed-microwave thought transmissions (the "Voice of God," humanoids from Alpha Centauri, a dead relative, any of the cover stories concocted by post-PANDORA researchers and operatives) and words commenced in the auditory tract.[91]

The "voices" descended on Marti Koskii in the mid-1970s. A welder by trade and a resident of Edmonton, Canada, he charges the CIA, Canadian police and Litton Moffat with "telepathic terrorism":

> First I was prepared-sensitized for microwave telepathy. In my case the "talk" was initially the next-door neighbors.... This went on for approximately four years, twenty hours a week. Also, after this they were capable of some kind of mind reading and discovered the key to the function of various control centres of the body. Now they were able to more or less control my sleep, feelings, sense of taste (saltiness, acidity of food), sexual functions (erection, ejaculation), sense of smell, urination, bowel movement and metabolism.[92]

Koskii dismissed the "voices" visiting him a few hours a day as a "harmless schizophrenia." Not exactly. After the four-year preliminary period, his life was gradually ruined. Carbon dioxide caused him to foam at the mouth, making his work impossible. The "voices" hazed him every waking minute. He was allowed one hour of sleep a day. On one occasion, his heart beat stepped up "faster and stronger till I had a heart attack and had to be hospitalized." Twice, nerves in his lower bodily strata were deadened and his bladder ruptured. He was plagued by impotence and partial loss of memory.

Koskii hasn't a clue why he was chosen, but the motive may be political. "In an elaborate and excruciating experiment that involved hypnosis and supporting special effects," he recalls, "I was presented with a program of indoctrination to convince me criticism of the American society was a 'cancer' and a threat to us all. I was told I was 'unclean' and 'contaminated' with this 'cancer.'"

Experimenting overseas narrowed the odds of exposure. Robert Naeslund describes two independent cases that surfaced in Sweden:

> Rolf Sundwall was anesthetized while in police custody around 1974. Subsequently a strong radio signal entered his body day and night. After about one year, he was admitted to a mental asylum. Circumstances destroyed his life and he died in a fire in his home in 1978.
> The insertion of a brain transmitter in Gote Josefsson's head

was also performed while in police custody in 1975. The pain caused by the frequencies entering Josefsson's head were so strong that he was admitted to Ulleraker Mental Asylum... The court was provided with information regarding the criminal utilization by the police of brain transmitters in Josefsson's case, but refused to have him properly medically examined.[93]

The emphasis on pulsed microwaves stemmed from a 1972 Army study, supposedly concerning Soviet experimentation. Titled *Controlled Offensive Behavior, USSR,* the report mainly concerned itself with the targeting of individuals, not groups, and foreshadowed the government's microwave experiments on heedless human subjects, often political activists, during the Reagan/Bush administrations. The aim of developing microwave anti-personnel weapons and "mind altering techniques," according to the study, was "the total submission of one's will to some outside force."[94]

Pointing fingers at the Soviets is Washington's way of justifying domestic human rights violations. Electromagnetically "controlled offensive behavior" has lurked behind a long line of murders and suicides throughout the western hemisphere.

Sometimes at the doorstep of the intelligence establishment. On February 17, 1989, the *Washington Post* reported:

BANK KILLER TORMENTED BY "VOICES"

concerning Emmanuel Tsegaye, an Ethiopian-born bank teller in Bethesda, Maryland. The 33 year-old Tsegaye was the proverbial "disgruntled employee," depressed, suicidal, "tormented by voices that only he could hear." He murdered three coworkers at Chevy Chase Federal Savings, yet Tsegaye, the *Post* noted, "who attempted suicide numerous times and often spoke of hearing disembodied voices, rarely was violent to others."[95] He'd been institutionalized for depression several times, and received treatment at St. Elizabeth's Hospital, long a haunt of CIA psychiatry.

"I used to hear... voices both from space and as... exact repeated words" (a fair description of psychic driving), he wrote in a letter to the judge who committed him in 1984. "I used to hear a person speaking from (the) distance about the things I was thinking." After one suicide attempt, he wrote, "I was depressed, mentally and physically weak... from the voices I used to hear and inadequate sleeps." The "voices" were so real to Tsegaye that he tried several times to tape record them "from the air."

Evidence of gigahertz mind control often passes unnoticed in the background of public spectacles like the Tsegaye carnage. Political and financial conspiracies are just as often at play. The unfortunate Rex Niles, a former Southern California electronics salesman, learned the hard way. Niles was a federal informant in a kickback ring of Pentagon contractors. But before he could produce testimony in court, he fell prey to a malicious MASER attack.[96]

To a *Los Angeles Times* reporter, he complained that noises were keeping him awake at night:

> "You know, in the middle of the night, at 2 in the morning, when they wouldn't allow me to sleep, when they were aggravating my conscious as well as my subconscious mind, I would hear what sounded like large groups of people down on the street— yelling, talking, and they would laugh and throw something that sounded like a bottle breaking on the street. "So I would go to the window, or one time I was dressed because I couldn't sleep, so I went down, and the street was absolutely empty.

Federal "marshals," he said, harassed him with microwave weapons and deprived him of rest to make him appear deranged. His sister testified that helicopters often circled her home, and 250 watts of atmospheric microwaves in the Niles home were gauged by an engineer.

A lifelong friend of Niles insists that her computer "went haywire" when Niles approached it. For the *Times* photographer, he held up an aluminum foil hat—*pierced through with small holes:* "proof that the government is bombarding him with microwaves in an attempt to kill him."

The Microwave Mafia Murders

A particularly nasty flare-up of the mind control underground was the 1978 "disappearance" of Andrija Puharich, owner of the Intelectron Corp., a medical technology firm, and a Merry Prankster on the techno-parapsychological fringe of the CIA.

Puharich was a veteran of MKULTRA. According to journalist Steven Levy:

> The details of his assignment are clouded in a murkiness he has come to wear like some exquisite garment. In any case, his activities have raised the perception among many that under the auspices of the U.S. government, Puharich had been involved in actual experiments in parapsychology and psychedelic drugs. Those with a conspiratorial bent have often assumed Puharich has dark intelligence connections.[96]

He was conversant in psychoactive weapons, and his "pet subjects" were mind control and the telepathic effects of extra low frequency (ELF) waves. Alas, he had breached the CIA's Cone of Silence by speaking openly of "weapons systems... that we have no defense against," as Ira Einhorn, a former cohort, phrased it. "That would be the last thing the CIA—or anyone in the military establishment—would even want us to breathe about." Shortly before Puharich vanished, his Ossining home was torched and destroyed. He told Einhorn that the CIA was responsible.[97]

The harassment of Puharich was reenacted wholesale with the weird deaths of 22 British scientists in the 1980s, otherwise known as the "Star Wars Killings." SDI really had little to do with the homicides. Star Wars, after all, was a cover story for the R&D of electromagnetic weapons. The deception is a premise of *The Zapping of America,* by Paul Brodeur, who, after puzzling over technical and strategic shortcomings of space-based defense, concludes that the program was (is?) "little more than an elaborate smokescreen designed to hide the fact that the United States is developing a directed-energy weapon that uses a high-power microwave pulse."[98]

While the public was permitted an occasional glimpse at Brilliant Pebbles on the evening news, the Pentagon and CIA pursued a sprawling, obscure initiative of its own.

Seven of the murdered scientists worked for Marconi, a subsidiary of General Electric—a fount of EMR brain control technology and microwave radiation projects[99]—and the largest military electronics contractor in the UK.[100]

Two of the deaths can be interpreted as grim warnings to others in the telemetric mind control netherworld. John Ferry, a Marconi executive, was ruled to have committed "suicide" by chewing on live wires. The corpse of Alistair Beckham, a software designer, was found coiled in bare wires—a message to others engaged in EM research and development?

One British engineer has been directly linked to the program. This was Frank Jennings of Plessey Defense Systems, dead of a heart attack.

The American Sons of ARTICHOKE

Until recently, as Naval Captain Paul Taylor wrote in a 1976 essay, "The Electromagnetic Spectrum in Low-Intensity Conflict," most scientists assumed that "a microwave is a microwave."[103] Captain Taylor's survey of covert warfare applications discussed radio frequencies "disruptive to purposeful behavior," and the brain as "an electrically mediated organ." A "speed-of-light weapons effect" could be achieved, he said, with "the passage of approximately 100 milliamperes through the myocardium (leading) to cardiac standstill and death." EM devices with stun or kill settings could sweep across entire armies (or cities).[104] The genocidal "death ray" had arrived.

The Reagan administration used it as a hidden bargaining chip in arms negotiations with the Soviets.[105] But the technology was tested at home on private citizens.

The entire city of Eugene, Oregon was doused in microwave radiation in March, 1978. The *Oregon Journal* reported:

MYSTERIOUS RADIO SIGNALS
CAUSING CONCERN IN OREGON

The signals were recorded throughout the state. Naturally, the federal government was called in "to help solve the problem." [106] One Oregonian who could do without the government's "help" was Marshall Parrott, chief of the state Health Division's radiation control section. Parrott posited that the cause of the microwave pulses "could be any thing from sunspots to our own federal government." [106] Paul Brodeur reports that TRW has proposed constructing a Naval communications system along an existing 850-mile power line with its terminus in Oregon. He attributes the microwave assault on Eugene to the interplay of Naval ELF beams and Soviet jamming.[107] Ranking government specialists blamed the Soviets, but even the FCC has concluded that the signal came from a Navy transmitter in California. Microwaves, the FCC report concluded, were the likely cause of several sudden illnesses among faculty researchers at an Oregon State University laboratory.[108]

Oregonians complained of headaches, fatigue, inability to sleep, reddening of the skin, anxiety, "clicks" in the head and a "buzz" harmonizing with a high-pitched wail.

Andrew Michrowski, a concerned Canadian researcher, wrote to Prime Minister Pierre Trudeau on September 19, 1978, citing a Pacific Northwest Center for Non-Ionizing Radiation study that found the "Soviet" signals *"psychoactive"* and *"very strongly suggestive of achieving the objective of brain control."* An EEG examination of a Eugene resident recorded 6 Hz brainwaves, indicating "irritability." The radiation, Michrowski observed, was "dangerous in the... shadow of planetary-scale brain control that is growing into a reality with each passing week." [109]

A similar ELF experiment raised the mental morbidity rate of Timmons, Ontario.[110]

The callously haphazard testing of EMR "non-lethal" effects around the world inspired researcher Harlan E. Girard, at a 1991 NATO conference, to report that a principal feature of the weapons system "is its ability to produce auditory effects." It is also capable of producing visual hallucinations, described to Girard "by a German artist, on whom this equipment is being tested involuntarily, as having the quality of 35mm slides." The equipment, he said, "can be used to block all sensation." Girard considers long-range mind control "truly *satanic*" in its moral implications. "Considering how recklessly, wantonly and indiscriminately America's new weapons have been used," he said, "physicians attending the dead and dying should consider the patient's own political views and associations before making a diagnosis or conducting an autopsy.[111]

An especially brutal turn in federal mind control experimentation involves children. A Southern California child therapist (requesting anonymity) tells of treating a young patient who'd undergone an obscure brain operation at the aforementioned UCLA Neuropsychiatric Institute at the age of three. The therapist insists that the operation explains his present "psychosis."[112]

Another therapist—specializing in ritual abuse trauma—offered in a phone conversation that she'd ordered X-rays of a 3 year-old patient who, she suspected, had been implanted. An attending physician confirmed that there was a tiny electrical device fitted to the child's brain.

The fact is that the wave of ritual child abuse allegations that swept the country in the 1980s cloaked federal psychotronic and eugenics experiments on young children. As one adult survivor of psychotronic mind control concludes, "covert arms of government... have coined the term 'screen memories' to describe the obfuscational memories impressed by the abusers themselves." The so-called "False Memory Syndrome," he says, "is a scapegoat created by a consortium of federal 'spin doctors' bent on negating the believability and viability of the more than 12,000 unwitting citizens who have been on the receiving end of this technology." The CIA and military establishment "must at all costs disguise their abuse in order to continue experimentation with psychotronics," he argues.

The "false memory" bromide has been popularized largely by organized pedophiles, cultists and hired guns of psychiatry. It has been adopted as the status quo position of the press. But the cover story originated with the CIA's mind control netherworld. "Nazi-inspired scientists," the survivor says, "perform medical tests during the abuse event, such as *implantation of biotelemetric tracking devices* into nasal cavities and ear canals."

The brain transmitters can be tracked by Global Positioning System satellites. The subject therefore cannot hope to escape the mind control network.[113]

Screen memories of abuse, created by hypnotic or psychotronic visualization, a "novelty effect," are offered by UFO researcher Martin Cannon as a probable explanation for the weirdness surrounding most "alien" abductions. Again the government, shielded by an unbelievable cover story, escapes detection. EM technology (and testing on humans) remains classified.

No doubt, UFOs exist and have traumatized thousands of "contactees" —the military has been building them since the 1940s. To be sure, *U.S.*

News & World Report (April 7, 1950) declaimed:

FLYING SAUCERS—THE REAL STORY
U.S. BUILT FIRST ONE IN 1942
—JET-PROPELLED DISKS CAN OUTFLY OTHER PLANES—

The "sky disks" could already "hover aloft, spurt ahead at tremendous speed, outmaneuver conventional craft," the article reported. The 1942 prototype was elliptical. It had a maximum speed of 400–500 miles an hour, and lifted from the ground almost vertically.[114]

Imagine what "UFOs" can do fifty years later.

Cannon posits that government saucers account for the countless sightings and abductions reported around the world. Screen memories explain the bug-eyed monsters. "All the powers of the espionage empire and the scientific establishment have entered into an unholy alliance," Cannon says, "psychiatrist and spy... microwave specialists and clandestine operators.[115] And then there are the cults. Between ritual molestation and "alien" abductions, there is this common connection. Cannon:

> Some abductees I have spoken to have been directed to join certain religious/philosophical sects. These cults often bear close examination. The leaders of these groups tend to be "ex" *CIA operatives,* or *Special Forces* veterans. They are often linked through personal relations, even though they espouse widely varying traditions. They often use hypnosis, drugs, or *"mind machines"* in their rituals. Members of these cults have reported periods of missing time during these ceremonies or "study periods."[116]

UFOs are stricly terrestrial, as one UFO abductee recognized. She phoned Julianne McKinney at the Microwave Surveillance Project in Washington to report her abduction, aware that it was government-directed. "Her house is being shot at," McKinney says, "and they are harassing her viciously, the target of massive microwave assault"[117] The abuse of psychoactive technology is escalating, unbeknownst to the American public. Recurrent hypno-programmed stalkers, ritual and "alien" outrages and psychotronic forms of political persecution are on the upswing at the hands of the DIA, CIA, FBI, NSA and other covert branches of government. Hired guns in media, law enforcement and psychiatry protect them by discrediting the victims. In effect, an ambitious but meticulously-concealed, undeclared *war* on American private citizens is in progress—a psywar.

And *anyone* is a potential casualty.

Footnotes

1. Nathaniel C. Nash, "Inner Voices Demanding Blood: Confession Diary in the Killings of 4 Women," *New York Times,* March 13, 1994, p. 12.

2. Pierre Thomas and Stephanie Griffith, "Navy Officer Fatally Shot at Pentagon," *Washington Post,* May 31, 1991, p. A-1. Also, "'Voices' Led to Tragedy for 2 Men," *Washington Post,* June 1, 1991, and "Suspect in Pentagon Killing is Found Unfit to Stand Trial," *Washington Post,* December 14, 1992, p. D-3.

3. Mediaeko Investigative Reporting Group, "Brain Transmitters: What They Are and How They are Used," October 1993, Stockholm, Sweden, p. 4: "Liquid crystals which are injected directly into the bloodstream" fasten to the brain.

4. Lincoln Lawrence, *Were We Controlled?,* University Books, New York Park, N.Y., 1967, p. 29.

5. Vance Packard, *The Hidden Persuaders,* David McKay, New York, 1957, pp. 239-40.

6. John Marks, *The Search for the Manchurian Candidate: The CIA and Mind Control,* Times Books, New York, 1979, pp. 202-3.

7. Harvey Weinstein, *A Father, a Son and the CIA,* James Lorimer & Co., Toronto, 1988, pp. 89-92.

8. Dick Russell, *The Man Who Knew Too Much,* Carroll & Graf/Richard Gallen, New York, 1992, p. 679.

9. Gordon Thomas, *Journey Into Madness: The True Story of Secret CIA Mind Control and Medical Abuse,* Bantam, New York, 1989, pp. 179-80.

10. Peter H. Breggin, "New Information in the Debate on Psychosurgery," *Congressional Record Extensions of Remarks,* March 30, 1972, pp. 3381 and 3387 fn. Dr. Freeman was also honorary president of the Second International Conference on Psychosurgery in 1970, which drew 100 participants and 41 papers from around the world.

11. Thomas, pp. 179-80.

12. David Remnick, "The Experiments of Dr. D. Ewen Cameron," *Washington Post,* July 28, 1985. Reprinted in the *Congressional Record,* U.S. Government Printing Office, August 1, 1985, p. S1008. Dr. Weinstein told the Post that the experiments left his father "a poor pathetic man with no memory, no life." It was "a nightmare that never ends."

13. Lawrence, p. 52.

14. Harlan E. Girard, "Effects of Gigahertz Radiation on the Human Nervous System: Recent Developments in the Technology of Political Control," a paper presented at the NATO Advanced Research Workshop in Coherent and Emergent Phenomena on Bio-Molecular Systems, University of Arizona, January 15-19, 1991.

15. Marks, pp. 201-02.

16. Julianne McKinney, director of the Electronic Surveillance Project of the Association of National Security Alumni, Silver Springs, Maryland. Telephone interview, April 4, 1994.

17. Thomas, pp. 275-78.

18. Ibid., pp. 275.

19. Donald Freed with Dr. Fred Simon Landis, *Death in Washington: The Murder of Orlando Letelier,* Lawrence Hill, Westport, Connecticut, 1980, p. 90: Former CIA operative William Peter Blatty worked for years beside David Atlee Phillips, who "had been much influenced by the secret dialectic of Blatty's opus *The Exorcist.*" Blatty, like Phillips and H.L. Hunt, another writer of popular fiction, "and a generation of spies, (were) obsessed with communism and the Devil."

20. Marks, p. 209.

21. Lawrence, pp. 53-54.

22. Ibid., p. 34.

23. Walter Bowart, *Operation Mind Control,* Dell, New York, 1978, pp. 261-64.

24. Russell, p. 677.

25. Hugh MacDonald, *Appointment in Dallas,* Zebra, New York, pp. 107-08. Quoted in Russell, p. 675.

26. Russell, pp. 675-76.

27. Bowart, pp. 192-93.

28. Burton Hersh, *The Old Boys: The American Elite and the Origins of the CIA,* Scribner's, New York, 1992, p. 160. For the early brainstorming of Richard Helms on the creation of a hypno-assassin, see Thomas, p. 252.

29. Russell, p. 459.

30. Ruby Keeler, "Remote Mind Control Technology," *Full Disclosure #15.* For a partial reprint, see Jim Keith, ed., *Secret and Suppressed,* Feral House, 1993, p. 16.

31. Bowart, p. 264.

32. Ibid., p. 256.

33. A.J. Weberman, "MIND CONTROL: The Story of Mankind Research Unlimited, Inc.," *Covert Action Information Bulletin,* No. 9, June 1980, p. 20. The directive is provided by MRU upon request.

34. Walter Bowart and Richard Sutton, "The Invisible Third World War," undated *Freedom,* p. 7.

35. Paul Brodeur, *The Zapping of America: Microwaves, Their Deadly Risk and the Cover-Up,* Norton, New York, 1977, p. 291.

36. Ibid., p. 60.

37. Susan Schiefelbein, "The Invisible Threat: The Stifled Story of Electric Waves," *Saturday Review,* September 1, 1979, pp. 17-18.

38. Ibid.

39. Jose M.R. Delgado, "Intracerebral Radio Stimulation and Recording in Completely Free Patients," *Psychotechnology,* Robert L. Schweitzgebel and Ralph K. Schweitzgebel, eds., Holt, Rinehart and Winston, New York, 1973, p. 195.

40. Thomas, p. 250.

41. Larry Collins, "Mind Control," *Playboy,* January 1990, p. 204.

42. Martin Cannon, *The Controllers: A New Hypothesis of Alien Abductions: "Preliminary Version."* Manuscript available from Prevailing Winds Research, Santa Barbara, California, 1989. See pp. 17-29 for a discussion of radio frequencies trained on "alien" abductees.

43. News brief, *Los Angeles Times,* June 5, 1989, p. 2.

44. Subcommittee on Department of Defense Appropriations, "Hearings Before a Subcommittee on Appropriations," House of Representatives, Department of Defense Appropriations for 1966: Part 5: "Research, Development, Testing and Evaluation," U.S. Government Printing Office, 1965, p. 760.

45. Ibid.

46. Weberman, p. 15.

47. Ibid., p. 16.

48. William M. Turner and Jonn G. Christian, *The Assassination of Robert F. Kennedy: A Searching Look at the Conspiracy and Cover-Up 1968-1978*, Random House, New York, p. 197.

49. Dr. Eduard Simson-Kallas, *Affidavit in Behalf of Sirhan Sirhan Presently Serving Time in San Quentin Prison*, March 9, 1973, p. 23.

50. Ibid., p. 15.

51. Christian and Turner, p. 166.

52. Anthony Sampson, *The Arms Bazaar: From Lebanon to Lockheed*, Viking, New York, 1977, p. 276.

53. Christian and Turner.

54. Ibid., pp. 210-11.

55. For an oblique discussion of psychic driving, see D. Ewen Cameron, Leonard Levy and Leonard Rubenstein, "Effects of Repetition of Verbal Signals Upon the Behavior of Chronic Psychoneurotic Patients," *Journal of Mental Science*, vol. 106: no. 443, April 1960, pp. 742-54.

56. Christian and Turner, pp. 225-26.

57. Ibid., pp. 215-16.

58. R.E. Holzer and O.E. Deal, "Low Audio-Frequency Electromagnetic Signals of Natural Origin," *Nature*, vol. 177: no. 4507, March 17, 1956, pp. 536-37.

59. Allan H. Frey, "Technical Note," *Aerospace Medicine*, December 1961, p. 1140. Frey's data were presented at the Aerospace Medical Association Meeting in Chicago, April 14, 1961.

60. Allan H. Frey, "Human Auditory System Response to Modulated Electromagnetic Energy," *Journal of Applied Physiology*, vol. 17: no. 4, July 1962, pp. 689-92.

61. Ibid., p. 692.

62. Ibid., p. 689.

63. Brodeur, pp. 50-53.

64. Ibid., pp. 256-58.

65. Robert O. Becker and Gary Selden, *The Body Electric: Electromagnetic and the Foundation of Life*, William Morrow, New York, 1985, p. 325.

66. Jose M.R. Delgado, *Physical Control of the Mind: Toward a Psychocivilized Society*, Harpers, New York, 1969.

67. Ibid., pp. 89-93, laying down a methodology for "direct communication with the brain."

68. Ford Rowan, *Technospies: The Secret Network that Spies on You*, G.P. Putnam's, New York, 1978, p. 235.

69. Ibid., p. 235.

70. Robert Naeslund, "Brain Transmitter," privately-circulated samizdat, Stockholm, October 1982.

71. Brodeur, p. 298.

72. Rowan, pp. 233-35.

73. Ibid., pp. 232-33.

74. Barton L. Ingraham and Gerald W. Smith, "The Use of Electronics in the Observation and Control of Human Behavior and its Possible Use in Rehabilitation and Parole," *Issues in Criminology,* no. 35, 1972, p. 7.

75. Alan Scheflin, "Freedom of the Mind as an International Human Rights Issue," *Human Rights Law Journal,* vol. 3: no. 1-4, 1982, p. 20. The paper derives from lectures at study sessions of the International Institute of Human Rights, 1981-82. In the introduction, Scheflin maintains that "research designed to explicitly control the thoughts and conduct of free citizens is now not only a reality but the evidence is clear that this research is growing in scope, intensity and financing."

76. Peter Schrag, *Mind Control,* Delta, New York, 1978, p. 3.

77. Rowan, p. 231.

78. Ibid., p. 233.

79. Dale F. Med, "Report Says Loving Machine Could Herald 21st Century," *San Jose Mercury,* August 24, 1973, p. 29. The report was issued at the Third International Joint Conference on Artificial Intelligence at Stanford University.

80. Jean Dietz, "A Suit Over Brain Surgery," *Los Angeles Herald Examiner,* March 21, 1979, p. A-26.

81. Thomas, p. 265.

82. Ibid.

83. Mind control notes of the late Mae Brussell, repositoried in Santa Barbara, California at Prevailing Winds Research.

84. Dietz.

85. Peter Breggin's expose appeared in *Rough Times,* vol. 3: no. 8, Nov.-Dec., 1973, and *Issues in Radical Therapy,* August, 1973. Also see, "Two Boston Doctors Paid to Pacify the 'Violent'—By Cutting Into Their Brains," *The Real Paper,* May 30, 1977.

86. Details of the operation are from the Dietz article and the notes of Mae Brussell.

87. Becker and Seldon, pp. 319-21.

88. "Psychotronics in Engineering" file, *Joint Publications Research Service,* Arlington, Va., September 6, 1974. A copy of the conference proceedings, according to a note on the file, is "available to U.S, Government recipients only."

89. Weberman, p. 16.

90. Michael Hutchinson, *Megabrain: New Tools and Techniques for Brain Growth and Mind Expansion,* Beech Tree, New York, 1986, p. 122.

91. Keeler.

92. Martii Koski, letter to "Mr. Ambassador," August 5, 1980, Edmonton, Alberta, Canada.

93. Naeslund letter.

94. Girard's 1991 NATO address.

95. Kim Murphy, "A Fearful Fix Grips Figure in Kickbacks," *Los Angeles Times*, March 28, 1988, p. B-1.

96. Steven Levy, *The Unicorn's Secret: Murder in the Age of Aquarius*, Prentice Hall, New York, 1988, pp. 242-43.

97. Ibid., pp. 242-43.

98. Bowart, "Invisible Cold War," and Julianne McKinney, telephone interview, April 4, 1994.

99. Larry Wichman, "Who's Killing the *Star Wars Scientists*, *Hustler*, June 1989, p. 70.

100. "Darth Vader's Revenge," *Penthouse*, August 1988.

101. Wichman, p. 68.

102. "Doubts surface over 'suicide' of Defence scientist," *Independent*, September 5, 1989.

103. Capt. Paul E. Taylor, MC, USN, "The Electromagnetic Spectrum in Low-Intensity Conflict," *Low-Intensity Conflict and Modern Technology*, Lt. Col. David J. Dean, USAF, ed., American University Press, 1986, p. 256.

104. Ibid., p. 250.

105. Keeler.

106. "Mysterious radio signals causing concern in Oregon," *Oregon Journal*, March 8, 1978, p. 1.

107. Becker and Seldon, p. 323.

108. "EPA Joins Probe of Odd signals," *Chico Enterprise-Record*, March 28, 1978, p. C-3.

109. Andrew Michrowski, letter to "The Right Honourable Prime Minister Pierre E. Trudeau," Ottawa, September 19, 1978. Michrowski notes, "it is 'official policy' at NRC (the National Research Council) to refute any psycho-physiological effects of ELF phenomena."

110. Levy, p. 242.

111. Girard (see fn. 14).

112. Julianne McKinney, Association of National Security Alumni, in correspondence with Catherine Gould, chairwoman of the Los Angeles County Commission for Women's Task Force on Ritual Abuse, February 8, 1993.

113. An Awakened Sleeper Unit, "Secret Service Masers Kill and Make Whores!" *Steamshovel Press*, Spring 1994, pp. 26-27.

114. "Flying Saucers—The Real Story: U.S. Built One in 1942," *U.S. News and World Report*, vol. 28: no. 14, April 7, 1950, p. 13.

115. Cannon ms.

116. Ibid.

117. Julianne McKinney interview, April 4.

Chapter Two

Blue Smoke & Lasers

SDI as a Cover Story for the R&D of Electromagnetic/Cybernetic Mind Control Technology

In 1976 William Bise, director of the Pacific Northwest Center for the Study of Non-Ionizing Radiation in Portland, compiled a report on "Radio-Frequency Induced Interference Responses in the Human Nervous System." Dr. Bise's experiments demonstrated that the irradiation of four of his human subjects in an electromagnetic field of 65-90 microvolts per meter caused impairment of memory and concentration. The Pacific Northwest experiments were a small part of a sprawling research effort, conceived by the Department of Defense toward the development of an arsenal of electromagnetic (EM) weapons, often sweetened in public by military spokesmen as "non-lethal."[1]

True, the biological effects of low-intensity EMR are scarcely more than an annoyance. The famous Taos hum, a baffling low-frequency vexation first reported in 1989 by residents of northern New Mexico, was one of several incidents of urban radio-frequency (RF) saturation. At the time, scientific investigators were unable to explain the low-pitch rumble blamed for a sudden outbreak of headaches, nosebleeds, dizziness and a general feeling of discomfort.[2] (A few years later, it emerged that Los Alamos Labs in Albuquerque had in development EM weapons capable of producing the same effects. The non-lethal defense program is run by John Alexander, an Army veteran, psychic enthusiast and walking *Terrorist's Cookbook* with a doctorate in Thanatology, the study of death.[3])

But "non-lethal'" weapons are potentially no more "humane" than the conventional type—a simple RF pulse can kill as readily, and as painfully, as a fusillade of black talons.

Columnist Jack Anderson mused in 1985: "Can the human mind be short-circuited or even destroyed by extremely low-frequency radio waves? Preposterous as such an idea may seem, scientists on both sides of the Iron Curtain have been conducting secret tests. Reputable scientists say they could be developed into yet another grisly weapon of mass destruction."[4]

Brain researchers told Anderson that American and Soviet scientists were close to perfecting a mechanism that interferes with the electrical signals of the brain with remote transmissions of EM radiation. "This interference," Anderson reported, "could extend to 'switching off' the brain's vital functions—that is, killing the targeted victims."

But scientists with CIA and military contracts have, for forty years, made it apparent they could produce devastating biological effects with EM radiation much earlier than Anderson's sources let on. In the mid-60s, for instance, State University of New York Professors Howard Friedman and Robert O. Becker, the Nobel laureate, and Charles Bachman, a physicist at Syracuse University, studied the effects of EM radiation on 28,642 patients at seven veterans' hospitals.[5] (However churlish, the study was the norm for a government now known to have tested radioactive isotopes on mental patients, and chemical warfare agents billeted from the Golden Gate Bridge.) Scientists at UCLA probed the brain in the 1960s, mapped out the synapses responsive to electromagnetic stimulation. Today, the university oversees experimentation at Los Alamos and Lawrence Livermore labs. Both have developed radio-biological weapons that appear to be a continuation of the brain studies, realizing their dystopian potential. Livermore, of course, has been a central participant in SDI since September 1982 when Edward Teller, the lab's founder, suggested the laser shield concept to Reagan. (The Father of the H-Bomb had coincidentally received 40,000 shares in a company engaged in laser research, later found to have defrauded investors.[6])

Remote mind control is not a recent breakthrough in "non-lethal" technology.

In 1965 the Pentagon's Advanced Research Project Agency set up Project PANDORA, the top-secret search for military applications of microwaves. Seven years later, the Army issued a classified report, noting: "it is possible to field a truck-portable microwave barrier system that will completely immobilize personnel in the open with present-day technology and equipment."[7]

Only recently has the barrier cannon been rolled out of the Pentagon's burgeoning vault of black projects. One NASA report written in 1970 by Thomas Fryer of Ames Research Labs concerned "Implantable Biotelemetry Systems" (the gadgets that turn up with unnerving regularity in the bodies of UFO abductees).

A 1976 DIA report mentions "anti-personnel applications" of pulsed microwaves that carry "sounds and possibly even words which appear to be originating intercranially."[8]

The Reagan administration intensified the push into EM weapons development. Dr. Michael Persinger, a neurologist at Ontario's Laurentian University, found that extremely low frequency fields could induce nausea, depression, panics, etc. Persinger's research was mustered under Reagan's secret, brain-scrambling Project S Sleeping Beauty.[9]

Other experiments were cloaked by the Strategic Defense Initiative— hardly inconsistent for a country with a long history of political scandals rising like a bad smell from the national security branch of government, from the U-2's Soviet adventure to Watergate to uranium testing on urban populations to the landing of cocaine shipments in Mena, Arkansas. Star Wars is, in fact, a cover story.

Paul Brodeur, in *The Zapping of America*, dissects available SDI data at length, concluding:

> "All the talk about death rays and charged particle beams has been little more than an elaborate smokescreen designed to hide the fact that the United States is developing a directed energy weapon that uses a high-power microwave pulse."[10]

If Star Wars is indeed a superficial public relations effort conceived to obscure a massive military push into mind control technology, the evidence must lie just beneath the surface, a colossal shadow R&D effort difficult to completely conceal. Behind the Star Wars front, funds would flow from legitimate to illicit programs, dropping through a hole in the floor.

That's precisely what happened. SDI funding was channeled into hidden research efforts. In early 1993, Aldric Saucier, a scientist for the Army's ballistic defense command with long experience in space research, complained to the House Government Operations Committee that Star Wars was cursed by a chronic diversion of funds. He estimated that as much as *half* of the entire SDI budget had disappeared into classified projects. "Millions of dollars in research awards were shifted from one program to another," he testified. Participants in the covert R&D effort even spoke in code words, referring to the diversions as "taxes" or "I.O.U.'s."

Saucier's blast at Star Wars appeared in the March 9, 1993 *New York Times*. He blew a shrill whistle at the "hundreds of millions diverted to secret programs." Yet Congress was assured that the funds had been used as directed. Dr. Saucier summed up SDI as a "high-risk, space-age national security pork barrel for contractors and top government managers," and a "serious obstacle to a strong national defense because of systematic illegality." He complained of egregious abuses of power, "the substitution of political method for the scientific method."[11]

Slippery accounting aside, if the true aim of SDI is the development of pulsed-microwave weapons, key defense firms would quietly merge to combine the fields of microwave technology and biology, a dangerous liaison in the shadow of Brilliant Pebbles. In fact, corporate shuffling behind SDI *does* reveal the hybrid and the technocracy behind it. A scandalous case in point is the move by Fiat, the most powerful corporation in Italy, into the American circle of competition for SDI contracts. On September 25, 1986, John Maresca, deputy assistant secretary of defense, wrote a memo to Richard Perle, then assistant secretary in charge of international policy, about legal papers drawn up a month earlier setting up "the FIAT Trading Company of North America as FIAT's sole conduit for doing business with DoD," an accord "sufficient to allow FIAT and its subsidiaries to compete for SDI research contracts.... It remains to be seen what reaction Congress will have to the situation."[12]

But the Congressional response was predictable enough. Muommar Ghaddaffi was an outgoing director of Fiat. His shares were abruptly snatched up by the company for $3.1 billion under arrangements made by Germany's Deutsche Bank. Some of the funds were laundered by a Fiat front company used since the early '80s to ship missile parts to Argentina and Libya in violation of an international ban on the transfer of high technology components through Germany's Bayerische Hypotheken and Weschel und Chase Manhattan, as detailed in an affidavit filed by a U.S. Customs agent in the eastern district court of California in 1988.[13]

Under the control of Italy's Agnelli family, Fiat has since the turn of the century been cozy with totalitarian political regimes, Hitler's and Mussolini's among them.[14]

The EM mind control initiative lurking behind the Star Wars cover story would appeal to a man of Fiat chairman Gianni Agnelli's domineering temper. In fact, he positively lusted after after an SDI contract. The Fiat board's divestment of the Libyan interest was intended to reassure critics of Agnelli in Reagan's own administration that the company would not be a security risk.

United Technologies, a heavily-subsidized extension of the Pentagon and a Fiat partner, had already drawn the Italians into the Star Wars sphere. United is the former stomping ground of Knight of Malta Alexander Haig, Clark MacGregor, a campaign manager for Nixon, and Edward Hennessy, a senior VP groomed for corporate control—by Harold Geneen of ITT—who left in 1979 to run Allied Chemical Corp.

Agnelli proposed joining SNIA, a Fiat subsidiary (the very same stung selling classified electronic missile components to Libya and Argentina), with Star Wars. With Ghaddaffi off the board of directors, he paved the way by merging SNIA with Bioengineering International BV, a Dutch-held medical technology firm.

The multi-billion dollar question is this: What does a space-based, anti-ballistic defense system have to do with biotechnology?

The SNIA board of directors was apprised by Chairman Cesare Romiti, according to Alan Friedman in a biography of Agnelli, that the merger was a "diversification from arms to the high-tech medical field."[15]

Yet SNIA was the subsidiary upon which Agnelli had been pinning his hopes of a role in SDI. SNIA is a space contractor, a producer of orbital transfer and guidance systems. The merger with Bioengineering was altogether inconsistent with space-based defense, but not with the Defense Department's classified EM weapons program.

It might be argued that the Fiat subsidiaries play a minor role in SDI, a small satellite in a big sky. But a report of the Council on Economic Priorities found that 87% of the SDI contracts awarded in 1983–84 went to only ten major defense firms. Eight of these were selected from among the DoD's twenty leading private contractors.[16]

Critics of Star Wars give further credence to Brodeur's argument that the program is a smokescreen. Most major news outlets, Mark Hertsgaard finds in *On Bended Knee,* have been "implicitly critical, if only because [reporting on SDI] exposed unwelcome truths about the system; most tellingly, that it would not work the way Reagan said it would, and that it would cost a fortune to develop. SDI was such an obviously flawed and perilous idea that it provoked considerable unease among influential members of the American academy, Congress and foreign policy and arms control communities.... A survey of National Academy of Science members found top scientists opposed to SDI developments by an eight-to-one margin."

Reagan's SDI proposal was conceived in a scientific vacuum. Historian A. Hunter Dupree wrote in a 1986 *Nature* article that the decision to fund SDI "was made without peer review, and no advice from scientists was sought or received." The funds were allocated, scarce specialists mustered, "without the slightest review or evaluation by the scientific community as to whether the project should be undertaken at all. This dangerous departure from postwar practice is unique."[17]

To quell opposition, Star Wars officials falsified research data. Four anonymous officials of the Reagan administration admitted in August 1993 that the deception was approved by then Secretary of Defense Caspar Weinberger, according to the *New York Times,* "to persuade the Soviet empire to cripple itself with debt."[18] This is sheer spin. If the motive was to deceive the Soviets, the Pentagon had no reason to submit falsified test data to closed Congressional briefings. A total of $36 billion has been spent on SDI development, much of the expenditure based on erroneous trials.

After three dismal failures, one test was rigged in June 1984, supposedly to fool the Kremlin. But it was clear in an account given by a project scientist that fudging test data was not an economic warfare gambit. "We would lose hundreds of dollars in Congress if we did not perform it successfully," the scientist said. "It would be a catastrophe. We put a beacon with a certain frequency on the target vehicle. On the interceptor, we had a receiver. The hit looked beautiful, so Congress did not ask questions."

The flimflam was inspired by sheer, self-serving financial expediency. SDI technocrats lied to their Congressional paymasters while the public watched panoramic cartoons of Brilliant Pebbles decimating a swarm of nukes on the evening news.

John Tirman, a director of the Winston Foundation for World Peace and an SDI critic, responded by editorializing that the entire program was a "hoax." Tirman: "The very idea of 'Star Wars'—an 'umbrella' that would shield America from Soviet nuclear warheads—was itself a massive deception. No knowledgeable scientist thought for a moment that such a shield was feasible. Yet the Pentagon proceeded with this fraud as if Reagan's fanciful notion had merit. What's more, other faked tests followed in 1990 and 1991, after the Soviet 'threat' had disappeared."[19]

Even the lofty Edward Teller has been charged with falsifying test data on "Super Excalibur," a nuclear-powered X-ray laser built by Lawrence Livermore Labs, in actuality a space-based red herring for the oversight committees to chew on.[20]

In 1988, investigators from a score of federal agencies and Congressional offices searched the premises and interviewed Livermore staffers. "For the first time in the lab's history," the *Los Angeles Times* reported, "key members of its leadership have broken ranks and gone public with tales of internal disarray." Roy Woodruff, formerly the director of Livermore's weapons program, accused Teller of deceiving Washington and the public with false information on the X-ray laser, the "centerpiece of the Strategic Defense Initiative." (Super Excalibur was killed in July 1992 anyway when the Energy Department canceled the tests without making a public announcement.[21] The official explanation was that the Bush administration, by abandoning the X-ray laser, code-named "Greenwater," was implementing a policy of nuclear test limitations after tens of millions of dollars had been spent.)

Critics of SDI, Woodruff said, "were saying that a system couldn't be based in space because it would require a tremendous energy supply and would be vulnerable to attack." Disinformation on "Greenwater," he said, was intended to curtail scientific objections. "They needed a little magic, and aha! Guess what? A little magic! Very classified so you can't review it or talk about it. No power-supply problem because it uses a hydrogen bomb."

Super Excalibur was fraudulent even in conception as an anti-missile system. "It has little potential for actually defending against ballistic attack," Woodruff emphasized. "It just wasn't that capable a laser. So if the program goals had been met, if indeed we were entering the engineering phase, as Teller said, what we would've had was a weapon that was capable of attacking satellites and defending satellites at great distances. If you have a very big satellite—a neutral particle beam accelerator, a big chemical laser, a garage full of kinetic-kill vehicles—this X-ray laser weapon has the potential to destroy those things." In other words, the weapon was not even an anti-ballistic system, as Teller claimed.[22]

Besides, there was nothing original about Lawrence Livermore's X-ray laser, which smelled suspiciously like the "Modulated Electron-Gun X-Ray Nuclear Booster" patented by the McFarlane Corporation, a private engineering firm, in 1965. The schematics and a prototype of the device were pirated by NASA, according to a McFarlane executive in hearings before the House subcommittee on DoD appropriations the following year. Company literature explained that the orbital laser was suited, among other things, to "electromagnetic radiation telemetering and death ray applications", a design, again, never intended for anti-ballistics.

Teller sold the citizenry a costly bill of goods. Aldric Saucier recalls that he "was present once when Dr. Edward Teller of the University of California National Laboratory said he needed $20 million for more studies of an already-completed experiment on the X-ray laser. Then S.D.I. director Gen. James Abrahamson responded to the effect that he could go ahead."[23]

Teller's interests, beyond capricious misapplications of nuclear technology, include "non-lethal defense." In November 1993, Dr. Teller was a featured speaker at a conference on electromagnetic weapons at Johns Hopkins University in Laurel, Maryland, sponsored by Los Alamos National Laboratory, chaired by the aforementioned Doctor of Death, John Alexander. Another key speaker at the conference was Clay Easterly of the Oak Ridge National Laboratory, addressing the fine points of the "Application of Extremely Low Frequency Electromagnetic Fields to Non-Lethal Weapons."[24]

The military-industrial sector was heavily represented at the conference by McDonnell Douglas, Tracor Aerospace, Martin Marietta, Northrop, Lockheed, Westinghouse and Boeing's defense and space groups.[25]

The major multinational SDI contractors held much more than a passing interest in orbital EM weapons technology capable of controlling and switching off the brain. So does the Pentagon, represented at the EM weapons conference by scientists from the U.S. Army Research Lab, the Special Operations Command, the Marine Corps Intelligence Center and the Advanced Research Projects Agency (ARPA).

Further evidence that Star Wars covers for radio-biological warfare is the staggering mortality rate of scientists involved in the program, particularly the colorful "suicides" of 23 SDI engineers in Great Britain. Harlan Girard, a scientist and subject of continuous microwave harassment by the military for his outspoken criticism of electromagnetic mind control projects, told high-brow attendees of a 1991 NATO conference on emergent technologies that the British technocrats had in common connections to the U.S. Navy.[26] Not improbable. The Navy has funded academic research on distant evoked responses and the brain-manipulating effects of gigahertz radiation on human subjects, in coordination with the

CIA, for decades. (Out of this research came the 10 milliwatt safety standard, set in the early 1950s by Herman Schwan, a repatriated Nazi scientist. Schwan hailed from the Kaiser Wilhelm Institute of Biophysics in Germany, and settled in the U.S. after the war to teach bio-engineering and physical medicine at the University of Pennsylvania.)[27]

The enduring mystery of the Star Wars "suicides" was foreshadowed on July 9, 1986 with the murder-by-bombing of the research director of West Germany's Siemens Co., yet another electronics conglomerate, said to have been negotiating with the Pentagon on an SDI contract. Next to go was a German bureaucrat, a diplomatic liaison to the Strategic Defense Initiative Organization, shot dead, quickly followed by an Italian Star Wars consultant.[28] A leftist brigade of terrorists was held responsible for the murders, but no arrests were made.

A pattern to the killings in Great Britain begins with the fact that seven of the scientists worked for Marconi, a subsidiary of General Electric. At the time, Marconi was under investigation for bribing and defrauding ministers of government. But Britain's MoD found "no evidence" linking the deaths. Blame for the sudden outbreak of suicides among Marconi engineers was laid on stress.[29] (Another unlikely explanation was given for the "hum" in Bristol, home of Marconi, a low-frequency noise like that in Taos, New Mexico, in this instance blamed on "frogs.") Jonathan Walsh. a digital communications specialist at Marconi, was assigned to the secretive Martlesham Heath Research Laboratory under a General Electric contract.[30] (GE has long led the field in the development of anti-personnel electronic weapons, an interest that gestated with participation in Project Comet, the Pentagon-based research program to explore the psychological effects of frequencies on the electromagnetic spectrum.) Walsh dropped from his hotel window in November 1985.

None of the Star Wars "suicides" were specialists in laser research or space-based missiles. All worked in advanced electronics or computer systems with military applications. Many were attached to the Royal Military College of Science, an authority on electronic surveillance, communications and weaponry.[31] They were employed on secret projects. Supposedly Star Wars was an open book. From the start, Reagan invited all friendly nations to contribute to the defense system. Major developments were to be publicized, not squandered in secret laboratories.

As is... oh, for instance... microwave brain telemetering from a remote source. *That* technology was *very* secret. John Alexander wrote in the December 1980 number of *Military Review* that "there are weapons systems that operate on the power of the mind and whose lethal capacity has already been demonstrated."[32] Star Wars was an ideal cover story, because the technology of radio-biological (or "psychic") warfare was in part a spin-off of the advanced physiological monitoring instruments used in space flight.[33]

EM-pulse mind control experimentation takes place inside a fog of secrecy and disinformation. Behind the Star Wars murders, if not an inside job or the work of the CIA, are other likely culprits. Iran, for instance, then at war with Iraq, had highly-placed connections in British intelligence, among them Michael Heseltine, soon to be England's Minister of Defense. Heseltine was the sole shareholder of Royal Ordnance, Inc., a military explosives manufacturer that traded with the Khomeini regime in violation of a ban on on the export of sensitive technology to Third World dictatorships.[34] (Heseltine was also Gianni Agnelli's British supplier in the aforementioned sale of missile components to Muommar Ghaddaffi.)

Iraq was preparing to graduate from conventional to "non-lethal" EM weapons. Khomeini's intelligence operatives may have learned of Iraq's trade with Marconi and the transfer of secret technology through an intelligence source in the British government. Iranian terrorists were already active in the UK. The stresses in the background of the Iran-Iraq war could explain the attacks on electromagnetic weapons designers and programming specialists.

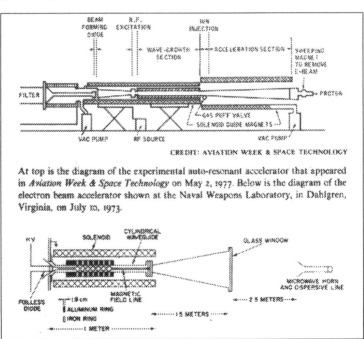

At top is the diagram of the experimental auto-resonant accelerator that appeared in *Aviation Week & Space Technology* on May 2, 1977. Below is the diagram of the electron beam accelerator shown at the Naval Weapons Laboratory, in Dahlgren, Virginia, on July 10, 1973.

Physicist Paul Brodeur, mystified by Pentagon disinformation regarding SDI, examined a schematic for an "Electron Beam Accelerator" of the type to be incorporated—supposedly—in space-based defense. Brodeur discovered that the weapon was in reality a device capable of generating a powerful EM pulse. All of this is recounted in Brodeur's *Zapping of America*, which features a chapter on mind control technology.

An Iranian backlash was predictable since, according to the *London Times*, "the twin focuses of British and American policy towards the arming of Iraq lay in the identification of Iran as the enemy," with diversions of cash to defense companies in England and the U.S. "supplying Baghdad through the Banca Nazionale del Lavoro (BNL) branch in Atlanta."[35]

The intrigue was heightened by fierce competition among the multi-nationals for Star Wars contracts. Many of these shared with Fiat and GE sordid histories of selling advanced military technology to repressive military regimes. Saddam Hussein placed a priority on microwave weapons. His strategy of waging "unconventional" warfare was not possible without support from executives of the major defense firms in NATO countries. One of England's closest competitors in the microwave communications business is Thomson-CSF, an electronics conglomerate run by the French government. In the 1980s, Thomson, pitted against Plessey Defense Systems in England, won a lucrative contract with Iraq. Initial payments were made by the infamous BNL, which collapsed in 1989.

In *The Death Lobby,* Kenneth Timmerman describes how Thomson and BNL assisted Iraq's expansion into electronic warfare. "The project was given the code name Saad 13. The $1 billion contact was barely mentioned in the French press and was treated as a virtual state secret in times to come. At one point Thomson even tried to deny it had ever signed such a deal, although thousands of Thomson engineers were involved at different times." The idea, a Thomson vice president said, was to "give the Iraqis a tool for the future. It was certainly the most ambitious project of its kind undertaken in a Third World country."[36]

The carnage among Star Wars scientists was coincident with the rivalry between Marconi and Plessey in Great Britain, and Thomson-CSF in France. Two of the deceased were employees of Plessey: Michael Baker, a digital communications specialist, killed in May 1987 when his BMW careened through a road barrier, and Frank Jennings, an electronic weapons engineer, dead of a heart attack a month later. The British gained the upper hand over France in dealings with Iraq by loaning Saddam Hussein a unit of Special Air Service (SAS) commandos to train his secret police, the Iraqi Special Forces. Timmerman: "In 1985 the French had lost two large contracts to British electronics companies. Marconi signed a contract to supply 'troposcatter' microwave transmitters that Thomson-CSF thought it had won. The transmitters allowed Iraqi forces to dispatch orders from Baghdad to the southern front without relying on telephone lines (and they confounded allied intelligence during Operation Desert Storm.)"[37] Intense competition among defense firms, and illicit trade in secret technology with warring dictatorships, was the backdrop to the British deaths. Conditions were rife for such skullduggery.

So were the microwave devices sold to Iraq. The troposcatter microwave transmitter, with a few modifications, could be transformed into a powerful offensive weapon. Myron Wolbarscht, an ophthalmologist at Duke University and the author of a book on emergent technologies, warns: "Microwave weapons used to disrupt an opponent's communications could 'fry' any soldiers hit by them as well."[38]

Marconi and Thomson-CSF share a common interest in microwave communications. Devices like the troposcatter are in the same technical genus as the Gyrotron resonance maser, a machine that talks to the brain. An article in *21st Century Science & Technology* outlines the workings of a resonance maser. The device surrounds and penetrates the entire body in an EM flux, and beams into it a microwave communications field. A laser, like the needle of light on a compact disk, reads changes in electrons after passing through the body. A computerized CAT scan sorts the frequencies of the brain and five senses. The maser, with pulsed-power source, fits inside a truck. With it, the encyclopedia claims, "special forces trained in radio-biological warfare could wipe out entire officer corps, divisions and battalions."[39]

Masers, not lasers, are the hidden thrust of "Star Wars." The weapon is an extremely sophisticated mind and body machine capable of thought transfer, manipulation of emotions and muscle control. Images, even dreams, can be beamed to the subject. A human or cybernetic controller can carry on a conversation telepathically, and at the same time instill physical sensations, subliminal commands, emotions and visual and aural hallucinations. Computerized EM devices that talk and transmit images to the brain were current when Reagan delivered his first SDI pitch in 1983. Harlan Girard, in his NATO address on emergent technologies eight years later, said: "Experiments had produced some communications equipment that far exceeded the ability to broadcast defeat into the minds of the enemy," an objective of DoD brass. "It is not only capable of producing auditory hallucinations, but visual hallucinations as well."[40]

"Is it possible," asks John Lambros, a prisoner at Leavenworth and mind control experimentee (a claim he corroborates with an X-ray of four strand-shaped foreign objects in his head) "that the particle beam intended for enemy missiles alone might now be intended for human minds?"[41]

The electronic battlefield has been armed for some time. GTE, for instance, has had an electronic weapons division since the 1950s, then headed by William Perry, Clinton's secretary of defense. And in the 1960s executives of Honeywell, the Franco-American computer firm (and Star Wars contractor), told author Lincoln Lawrence that the company was experimenting with machines that "penetrate a man's mind and control his brain waves over long distance."[42]

The Microwave Mafia often rely on the implantation of miniaturized radio receivers. The technique is known as intra-cerebral control and uses radio or ultra-sound. It was developed by the CIA's MKDRACO and

HATTER brain telemetry projects. The implantation of a micro-receiver in the frontal or temporal lobes by trained teams of operatives is done with an "encaphalator," usually through the sinuses of a drugged subject.[43]

But the current state of the art in Radio-Hypnotic Intracerebral Control (RHIC) depends upon "Personal Radio and Electromagnetic Frequency Allocation," or PREMA, a frequency unique to the subject's brain. A "reading wand" is hidden near the victim, who is scanned by an instrument smaller than a briefcase. Once the "Freak" is determined, the brain becomes a link in a cybernetic system, and the subject (or a group) can communicate, be surveilled, guided, manipulated, harassed or controlled from afar.[44]

The mind-invasive technology lurking behind the Star Wars cover story became the fascination of Brian Wronge, a victim of prison experiments in New York state.[45] Wronge claims that the mind control fraternity has developed a "gallium scan" to map electrical activity of the brain, and in concert with a transmitter linked to the nervous system, beam radio-biological signals to an analog computer or satellite.

Skeptics should note that that implant technology is not strictly the domain of covert federal agencies. On October 17, 1994 the *London Times* ran a story on medical advances in microchip implantation, "Bionic Man Comes of Age," no less futuristic than gyrotronic mind taps or PREMA Freak scanners. "Over the past decade," the *Times* reported, "more than 15,000 people worldwide have had electronic components implanted into their brains. In a procedure confined until recently to the fantasies of science fiction, microchips are now being routinely placed beneath the skull into brain stems. In many cases, these devices are connected to platinum wires, which are then fused and buried in the brain."

Some of the *commercially* available implants can "think": "Through the use of microchip technology, they can interface with the brain, provide complex instructions to mechanical parts and monitor brain activity." In the last ten years, progress in microtechnology has made possible "artificial vision," and paralyzed patients have only to think to produce "a characteristic electrical wave pattern that is detected by sensors implanted in the brain. The sensors then send an electrical signal to a microprocessor chip implanted in the patient's shoulder." The chip responds with electrical instructions to a mass of tiny implants linked to several dozen nodes in the right arm. The paralyzed muscle fibers contract, and the arm lifts.[46]

The monitoring of a patient's vital signs from a remote source, discussed in the *Journal of Biomedical Engineering* in 1993, relies on an advanced VHF telemetry station, another commercially-available system. A computer amplifies and digitizes the signal from an implanted transmitter, analyzes it and displays the data on a personal computer monitor.[47]

But not all commercially-sold brain machines are approved by the AMA. Anyone with a bank account and a score to settle can order by mail the schematics for a crude "Electronic Brainblaster" from a small electronics firm in Alamogordo, New Mexico. The company bills itself as "the national clearinghouse for survival information," and claims that the machine was developed "to produce healing and curative effects." But "we coincidentally discovered that, if you use certain EM coil configurations, wave forms and intensities, a powerfully destructive, deadly-silent and instantaneous weapon is produced!"

The Brainblaster is a true electromagnetic-pulse weapon and—like the EM devices in the Pentagon's "non-lethal" arsenal—interferes violently with brain waves. The heart of the machine, according to company literature, is the formidable "Cycle Slicer": "simple and inexpensive to build... basically a crude, bludgeoning device used primarily to inflict physical pain and cause brain hemorrhaging." With exposure to the Brainblaster's EMFs, "severe behavioral changes, some associated with mental illness, can result. Behavioral changes include bizarre and erratic behavior, increased reaction times, panic, confusion, hyperactivity, manic-compulsive behavior, dizziness, hallucinations, personality disassociations, delirium, incoherence, frenzy, tremors and jerkiness, headache, ears ringing, nausea," and so on. The company recommends testing the Brainblaster on animals, since "the life of one strong, intelligent, and capable Freedom-loving patriot is more important than the lives of many animals." An EM Brainblaster, of course, "can provide the patriot and his loved ones with an effective weapon for destroying the enemies of his family, region, nation or culture."

If a neo-Nazi mail-order house can openly hawk the EM Brainblaster, the comic-book technology at the far end of the classified military technology lag must be breathtaking. Word of remote-viewing devices and cybernetic surveillance systems has leaked to the surface of the national security underground.

And the technology isn't gathering dust. Since the advent of SDI, reports of sadistic EMR harassment of private citizens have escalated. One report filed with the Association of National Security Alumni in February 1992 concerns "a woman in Dayton, Ohio, whose husband is employed at Wright-Patterson AFB as a civilian electronics engineer. Coincidentally, he works in a top secret vault on a project focusing on 'transitional technologies.'" The husband's top-secret work took him to the Industrial College of the Armed Forces (ICAF) in Fort McNair, Virginia in the mid-1980s. While he was away, college administrators insisted that his wife undergo extensive psychological evaluation. She was told that "data obtained from these exams would be used to keep their marriage and family intact, since her husband's job tended to be stress-inducing." She returned home from college and "became the target of massive electronic harassment and may have been drugged on recurrent occasions." She talked to doctors. None of them could explain her physical and psychological pain. Her husband took no interest. She asked him to sweep their home electronically, but he claimed to know nothing about the necessary equipment.

She contacted McKinney's Electronic Surveillance Project in Silver Spring, Maryland, a group that monitors EM harassment, in November 1992. (McKinney's project is a spin-off of the Association of National Security Alumni, an organization that opposes excesses of the intelligence community. Members on the ANSA board have written and lectured widely on America's covert misadventures, including Phillip Roettinger, David MacMichael, Peter Dale Scott, Phillip Agee and Daniel Ellsberg.) "Within two days," McKinney says, "her husband had her forcibly hospitalized in a psychiatric ward at Good Samaritan, claiming that she had established contact with a 'Jonestown'-type network and had become suicidal as a consequence. Her husband cooperated by lying in a court-approved affidavit for purposes of prolonging her hospitalization." During her forced restraint, the hospital ward was "flooded with patients who were complaining of 'hearing voices.'" They were prescribed stupefying drugs and left to their own devices. The electrical engineer's wife has since moved to Columbus, Ohio, but the EM assault on her continues.[48]

In this instance, the subject's torment was linked to a military base, but experimentation and harassment with classified EMR weapons can occur anywhere. The technology itself derives from any academic or commercial military-industrial sector. McKinney speaks of "active involvement on the part of the DoD and certain DoD contractors — the Boeing Corporation being one of many." She alleges that intensive R&D is also underway at Northrop, the Newbury Park, California aerospace firm. She suspects that EM stimulation from a remote source drove Alan Winterbourne, a computer systems engineer, to his killing spree at a Ventura County unemployment office on December 2, 1993.[49] Winterbourne, like the berserker SDI "suicides" in England, was engaged in highly-classified projects. He hinted darkly to his sister Carol, "they're working on terrible things at Northrop that would kill millions of innocent people. Things you can't imagine." Before resigning from Northrop, Winterbourne had complained that his co-workers were harassing him. He suspected that his phone was tapped. The paranoia began after he'd written a letter to his Congressman maintaining that the company was engaged in illegalities, and requested a federal investigation.[50]

McKinney has also found secret EMR weapons development at General Electric, Northern Telecom, TRW and other engines of the Defense Department. The number of firms engaged in mind control R&D is kept small by the need for secrecy. But "non-lethal" technology is increasingly in demand by police agencies. Army officials have taken to touting the new "dual-use" technology—a euphemism for weapons with military and law enforcement applications. (*The Los Angeles Times* noted without so much as a giggle that "experts" believed domestic proliferation of "non-lethal" weapons "could provide jobs for smaller firms.")[51]

But on inevitable occasions, the technology has found its way into the hands of terrorists. In September 1984, for example, the neo-Nazi cadre known as The Order launched the "Reliance Project" EM mind control operation. According to an FBI affidavit reprinted in *The Brotherhood of Murder,* by Thomas Martinez and John Guinther, Order leaders paid $100,000 to "two former government scientists who had been involved in a secret United States scientific experiment dealing with the transmission of electronic signals or waves at particular frequencies which serve to render people more docile and subservient." And "experiments were being conducted that will allow persons with the knowledge to take a lock of hair from another and by some scientific process, project a chemical imbalance in that person."[52]

The hinges of PANDORA's box creak in the wind. The American arsenal of psychoactive weapons, Michael Hutchinson writes in *Megabrain,* is the product of "a vast underground network of bio-electricians busily tinkering away with electromagnetic devices that could potentially change the world."[53] Instead, the technology is applied to "mind control, moving objects with mind power," to "the potential for mentally shutting down computers, missile-guidance systems, satellites." Hutchinson, once a mind control skeptic, concludes that his worst paranoid fantasies were "accepted by electronics experts as facts of life."

The growing importance of EM weapons to the DoD was implied in the promotion of William Perry to Secretary of Defense by Bill Clinton in 1994. Perry was "the favorite of the Joint Chiefs of Staff," noted the *Los Angeles Times.* He was chosen in 1954 by GTE to direct the company's electronic defense lab.[54] Twelve years later he was installed as president of ESL, Inc., an electronics company engaged in some of the Pentagon's murkiest black projects—including Area 51, the secret military base in the sprawling desert wasteland north of Las Vegas. (ESL has since been acquired by TRW, a key Star Wars contractor.)[55]

Periodically, Congress beats the drum for "strategic defense." If SDI advocates have their way, the EM-frustrating Faraday Cage may someday become all the rage, like the backyard bomb shelter of old.

Footnotes

1. Paul Brodeur, *The Zapping of America: Microwaves, Their Deadly Risk and the Cover-Up* (New York: Norton, 1977), p. 299.

2. Matt Creenson, "Taos Hum not just in your head, Survey confirms mystery noises," *Knight-Ridder News Service,* message #20758, AEN News computer network.

3. Armen Victorian, "Non-Lethality: John B. Alexander, the Pentagon's Penguin," *Para/Net,* Cairn, Queensland, p. 40.

4. Jack Anderson, "Exotic Weaponry is Checked," reprint from July, 1985.

5. Lincoln Lawrence, *Were We Controlled?* (New Hyde Park: University Books, 1967), p. 40.

6. "Physicist Teller's Denial in a Story of Free Stock," *San Francisco Chronicle,* June 1, 1983.

7. Brodeur, p. 296.

8. Ibid., p. 295.

9. Joe Vialls, "Real Life Death Rays," *AEN News Computer Network,* 1994.

10. Brodeur, p. 279.

11. "Scientist Said to Assert Fraud in 'Star Wars,'" *New York Times,* March 2, 1992, p. A-1. Also see, John Cushman, Jr., "Whistleblower Wins Study of 'Star Wars' Program," *New York Times,* March 3, 1992, p. A-13, and Aldric Saucier, "Lost in Space," *New York Times,* March 3, 1992, p. A-17.

12. Alan Friedman, *Agnelli and the Network of Italian Power* (London: Harrap, 1988), p. 191.

13. Ibid., p 232.

14. Jeff Madrick, *Taking America: How We Got from the First Hostile Takeover to Megamergers, Corporate Raiding, and Scandal* (New York: Bantam, 1987), pp. 36-39.

15. Friedman, pp. 204-7.

16. Mark Hertsgaard, *On Bended Knee: The Press and the Reagan Presidency* (New York: Farrar Straus Giroux, 1988), p. 285.

17. Ibid., pp. 285 and 295.

18. Phil Reeves, "Star Wars 'Fake' Fooled the World," *London Independent,* August 19, 1993, p. 8 (based on the *New York Times* story).

19. John Tirman, "A Big Hoax to Match a Big Lie," *Los Angeles Times,* August 20, 1993, p. B-7.

20. Robert Scheer, "The Man Who Blew the Whistle on 'Star Wars,'" *Los Angeles Times,* July 17, 1988, pp. 7, 8 and 30.

21. Michael R. Gordon, "Star Wars' X-Ray Laser Weapon Dies as Its Final Test is Canceled," *New York Times,* July 7, 1992, p. A-1.

22. Scheer, p. 11.

23. Saucier.

24. "Updating and Ongoing" section, *Lobster* (UK), Winter-Spring 1994, no. 26, p. 24.

25. "Attendee and Exhibitor Roster," Non-Lethal Defense Conference, Johns Hopkins Applied Research Lab, Laurel, MD.

26 Harlan E. Girard, "Effects of Gigahertz Radiation on the Nervous System: Recent Developments in the Technology of Political Control," a lecture at the NATO Advanced Research Workshop on Coherent and Emergent Phenomena on Bio-Molecular Systems, University of Arizona, January 15-19, 1991.

27. Susan Schiefelbein, "The Invisible Threat: The Stifled Story of Electrical Waves," *Saturday Review,* September 15, 1993, p. 17. Schiefelbein notes that Schwan was "a highly-funded researcher in electromagnetics. His research funds came primarily from the Department of Defense."

28. "Darth Vader's Revenge," *Penthouse,* August 1988.

29. Larry Wichman, "Who's Killing the Star Wars Scientists?" *Hustler,* June 1989, pp. 67-92.

30. Ibid., pp. 88-92.

32. John Alexander, "The New Mental Battlefield," *Military Review,* Vol. LX, no. 12, December 1980. Reprinted in *Psychic Warfare: Fact or Fiction,* John White, ed., (Surrey, UK: Aquarian, 1988), p. 69.

33. Michael Rossman, "On Some Matters of Concern in Psychic Research," *New Age Blues* (New York: EP Dutton, 1978). Reprinted in White, p. 130.

34. Paul Brown and David Pollister, "Heseltine Link with Iran," *The Guardian,* December 20, 1993, p. 1.

35. David Watts, "West 'well served' by Iran and Iraq at war," *London Times,* November 10, 1993, p. 3.

36. Kenneth R. Timmerman, *The Death Lobby: How the West Armed Iraq* (New York: Houghton Mifflin, 1991), p. 80.

37. Ibid., p. 340.

38. Art Pine, "Not So Deadly Weapons," *Los Angeles Times,* May 18, 1993, p. A-1.

39. Copy from John G. Lambros in an unpublished samizdat.

40. Girard (see fn. 27).

41. Lambros.

42. Lincoln Lawrence, *Were We Controlled?* (New Hyde Park, NY: University Books, 1967), p. 52.

43. Ibid.

44. Ibid.

45. T.F. Maitefa Angaza, "SCI-FACT—NOT FICTION: High-Tech Slavery is Here," *New York City Sun,* December 15, 1993, p. 4.

46.. Simon Davies, "Bionic Man Comes of Age," *London Times,* October 17, 1994, p. 16.

47. Andreasen, et.al., "Seven-channel digital telemetry system for monitoring and direct computer capturing of biological data," *Journal of Biomedical Engineering,* September 1993, pp. 435-40.

48. Julianne McKinney, Association of National Security Alumni, Silver Springs, MD, in private correspondence with an Air Force general, February 1, 1993, pp. 1-3.

49. Julianne McKinney, telephone conversation, April 4, 1994.

50. Mark Nollinger, "Rage," *Wired,* June 1994, pp. 102.

51. Art Pine, "Not So Deadly Weapons," *Los Angeles Times,* May 5, 1993, p. A-1.

52. Thomas Martinez with John Guinther, *The Brotherhood of Murder* (New York: McGraw-Hill, 1988), p. 230.

53. Michael Hutchinson, *Megabrain: New Tools and Techniques for Brain Growth and Mind Expansion* (New York: Beech Tree, 1986), pp.123-24.

54. Art Pine, "Low-Key Perry Being Asked to Master High-Flying Job," *Los Angeles Times,* January 25, 1994, p. A-26.

55. Ed Vulliamy, "Dying for an American Dream," *London Observer,* December 4, 1994.

Section Two

CIA, Satanism & Cult Abuse of Children

CIA, Satanism & Cult Abuse of Children

Chapter Three

The False Memory Hoax

Part I: CIA Connections to the Mind Control Cults

Swiss newspapers described the carnage inside the charred farmhouse as a "wax museum of death." Within hours, 27 other members of the Sovereign Order of the Solar Temple were found dead at chalets in Granges, Switzerland and Morin Heights, Quebec. Luc Jouret, the Temple's grand master, the *London Times* reported, "espoused a hybrid religion that owed more to Umberto Eco's novel *Foucault's Pendulum* than to any bible. His followers called themselves 'Knights of Christ.' The crusading codes of the Knights Templar, the rose-and-cross symbolism of the medieval Rosicrucian Order, Nazi occultism and new age mysticism were joined together into a mumbo-jumbo mishmash that seemed more designed for extracting money from disciples than saving souls."

Jouret, born in the Belgian Congo in 1947, set out in youth as a mystic with communist leanings, but his politics apparently swung full circle. He has since been linked to a clutch of neo-Nazis responsible for a string of bombings in Canada. He told friends that he had once served with a unit of Belgium paratroopers.

French-Canadian journalist Pierre Tourangeau investigated the sect for two years. A few days after the mass murder, he reported that the sect was financed by the proceeds of gun-running to Australia and South America. Simultaneously, Radio Canada announced that Jouret's Templars earned hundreds of millions of dollars laundering the profits through the infamous Bank of Credit and Commerce International (BCCI), closed by authorities worldwide in 1991. Montreal's *La Presse* observed: "each new piece of information only thickens the mystery"—but the combination of international arms smuggling and BCCI presented a familiar enough picture of CIA sedition. The Manhattan D.A. who closed the American branch announced that 16 witnesses had died in the course of investigating the bank's entanglements in covert operations of the CIA, arms smuggling to Iraq, money laundering and child prostitution.

The average coffee table would crumple under the weighty BCCI Book of the Dead. Journalist Danny Casalaro and Vince Foster appear in it—grim antecedents to the Solar Temple killings. The cult's connection to BCCI (reported in Europe but filtered from American newspaper accounts) fed speculation among Canadian journalists that followers of Jouret were killed to bury public disclosures of gun-running and money laundering.

But the fraternizing of America's national security elite and the cults did not begin in Cheiry, Switzerland. Jouret's Order of the Solar Temple was but the latest incarnation of mind control operations organized and overseen by the CIA and Department of Defense.

> In a sense, we are in the same ethical and moral dilemma as the physicists in the days prior to the Manhattan Project. Those of us who work in this field see a developing potential for a nearly total control of human emotional status.
>
> —Dr. Wayne Evans
> *Army Institute of*
> *Environmental Medicine*

Scientists in the CIA's mind control fraternity lead double lives. Many are highly respected, but if the truth were known they would be deafened by the public outcry and drummed out of their respective academic haunts.

Martin T. Orne, for example, a senior CIA/Navy researcher, is based at the University of Pennsylvania's Experimental Psychiatry Laboratory. He is also an original member of the False Memory Syndrome Foundation's advisory board, a tightly-drawn coterie of psychiatrists, many with backgrounds in CIA mind control experimentation in its myriad forms. The Foundation is dedicated to denying the existence of cult mind control and child abuse. Its primary pursuit is the castigation of survivors and therapists for fabricating accusations of ritual abuse.

Dismissing cult abuse as hysteria or false memory, a common defense strategy, may relieve parents of preschool children. In a small percentage of cult abuse cases its possible that children may be led to believe they've been victimized.

But the CIA and its cover organizations have a vested interest in blowing smoke at the cult underground because the worlds of CIA mind control and many cults merge inextricably. The drum beat of "false accusations" from the media is taken up by paid operatives like Dr. Orne and the False Memory Syndrome Foundation to conceal the crimes of the Agency.

Orne's forays into hypno-programming were financed in the 1960s by the Human Ecology Fund, a CIA cover at Cornell University and the underwriter of many of the formative mind control experiments conducted in the U.S. and abroad, including the gruesome brainwashing and remote mind control experiments of D. Ewen Cameron at Montreal's Allan Memorial Institute. Research specialties of the CIA's black psychiatrists included electroshock lobotomies, drugging agents, incapacitants, hypnosis, sleep deprivation and radio control of the brain, among hundreds of sub-projects.

The secondary source of funding for Dr. Orne's work in hypnotic suggestion and dissolution of memory is eerie in the cult child abuse context. The voluminous files of John Marks in Washington, D.C. (139 boxes obtained under FOIA, to be exact, two-fifths of which document CIA interest in the occult) include an Agency report itemizing a $30,000 grant to Orne from Human Ecology, and another $30,000 from Boston's Scientific Engineering Institute (SEI)—another CIA funding cover, founded by Edwin Land of the Polaroid Corporation (and supervisor of the U-2 spy plane escapades). This was the year that the CIA's Office of Research and Development (ORD) geared up a study of parapsychology and the occult. The investigation, dubbed Project OFTEN-CHICK-WIT, gave rise to the establishment of a social "laboratory" by SEI scientists at the University of South Carolina—a college class in black witchcraft, demonology and voodoo.

Dr. Orne, with SEI funding, marked out his own mind control corner at the University of Pennsylvania in the early 1960s. He does not publicize his role as a CIA psychiatrist. He denies it, very plausibly. In a letter to Dr. Orne, Marks once reminded him that he'd disavowed knowledge of his participation in one mind-wrecking experimental sub-project. Orne later recanted, admitting that he'd been aware of the true source of funding all along.

Among psychiatrists in the CIA's mind control fraternity, Orne ranks among the most venerable. He once boasted to Marks that he was routinely briefed on all significant CIA behavior modification experiments: "Why would they come to him," Martin Cannon muses in *The Controllers,* which links UFO abductions to secret military research veiled by screen memories of "alien" abduction, "unless Orne had a high security clearance and worked extensively with the intelligence services?"

To supplement his CIA income, the influential Dr. Orne has been the donee of grants from the Office of Naval Research and the Air Force Office of Scientific Research. "I should like to hear," Cannon says, "what innocent explanation, if any, the Air Force has to offer to explain their interest in post-hypnotic amnesia."

According to Army records, Orne's stomping grounds, Penn U., was a beehive of secret experiments in the Vietnam War period. The Pentagon and CIA—under the auspices of ORD's Steve Aldrich, a doyen of occult and parapsychological studies—conferred the Agency's most lucrative research award upon the University of Pennsylvania to study the effects of 16 newly-concocted biochemical warfare agents on humans, including choking, blistering and vomiting agents, toxins, poison gas and incapacitating chemicals. The tests were abruptly halted in 1972 when the prison's medical lab burned to the ground.

Testimony before the 1977 Church Committee's probe of the CIA hinted that, as of 1963, the scientific squalor of the CIA's mind control regimen, code-named MKULTRA, had abandoned military and academic laboratories, fearing exposure, and mushroomed in cities across the country. Confirmation arrived in 1980 when Joseph Holsinger, an aide to late Congressman Leo Ryan (who was murdered by a death squad at Jonestown) exposed the formation of eccentric religious cults by the CIA. Holsinger made the allegation at a colloquium of psychologists in San Francisco on "Psychosocial Implications of the Jonestown Phenomenon." Holsinger maintained that a CIA rear-support base had been in collusion with Jones to perform medical and mind control experiments at People's Temple. The former Congressional aide cited an essay he'd received in the mail, "The Penal Colony," written by a Berkeley psychologist. The author had emphasized: Rather than terminating MKULTRA, THE CIA SHIFTED ITS PROGRAMS FROM PUBLIC INSTITUTIONS TO PRIVATE CULT GROUPS, including the People's Temple.

Jonestown had its grey eminence in Dr. Lawrence Laird Layton of the University of California at Berkeley, formerly a chemist for the Manhattan Project and head of the Army's chemical warfare research division in the early 1950s. (Larry Layton, his son, led the death squad that murdered Congressman Leo Ryan, who'd arrived at Guyana to investigate the cult.) Michael Meiers, author of *Was Jonestown a CIA Medical Experiment?*, scavenged for information on the People's Temple for six years, concluding: "The Jonestown experiment was conceived by Dr. Layton, staffed by Dr. Layton and financed by Dr. Layton. It was as much his project as it was Jim Jones's. Though it was essential for him to remain in the background for security reasons, Dr. Layton maintained contact with and even control of the experiment through his wife and children." The African-American cult had at its core a Caucasian inner-council, composed of Dr. Layton's family and in-laws.

The press was blind to obvious CIA connections, but survivors of the carnage in Guyana followed the leads and maintained that Jim Jones was "an employee, servant, agent or operative of the Central Intelligence Agency" from 1963—the year the Agency turned to cult cut-outs to conceal MKULTRA mind control activities—until 1978. In October 1981 the survivors of Jonestown filed a $63 million lawsuit against Secretary of State Cyrus Vance and Stansfield Turner, former director of the CIA, currently a teacher at the University of Maryland and a director of the Monsanto Corporation. The suit, filed in U.S. district court in San Francisco, accused Turner of conspiring with Agency operatives to "enhance the economic and political powers of James Warren Jones," and of conducting "mind control and drug experimentation" on the Temple flock.

The suit was dismissed four months later for "failure to prosecute timely." All requests for an appeal were denied.

Ligatures of the CIA clung to the cults. Much of the violence that has since exploded across the front pages was incited by CIA academics at leading universities.

Small wonder, then, that Ted Goertzel, director of the Forum for Policy Research at Rutgers, which maintains a symbiosis with the CIA despite media exposure, should write that the most susceptible victims of "cryptomnesia" (a synonym for false memories) believe "in conspiracies, including the JFK assassination, AIDS conspiracies, as well as the UFO cover-up." The problem, Goertzel says, "may have its origins in early childhood," and is accompanied by "feelings of anomie and anxiety that make the individual more likely to construct false memories out of information stored in the unconscious mind."

This side of gilded rationalizations, the CIA's links to the cults are no manifestation of "cryptomnesia."

Like Jonestown, the Symbionese Liberation Army was a mind control creation unleashed by the Agency. The late political researcher Mae Brussell, whose study of The Firm commenced in 1963 after the assassination of John Kennedy, wrote in 1974 that the rabid guerrilla band "consisted predominantly of CIA agents and police informers." This unsavory group was, Brussell insisted, "an extension of psychological experimentation projects, connected to Stanford Research Institute, Menlo Park." (She went on to lament that "many of the current rash of 'senseless killings,' 'massacres,' and 'zombie-type murders' are committed by individuals who have been in Army hospitals, mental hospitals or prison hospitals, where their heads have been literally taken over surgically to create terror in the community.")

Evidence that the CIA conceived and directed the SLA was obvious. The SLA leadership was trained by Colston Westbrook, a Pennsylvania native. Westbrook was a veteran of the CIA's murderous PHOENIX Program in South Vietnam, where he trained terrorist cadres and death squads. In 1969 he took a job as an administrator of Pacific Architects and Engineers, a CIA proprietary in Southern California. Three of Westbrook's foot soldiers, Emily and William Harris and Angela Atwood (a former police intelligence informer), had been students of the College of Foreign Affairs, a CIA cover at the University of Indiana. Even the SLA symbol, a seven-headed cobra, had been adopted by the OSS (America's wartime intelligence agency) and CIA to designate precepts of brainwashing.

When the smoke cleared at SLA headquarters in L.A., Dr. Martin Orne was called upon to examine Patricia Hearst in preparation for trial. The government charged that she had participated voluntarily in the

SLA's gun-toting crime spree. Orne's was a foregone conclusion—he sided with the government. His opinion was shared by two other psychiatrists called to appraise Ms. Hearst's state of mind, Robert Jay Lifton and Louis Jolyon West. Dr. Lifton was a co-founder of the aforementioned Human Ecology Fund. The CIA contractor that showered Orne with research grants in the 1960s. Dr. West is one of the CIA's most notorious mind control specialists, currently director of UCLA's Neuropsychiatric Institute. It was West who brought a score of mind control psychiatrists of the ultra-right political stripe to the UCLA campus.

Drs. Orne, Lifton and West unanimously agreed that Patty Hearst had been "persuasively coerced" to join the SLA. She had been put through a grueling thought reform regimen. She'd been isolated and sensory deprived, raped, humiliated, badgered, politically indoctrinated with a surrealistic mutation of Third World Marxism. Ms. Hearst was only allowed human companionship when she exhibited signs of submission. Orne and his colleagues assured that attention was narrowed to their psychologizing, conveniently rendering evidence of CIA collusion extraneous to consideration by the jury.

Another psychiatrist called to testify at the trial of "Tania" surfaced with Dr. Orne in 1991 on the board of the False Memory Syndrome Foundation. (The FMSF board is almost exclusively composed of former CIA and military doctors currently employed by major universities. None have backgrounds in ritual abuse—their common interest is behavior modification.) Dr. Margaret Singer, a retired Berkeley Ph.D., studied repatriated prisoners-of-war returning from the Korean War at the Walter Reed Army Institute of Research in Maryland, 1952–58.)

Singer turned up in 1982 on the book jacket of *Raven*—the CIA's code-name for Jim Jones—by *San Francisco Examiner* reporters Tim Reiterman and John Jacobs, a thoroughly-researched account of the People's Temple that completely side-steps CIA involvement. Co-author John Jacobs was supposedly one of the country's leading authorities on CIA mind control, a subject he studied at length for a series published by the *Washington Post*. Reiterman had been the *Examiner* reporter on the Patricia Hearst beat. Yet both writers managed to avoid obvious intelligence connections. Dr. Singer commended the book as "the definitive psychohistory of Jim Jones." *Raven*, she opined, conveyed "the essence of psychological and social processes that Jim Jones, the ultimate manipulator, set in motion." The true "manipulators," of course, were operatives of the CIA, and the public disinformation gambit lauded by Dr. Singer was, according to Meiers, in tune with "a concerted attempt to suppress information, stifle investigations, censor writers and manipulate public information."

The CIA and Pentagon have quietly organized and influenced a long line of mind control cults, among them:

The Riverside Lodge of the Ordo Templis Orientis: Also known as The Solar Lodge of the OTO, which followed the teachings of cult messiah Aleister Crowley, whose fixed gaze on the astral equinox resulted in instructions from his deities to form a religious order. Crowley, high priest of the OTO and a British intelligence agent, gave Winifred T. Smith a charter to open an OTO lodge in Pasadena. The high priest of the lodge was Jack Parsons, a rocket expert and founder of the California Institute of Technology. Parsons, who took the oath of the anti-Christ in 1949, contributed to the design of the Pentagon under subsequent CIA director John J. McCloy. He was killed in a still unexplained laboratory explosion. There is a crater on the moon named after him.

The OTO's Solar Lodge in San Bernardino was presided over by Georgina "Jean" Brayton, the daughter of a ranking Air Force officer in the 1960s. The cult subscribed to a grim, apocalyptic view of the world, and like Charles Manson believed that race wars would precipitate the Big Cataclysm. In the Faustian Los Angeles underworld, the lodge was known for its indulgence in sadomasochism, drug dealing, blood drinking, child molestation and murder.

Candace Reos, a former member of the lodge, was deposed by Riverside police in 1969. Reos said that Brayton controlled the thinking of all cult members. One poor soul, she said, was ordered to curb his sexual urges by cutting his wrists every time he was aroused. Mrs. Reos told police, according to the report, that when she became pregnant, Georgina was angry and told her that she would have to condition herself to hate her child. Reos told police that children of the cult's 43 adult members were secluded from their parents and received "training" that took on "very severe tones."

"There was a lot of spanking involved," she said, "a lot of heavy criticism. There was a lot of enclosed in dark rooms." The teachers, she added, "left welts."

If so ordered, adult cultists would beat their children.

According to a Riverside County Sheriff's report, a six year-old child burned the group's school house to the ground. The boy was punished by solitary confinement in a locked shipping crate left in the desert, where the average temperature was 110 degrees, for two months. The boy was chained to a metal plate.

When police freed him, they were nauseated by the suffocating stench of excrement. The child was smothered in flies swarming from a tin-can toilet.

The Bhagwan Shree Rajneesh Movement: In 1985 the *Portland Oregonian* published a 36-part, book-length series linking the cult to opium trafficking, prostitution, money laundering, arson, slave labor, mass poisonings, illegal wiretaps and the stockpiling of guns and biochemical warfare weapons. The year-long *Oregonian* investigation revealed cult ties to CIA-trained mercenaries in El Salvador and the Far East. Domestically, Rajneesh's secret police force worked with Agency operatives.

Finders: On February 7, 1987 Customs agents raided a child-porn ring in Tallahasee, Florida. Eight suspects and six children were taken into custody. The children, according to a Customs Department memo, behaved "like animals in a public park," and "were not aware of the function and purpose of telephones, televisions and toilets."

The children told police that they were forced to live outdoors and were given food only as a reward. A check on the backgrounds of the adults turned up a police report, "specific in describing 'bloody rituals' and sex orgies involving children, and an as-yet unsolved murder." Customs agents searched a cult safe house and discovered a computer room and documents recording "high-tech" bank transfers, explosives, and a set of instructions advising cult members on moving children through jurisdictions around the country. One photographic album found in the house featured the execution and disembowelment of goats, and snapshots, according to a Customs report, of "adults and children dressed in white sheets participating in a bloody ritual."

An American passport was found. The investigating agents contacted the State Department and were advised to "terminate further investigation."

They investigated anyway, reporting that "the CIA made contact and admitted to owning the Finders ... as a front for a domestic training organization, but that it had 'gone bad.'" The late wife of Marion David Pettie, the cult's leader, had worked for the Agency, and his son had been an employee of Air America, the heroin-riddled CIA proprietary. Yet Pettie denied to a reporter for *U.S. News & World Report* any connection to the CIA. Police in Washington refused to comment. Officials of the CIA dismissed as "hogwash" allegations of any connection to the Finders cult.

MOVE: On May 13, 1985 MOVE's Philadelphia headquarters was firebombed by local police. Not only did the fire consume the cult's home—it devastated the entire neighborhood, leaving 11 dead and 250 homeless. The group was cofounded by Vince Leapheart, aka John Africa, a Korean veteran. His intellectual mentor and source of funding was Donald Glassey, a lecturer at the University of Pennsylvania's School of Social Work. Glassey was an admitted police "informant," but conducted himself like a paid provocateur. He purchased weapons for the cult with cash drawn from city coffers. John Africa, the cult's titular head, claimed to be a messiah, and like Jim Jones to have Godly "healing" powers and "total control" over his followers.

O.T.A.: The Order of the Temple of Astarte in Pasadena, California is a "hermetic" occult organization that practices "Magick in the Western Tradition." The cult is led by Fraters Khenemel, a police officer, and Aleyin, a veteran Green Beret. The cult's everyday language is unusual for a mystical order—one group schedule is laden with words like "operation," "sixteen-thirty hours," and "travel orders." Demonology is among the OTA's primary occult interests.

The police connection recalls the statement of Louis Tackwood, the former LAPD provocateur whose revelations of secret police subterfuge set off a political tempest in Los Angeles in 1973. "You don't know," he told journalist Donald Freed, "but there's a devil worship cult in Pasadena. Actually in Altadena." Tackwood alleged that the cultists were "on the LAPD payroll."

The CIA and Pentagon cooperate in the creation of cults. To be sure, the Association of National Security Alumni, a public interest veterans group opposed to covert operations, considers it a "primary issue of concern" that the Department of Defense has a "perceived role in satanic cult activities, which qualify in and of themselves as very damaging exercises in mind control and behavioral modification."

It is beginning to dawn on the psychiatric community at large that the CIA's mind control clique is a menace reminiscent of Nazi medical experimentation. In 1993, Dr. Corydon Hammond, a professor at the University of Utah's School of Medicine, conducted a seminar on federally-funded mind control experiments. Topics covered by Hammond included brainwashing, post-hypnotic programming and the induction of multiple personalities by the CIA. Hammond contended that the cult underground has roots in Nazi Germany, and that the CIA's cult mind control techniques were based upon those of Nazi scientists recruited by the CIA for Cold Warfare. (Researcher Lenny Lapon estimates in *Mass Murderers in White Coats* that 5,000 Nazis resettled in the U.S. after WW II.) Hammond was forced to drop this line of inquiry by professional ridicule, especially from the CIA's False Memory Syndrome Foundation, and a barrage of death threats. At a recent regional conference on ritual child abuse, he regretted that he could no longer speak on the theme of government mind control.

The psychological community is waking to the threat in its ranks, to judge by APA surveys and personal communications with ranking members of the mental health field, but the world at large remains in the dark. The "mass hysteria" and "false memory" bromides disseminated by the establishment press obscure federal and academic connections to the mind control cults, which are defended largely by organized pedophiles, cultists and hired guns of psychiatry. An ambitious disinformation gambit has led the world at large to side with cultists operating under federal protection. As at Jonestown and Chiery, Switzerland, the denouement of cult activity often ends in the destruction of all witnesses. This cycle of abuse and murder can only be ended by full public awareness of the federal mind control initiative.

Part Two: The CIA, The False Memory Syndrome Foundation & The Politics of Ritual Abuse

The conference session bears a passing resemblance to a 12-Step meeting. Assembled in a Portland religious retreat, members of the False Memory Syndrome Foundation (FMSF), all accused of child abuse, are encouraged to unload their anguish. Only women take the stage (they leave reporters with a sympathetic impression—men stigmatized by child abuse do not). Pamela Freyd, a Foundation founder, assures these victims of pernicious therapies they are not alone. The Foundation's office in Philadelphia, she says, takes 60 calls on a typical day from distraught adults hounded by their own confused children, rogue therapists and sensation-seeking pack journalists.

The number of dues-paying members (each contributes $100 a year) varies according to the source. The group reported in January 1993 that 1,200 families had made contact in its first year of operation. The same month, the *San Jose Mercury News* declared flatly that "nearly 3,000 families" from across the country had been recruited. The FMSF now claims 5,000 families. *Time* magazine raised the figure to "7,000 individuals and families who have sought assistance."

The Foundation's distinctive handling of statistics is incessant. In April of this year the FMSF claimed 12,000 families have been strained by false child abuse allegations. A month later, the figure dropped to "9,500 U.S. families." Yet the Foundation prides itself on accuracy. One FMSF newsletter advises members to insist the media "report accurate information. The rumors and misinformation surrounding the false accusations based on recovery of repressed memories are shocking." The same author regrets that "65% of accusations of abuse are now unsubstantiated, a whopping jump from 35% in 1976." This figure, once gleefully disseminated by such pedophile defense groups as NAMBLA (North American Man/Boy Love Association) and VOCAL (Victims of Child Abuse Laws) was debunked years ago. It was fabricated by Douglas Besherov of the American Enterprise Institute, a hard right-wing propaganda factory fueled by the Olin Foundation, a CIA funding cover. (Christian conservatives are often accused of propagating ritual abuse "hysteria," yet in the 1992 presidential election the para-conservative wing of the Republican Party slipped into its platform a strategy to put an end to investigations of child abuse.)

The FMSF selectively ignores child abuse data that disagree with their own. Judith Herman, author of *Trauma and Recovery,* reported in the *Harvard Mental Health Letter* that false abuse allegations by children "are rare, in the range of 2–8% of reported cases. False retractions of true complaints are far more common, especially when the victim is not sufficiently protected after disclosure and therefore succumbs to intimidation by the perpetrator or other family members who feel that they must preserve secrecy."

Other statistics shunned by the False Memory Syndrome Foundation include a survey presented at a 1992 psychiatric conference that found that a full 88% of all therapists in a large sampling consider ritual child abuse to be a very real social problem with devastating emotional effects. Another: In 1990 the State University of New York at Buffalo polled a national sampling of clinical psychologists on ritual abuse. About 800 psychologists—a third of the poll—were aware of treating at least one case. Only 5% of all child abuse cases ever enter the courtroom—half of these end with the child in the custody of the abusive parent.

The recovered memory debate was discussed at a 1993 conference on multiple personality disorder. Richard Lowenstein, a psychiatrist from the University of Maryland Medical School, argued that the Foundation is "media-directed, dedicated to putting out disinformation."

Other conference participants contemplated funding sources and "possible CIA connections."

San Jose Mercury News

SUNDAY
JANUARY 24, 1993

Therapists accused of implanting memories of abuse

■ **In depth:** Recollections of incest are questioned in court.

BY S.L. WYKES
Mercury News Staff Writer

Stanford University psychiatrist Saul Wasserman and his wife began a quick slide into parental hell a year ago. Their only child accused them and her grandfather of sexual abuse, the Wassermans say, and then she threatened to have her parents killed if they came near her.

Wasserman, a therapist who treats abused children, denies the charges and believes his daughter's claims were induced by improper psychological treatment — that she might be under the spell of false memory syndrome.

Characterized by a belief in events that never took place, the false memory syndrome label has emerged amid a wave of attitudinal change about sexual abuse.

For years, incest and sexual abuse were never discussed or admitted, but gradually the subject has come out in the open and gained understanding and legal and medical attention.

No one questions the legitimacy of many histories of incest and abuse, but a wave of litigation has begun to fill the courts as some accused parents challenge childhood memories dredged up during therapy.

An association of parents who say their children have accused them falsely of sexual abuse has grown in less than a year to nearly 3,000 families. The False Memory Syndrome Foundation has members from every state, including 366 Californians, and there are members from Canada, England, France and Germany.

Stanford psychiatrist Saul Wasserman contends improper psychological treatment caused his daughter to accuse him of abuse, then threaten to have him killed.

False recollections dredged up by psychologists, parents say

"It's going to become the psychologic quackery of the 20th century, without any doubt. It's a phenomenon of epidemic proportions and it's growing."

— Richard Ofshe, sociologist, University of California, Berkeley

The Devil Denuded

The CIA, in fact, has several designates on the FMSF advisory board. They have in common backgrounds in mind control experimentation. Their very presence on the board, and their peculiar backgrounds, reveal some heavily obscured facts about ritual child abuse.

Martin T. Orne, a senior CIA researcher, is an original board member of the Foundation, and a psychiatrist at the University of Pennsylvania's Experimental Psychiatry Lab in Philadelphia. In 1962 his forays into hypno-programming (the elicitation of "anti-social" behavior, dissolving memory and other mind-subduing techniques) were financed by a CIA front at Cornell University. He was also funded by Boston's Scientific Engineering Institute, another front, and a clearinghouse for the Agency's investigation of the occult.

The CIA and Pentagon have formed a partnership in the creation of cults. To be sure, the Association of National Security Alumni, a public interest veterans group opposed to clandestine ops, considers it a "primary issue of concern" that the Department of Defense has a "perceived role in satanic cult activities, which qualify in and of themselves as very damaging exercises in mind control."

The smoothing over of the national security state's cult connections is handled by academic "experts."

A forerunner of the Foundation is based in Buffalo, New York, the Committee for Scientific Examination of Religion, best known for the publication of *Satanism in America: How the Devil Got More Than His Due,* widely considered to be a legitimate study. The authors turn up their noses to ritual abuse, dismissing the hundreds of reports around the country as mass "hysteria." Cult researcher Carl Raschke reported in a March, 1991 article that he coincidentally met Hudson Frew, a *Satanism in America* co-author, at a Berkeley bookstore. "Frew was wearing a five-pointed star, or pentagram, the symbol of witchcraft and earth magic," Raschke says. Shawn Carlson, a contributor to the book, is identified by the media as a "physicist." Yet he runs the Gaia Press in El Cerrito, California, a New Age publishing house with an emphasis on witchcraft and occultic lore. Carlson is also a "scientific and technical consultant" to the Committee for Scientific Investigation of Claims of the Paranormal (a promoter of the "false memory" theory of ritual abuse and UFO abductions), publisher of the *Skeptical Inquirer.*

The FMS Foundation is no less eccentric. Within two years of its founding, it was clear that the Foundation leadership was far from disinterested on the workings of childhood memory, and concealed a secret sexual and political agenda.

FMSF founder Ralph Underwager, director of the Institute of Psychological Therapies in Minnesota, was forced to resign in 1993. Underwager (a former Lutheran pastor) and his wife Hollida Wakefield publish a journal, *Issues in Child Abuse Allegations,* written by and for child abuse "skeptics." His departure from the False Memory Syndrome Foundation was hastened by a remark in an interview, appearing in an Amsterdam journal for pedophiles, that it was "God's Will" adults engage in sex with children. (His wife Hollida remained on the Foundation's board after he left.) As it happens, holy dispensation for pedophiles is the exact credo of the Children of God cult. It was fitting, then, when Underwager filed an affidavit on behalf of cult members tried in France in 1992, insisting that the accused were positively "not guilty of abuse upon children." In the interview, he prevailed upon pedophiles everywhere to shed stigmatization as "wicked and reprehensible" users of children.

In keeping with the Foundation's creative use of statistics, Dr. Underwager told a group of British reporters in 1994 that "scientific evidence" proved 60% of all women molested as children believed the experience was "good for them."

Dr. Underwager invariably sides with the defense. His grandiloquent orations have graced courtrooms around the world, often by satellite. Defense lawyers for Woody Allen turned to him, he boasts, when Mia Farrow accused her estranged husband of molesting their seven year-old daughter. Underwager is a virtual icon to the Irish Catholic lobby in Dublin, which raised its hoary hackles against a child abuse prevention program in the Irish Republic. He was, until his advocacy of pedophila tarnished an otherwise glittering reputation, widely quoted in the press, dismissing ritual child abuse as a hysterical aberration.

He is the world's foremost authority on false memory, but in the courtroom he is repeatedly exposed as a charlatan. In 1988, a trial court decision in New York State held that Dr. Underwager was "not qualified to render any opinion as to whether or not (the victim) was sexually molested." In 1990 his testimony on memory was ruled improper "in the absence of any evidence that the results of Underwager's work had been accepted in the scientific community." And In Minnesota a judge ruled that Underwager's theories on "learned memory" were the same as "having an expert tell the jury that (the victim) was not telling the truth."

Peter and Pamela Freyd, executive directors of the Foundation, joined forces with Underwager in 1991, and their story is equally wretched. Jennifer Freyd, their daughter, a professor of psychology at the University of Oregon, openly leveled accusations of abuse against her parents at an August 1993 mental health conference in Ann Arbor, Michigan.

"My family of origin was troubled in many observable ways," she said. "I refer to the things that were never 'forgotten' and 'recovered,' but to things that we all knew about." She gave her father's alcoholism as an example. "During my childhood, my father sometimes discussed his own experiences of being sexually abused as an 11 year-old boy, and called himself a 'kept boy.'" Peter Freyd graduated to male prostitution as an adolescent.

At the age of 13, Jennifer Freyd composed a poem about her father's nocturnal visits:

> *I am caught in a web,*
> *A web of deep, deep terror.*

she wrote. The diaries of her youth chronicle the "reactions and feelings (guilt, shame and terror) of a troubled girl and young woman. My parents oscillated between denying these symptoms and feelings... to using knowledge of these same symptoms and feelings to discredit me."

"My father," she says, "told various people that I was brain damaged." The accusation was unlikely. At the time, Jennifer Freyd was a graduate student on a National Science Foundation fellowship. She has taught at Cornell and received numerous research awards. The "brain damage" apologia did not wash. Her mother suggested that Jennifer's memories were "confabulations," and faulted therapeutic intervention. Pamela Freyd turned to her own psychiatrist, Dr. Harold Lief, currently an advisory board member of the Foundation, to diagnose Jennifer.

"He explained to me that he did not believe I was abused," Jennifer recalls. Dr. Lief's diagnosis was based on his belief that Peter Freyd's fantasies were strictly "homoerotic." Of course, his daughter furrows a brow at the assumption that homoerotic fantasies or a heterosexual marriage exclude the possibility of child molestation. Lief's skewed logic is a trademark of the Foundation.

He is a close colleague of the CIA's Martin Orne. Dr. Lief, a former major in the Army medical corps, joined the University of Pennsylvania faculty in 1968, the peak of federally-funded behavioral modification experiments at Holmesburg Prison. Dr. Orne consulted with him on several studies in hypnotic programming. His academic writing reveals a peculiar range of professional interests, including "Orgasm in the Postoperative Transsexual" for *Archives of Sexual Behavior,* and an exploration of the possibility of life after death for a journal on mental diseases edited by Foundation fellow Paul McHugh. Lief is a director of the Center for Sexuality and Religion, past president of the Sex Information and Education Council.

And an original board member of the False Memory Syndrome Foundation. Two others, Jon Baron from Penn U. and Ray Hyman (an executive editor of the aforementioned *Skeptical Inquirer*), a professor of psychology at the University of Oregon, resigned from the board after Jennifer Freyd went public with her account of childhood abuse and the facetious attempts of her parents and their therapist to discredit her. They were replaced by David Dinges, co-director—with the ubiquitous Martin

Orne—of the Unit for Experimental Psychiatry at the University of Pennsylvania.

"At times I am flabbergasted that my memory is considered 'false,'" Jennifer says, "and my alcoholic father's memory is considered rational and sane." She does not, after all, remember impossible abuses: "I remember incest in my father's house.... My first memories came when I was at home a few hours after my second session with my therapist, a licensed clinical psychologist working within an established group in a large and respected medical clinic.

"During that second visit to my therapist's office, I expressed great anxiety about the upcoming holiday visit from my parents. My therapist asked about half way into the session, whether I had ever been sexually abused. I was immediately thrown into a strange state. No one had ever asked me such a question. I responded, 'no, but....' I went home and within a few hours I was shaking uncontrollably, overwhelmed with intense and terrible flashbacks." Jennifer asks herself why her parents are believed. "In the end, is it precisely because I was abused that I am to be discredited despite my personal and professional success?"

Pamela Freyd published an open letter defending her husband in Ralph Underwager's *Issues in Child Abuse Accusations* in 1991. It was reprinted in *Confabulations,* a book published a year later. Laced with lubricious sentiment, the book bemoans the "destruction of families" brought on by false child abuse accusations, and maligns "cult-like" support groups and feminists, or "lesbian cults." Executive director Freyd often refers to the feminist groups that have taken up the cause of child abuse survivors as "lesbians," after the bizarre Dr. Underwager, who claims, "these women may be jealous that males are able to love each other, be comrades, friends, be close, intimate."

Pamela Freyd's account of the family history, Jennifer insists, is patently false. In an electronic message from her father, he openly acknowledged that in his version of the story "fictional elements were deliberately inserted."

"'Fictional is rather an astounding choice of words," Jennifer observed at the Ann Arbor conference. The article written by her parents contends that Jennifer was denied tenure at another university due to a lack of published research. "In fact," Jennifer counters, "I moved to the University of Oregon in 1987, just four years after receiving my Ph.D. to accept a tenured position as associate professor in the psychology department, one of the world's best psychology departments.... My mother sent the Jane Doe article to my colleagues during my promotion year—that is, the year my case for promotion to full professor was being considered. I was absolutely mortified to learn of this violation of my privacy and this violation of truth."

Manipulative tactics are another Foundation imprimatur. Lana

Alexander, editor of a newsletter for survivors of child sexual abuse, observes that "many people view the false memory syndrome theory as a calculated defense strategy developed by perpetrators and the lawyers and expert witnesses who defend them."

A legitimizing barrage of stories in the press has shaped public opinion and warmed the clime for defense attorneys. The concept of false memory serves the same purpose as Holocaust denial. It shapes opinion. Unconscionable crimes are obstructed, the accused is endowed with the status of martyr, the victim reviled.

The emphasis on image is obvious in "How Do We Know We are Not Representing Pedophiles," an article written for the February 29, 1992 *FMS Foundation Newsletter,* by Pamela Freyd. In it, she derides the suggestion that many members of the group could be molesters because "we are a good-looking bunch of people, greying hair, well dressed, healthy, smiling; just about every person who has attended is someone you would surely find interesting and want to count as a friend."

Friendly Fire

> *People forget things. Horrible things. Here at the Foundation*
> *someone had a repressed memory, or what would be called a*
> *repressed memory, that she had been sexually abused.*
> —Pamela Freyd
> FMS Foundation Founder

The debate's bloodiest stage is the courtroom. The hired guns of Martin Orne's circle of psychiatrists are constantly called upon to blow smoke at the jury's gallery to conceal CIA mind control operations. This branch of the psychiatric community is steeped in the programming of serial killers, political assassins and experiments on involuntary subjects. Agency psychiatrists on the witness stand direct the press away from the CIA, and the prosecution to a predetermined end.

Orne's influence contributed to the outcome of a high-profile abuse case, the $8 million lawsuit filed by Gary Ramona of Napa, California against child therapist Marche Isabella and psychiatrist Richard Rose. Ramona charged that his daughter Holly's therapists elicited from her flashbacks of sexual molestation that never occurred, decimating his marriage and career as a vice president at Robert Mondavi wineries. His wife and employer, note, immediately believed Holly's accusations. In May of 1994 Ramona received a $500,000 jury award. He hailed the decision as a "tremendous victory."

Nevertheless, Holly Ramona still maintains that she was sexually abused by her father, though no criminal charges have been filed. Holly first confronted her father with the allegations on March 15, 1990, with her mother and Isabella present. She filed a civil action against him in Los Angeles County, but before it went to trial her father's suit got underway in Napa.

The suit turned on the use of sodium amytal to resurrect buried memories. Holly Ramona exhibited telltale symptoms of abuse—fear of gynecological examinations, a phobia of pointy teeth, like her father's—and asked to be treated with sodium amytal. Dr. Rose wrote in his notes that under the influence of the drug, Holly "remembered specific details of sexual molestation." But Orne, who has pioneered in the use of sodium amytal in hypnosis research, cautioned in a court brief that the drug is "not useful in ascertaining 'truth.' The patient becomes receptive to suggestions due to the context and to the comments of the interviewers."

Yet the jury foreman stated for the record that Isabella and Rose *did not* implant false memories of abuse, as Holly's father had complained, but were negligent in reinforcing the memories as Holly described them under the influence of the barbiturate. The court considered it irrelevant whether Holly actually suffered abuse, narrowing the legal focus instead to the chemical evocation of Holly's recollections and her therapist's leading questions.

Left hanging was the question of Ramona's guilt or innocence, not exactly an irrelevant issue. Orne offered no opinion. The "tremendous victory" in Napa, given these facts, begins to look like a manipulation of the court system, especially the use of "expert" testimony.

The therapists did not, contrary to most press reports, bear the full brunt of blame. The jury found that Ramona himself bore 5% of the blame for what happened to him, Holly's therapists 55%, and 45% by the girl's mother and the Robert Mondavi winery.

But the 55% solution is diluted by Holly's memories. Contrary to the impression left by the press, her past has not been explained away. "I wouldn't be here if there

Pamela Freyd, Ph.D

was a question in my mind," she testified in Napa.

False memory had no clinical history or symptomology (repressed memory has both), but the concept had held up in court.

All that remained was to provide a scientific explanation. The Foundation had spread the word that a "syndrome" was winding through society and "destroying families." But what is the origin of false (not inaccurate or clouded or fragmented) memories? What are the symptoms? It remained to supply a cognitive model for false memories of ritual molestation.

One of the most prolific and quotable popularizers of false memory is Elizabeth Loftus, a professor of psychology and law at the University of Washington in Seattle, and an advisory board member of the Foundation. Her dual academic interests have fueled suspicions that the organization is more committed to defending perpetrators than ferreting out the facts. Loftus testified in over 150 criminal cases prior to joining the Foundation, always on behalf of defendants. In 1991 she published a professional auto-biography, *Witness for the Defense,* a study of eight criminal trials in which she appeared as an expert witness. In her book, Loftus—billed as "the expert who puts memory on trial"—conceded that her critics deem her research "unproven in real-life situations," and her courtroom disserta-tions "premature and highly prejudicial."

One book reviewer for the *New York Times* grumbled: "Her testimony would be less controversial if she could distinguish between the innocent and the guilty and reserve her help for the former."

Elizabeth Loftus has two criteria for taking the stand. The first is when eyewitness identification is the sole or primary evidence against the defendant. Secondly, the accused must act innocent—she regrets testify-ing on behalf of Ted Bundy because the serial killer once smiled at the prosecutor, which she regards as an expression of guilt—and defense attorneys must believe it.

Loftus stood at the Harvard Medical School podium in May, 1994 to inform a conference on false memory of her research, "in which false memories about childhood events were created in 24 men and women ages 18 to 63." Dr. Loftus reported that the parents of volunteers "coop-erated to produce a list of events that had supposedly taken place in the volunteer's early life." Three of the events actually took place. But one, a shopping trip, never happened. Some of the volunteers had memories, implanted by suggestion, of wandering lost on the fictitious shopping expedition.

Karen Olio, the author of scores of articles on sexual abuse, complains that Loftus's memory studies "examine only the possibility of implanting a single memory with which most people could easily identify (being lost in a mall, awakened by a noise in the night). The possibility of 'implant-ing' terrifying and shameful memories that differ markedly from an individual's experience, such as memories of childhood abuse in individuals who do not have a trauma history," remains to be proven.

Psychiatrist John Briere of the University of Southern California has found that nearly two-thirds of all ritual abuse survivors report episodic or complete amnesia at some point after it occurred. The younger the child, the more violent the abuse, the more likely that memory lapses occurred. These findings have been duplicated at the University of California at San Francisco by psychiatrist Lenore Terr, who concluded that children subjected to repeated abuse were more likely to repress memories of it than victims of a single traumatic event.

Clinical psychologist Catherine Gould has treated scores of ritually abused children at her office in Encino, California. At the September 1993 National Conference on Crimes Against Children in Washington, D.C., Gould objected that the studies of Elizabeth Loftus ignore past research on trauma and its influence on memory.

"My concern about Elizabeth Loftus," Gould says, "is that she has stated in print, and correctly so, that her data tells us nothing about the nature of memory of traumatic events. And yet she has failed to protest the misapplication of her findings by groups who are involved in discrediting the accounts survivors are giving of their traumatic history. I believe that Dr. Loftus, like other psychologists, has an ethical responsibility to do everything possible to ensure that her research findings are interpreted and applied accurately, and are not manipulated to serve the political agenda of groups like the False Memory Syndrome Foundation. I question whether she has met this ethical responsibility."

Her study did not live up to its promise. But now that she had "proven" that a false memory could be implanted, friends of the Foundation at the Harvard conference announced they'd identified the neurological and cognitive causes of disorder. Daniel Schacter, a Harvard psychologist and conference organizer, claimed that the "confabulator" selects a fragment of a real memory, "but confuses its true context, and draws on other bits of experience to construct a story that makes sense of it." Dr. Morris Moscovitch, a neuro-psychologist at the University of Toronto, claimed that "brain damage" could also evoke false memories. He noted that mental patients with frontal lobe defects frequently confuse imaginary stories with actual memories.

A superficially plausible revelation was provided by Cornell psychologist Stephen Ceci, who reported on five studies of 574 preschool children. After 10 weeks of repeated questioning, 58% of them concocted a false account for at least one fictitious event.

But like the studies of Elizabeth Loftus, Ceci did not attempt to explain the supposed amnesiac effect of severe trauma on children and adults alike (veterans of WW II and Vietnam have been known to "forget" atrocities of war). Besides, the average preschooler is bound to invent at least one fantasy in 10 long weeks of repetitive questioning. Toddlers aren't known for their consummate adherence to objective reality. An invisible playmate and the Cat in the Hat are not "false memories."

The research results presented at the Harvard conference were not exactly staggering. All that had been proven was that children forget, become confused and make things up.

Seattle therapist James Cronin, one of the Foundation's harshest critics, believes that the false memory concept is promoted by "fact and artifice" to a public "conditioned to the fragmentation of knowledge, intellectual charades, elitism and the sterile abstractions that often pass for university education and expertise. The so-called experts now jumping on the side of false memory and therapist 'bias' are opportunists."

Yet the *New York Times* hailed the Harvard conference as "epic." The conference had given a gracious "scientific nod to the frailty of memory." Victims of aggravated child abuse had nothing to celebrate, but the *Times* reporter was ecstatic. At long last, scientists everywhere had arrived at "a consensus on the mental mechanisms that can foster false memories." A consensus? Actually, the "consensus" of psychologists, at least the 88% mentioned earlier—only a vast majority—believe it to be a very real scourge.

The *Times* story is typical of the scorn the press has shown ritual abuse victims and their therapists.

60 Minutes, for example, publicly exonerated Kelly Michaels, a day-care worker in New Jersey, of charges that she sexually molested dozens of youngsters in 1984. Michaels was sentenced to 47 years in prison for sodomizing the children in her care with kitchen implements, among related charges. Her conviction was overturned in March 1993 when the state appeals court ruled that Michaels had not had a fair trial.

But in its rush to present Michaels as a blushing innocent, the *60 Minutes* research department somehow overlooked a May 1991 *New York Times* story on the abuse trial, and the testimony of four Essex County corrections officers who witnessed Miss Michaels and her father kissing and "fondling" one another during jail visitations. Jerry Vitiello, a jailer, said that "he saw Ms. Michaels use his tongue when kissing his daughter, rub her buttocks and put his hand on her breasts." Similar incestuous liaisons were detailed in the courtroom by three women working in the jail. The bizarre sexual antics of Kelly Michaels—damningly chronicled in *Nap Time* by Lisa Manshel in 1990—were nixed from the one-sided *60 Minutes* account, which made her out to be grist for the meat grinder of wrong-headed child abuse laws.

The Forgettable "Remembering Satan"

The False Memory Syndrome Foundation made its collective debut in "Remembering Satan," a two-part story by Lawrence Wright in the *New Yorker* for April and May 1993. The story (republished in 1994 in book form) concerns a ritual abuse trial in Olympia, Washington that culminated with a 20-year prison sentence for Thurston County Sheriff Paul Ingram, chairman of the local Republican Party. Ingram has since filed motions to withdraw his guilty plea, a move rejected by an appellate court in 1992. Also charged, but not convicted, were Jim Rabie, a lobbyist with the Washington State Law Enforcement Association and a former police detective assigned to child abuse cases, and Ray Risch, an employee of the State Patrol's body-and-fender shop. Wright's conclusion, however, is based on the opinions of False Memory Syndrome Foundation psychiatrists: that accusations made by Ingram's two daughters, and his own confession to police, were fantasies misinterpreted by Ingram himself and his daughters as actual memories.

Wright fumigates any question of abuse with false memory theory. Among the authorities consulted by Wright was Foundation board member Paul McHugh, director of the department of psychiatry and behavioral sciences at Johns Hopkins. Like Margaret Singer, he is a veteran of the Walter Reed Army Institute of Research (1961–64) and moves in political circles. For three years (1986–89), McHugh was chairman of the bio-psychology study section of the National Institutes of Health, and a former member of the Maryland Governor's Advisory Commission.

McHugh is an unshakable skeptic of repressed memories. He told Wright that "most severe traumas are not blocked out by children but are remembered all too well." *Most,* in fact, are. But McHugh's own professional opinion leaves open the possibility that some severe traumas are repressed.

He cites as an example the children of Chowchilla, California, who were kidnapped in a school bus and buried alive. McHugh claims they remembered the horror "all too well." Not exactly. In fact, the FBI's subsequent use of investigative hypnosis was largely the result of the Chowchilla children's failure of memory. After their release, none of the children had a clear recollection of the kidnappers, could not identify them—and neither did the bus driver, Ed Ray, who managed to recite the license-plate number of the abductor's van under hypnosis.

Wright's defense of Ingram turns on the opinion of Richard Ofshe, a Berkeley psychologist, reputed mind control expert and friend of the False Memory Syndrome Foundation. Ofshe has written, Wright explains, "extensively about how the thought-control techniques developed in Communist china, the Soviet Union and North Korea had come to be employed and refined by various religious cults in the United

States." Pointing to mind control in Communist countries is a favorite tactic of the American mind control fraternity to divert attention from the highly sophisticated techniques employed in "democratic" countries (often in the form of experimentation on unknowing subjects). This historical revision is a fine example of "mirror imaging," the CIA technique of vilifying others, and ignoring the Agency's own role in the formation and manipulation of mind control cults. Ofshe has not been directly linked to the CIA, but his work parrots the writings of UCLA's Louis Jolyon West and other psychiatrists with Agency credentials.

Wright somehow failed to mention that Ofshe is sharply at odds with much of the American Psychological Association. He has filed a suit, with Margaret Singer, for $30 million against the APA for engaging in a "conspiracy" to "destroy" their reputations and prevent them from testifying in the courtroom. Both Ms. Singer and Richard Ofshe derive a significant part of their incomes as consultants and expert witnesses on behalf of accused child abusers. Their complaint, filed under federal racketeering laws—tripling any financial damages—claims that members of the APA set out with "repeated lies" to "discredit them and impair their careers."

The Association flatly denied the charges. Two courts quickly dismissed the case. The APA released a statement to the press stating that the organization had merely advised members against testifying in court on the subject of brainwashing with "persuasive coercion" (a concept, after all, used during the Korean war by the CIA to justify barbaric mind control experimentation on American citizens), and had in no way conspired to impair the careers of Ofshe, Singer or anyone else.

Many in Ofshe's own profession believe him to be a world-class opportunist. He is a constant in newspaper interviews and on the talk show circuit, where he claims there is "no evidence" to support ritual abuse allegations. His categorical denial ignore's Ingram's own confession and a number of jury decisions across the country. And then there are, to cite one documented example of evidence from the glut that Ofshe ignores, the tunnels beneath the McMartin preschool, the most widely-publicized case. And a raid on the Children of God compound in Argentina in 1993 turned up videos of ritual abuse and child pornography. Evidence does exist—Ofshe simply refuses to acknowledge the fact. A cult specialist with Ofshe's credentials would surely explore the abundance of evidence if he was a legitimate psychologist. Instead, he chirps a categorical "no evidence," perfectly aware that most mental health professionals will see through him. A credulous public will not.

On the December 3, 1993 *Rolanda* talk show, a woman was interviewed who'd had flashback memories of abuse before consulting with a therapist. Dr. Ofshe appeared on the program, his silver beard groomed, looking every inch the authority. Rolanda asked Ofshe if "a terrible childhood memory, as bad as child abuse, (can) actually be repressed?"

"There is absolutely no reason to think that that is true," Ofshe told her. "And it's not just what I say—this is the sum and substance of everything science knows about how memory works." This, of course, is a transparent lie. Ofshe dismissed repressed memories of abuse as the reigning "psychological quackery of the 20th century."

Dr. Daniel Lutzker, a psychologist at the Milton Erickson Institute, was sitting in the audience—turning crimson with rage at Ofshe's misrepresentations of the psychology of trauma. He stood up and argued that sex abuse can indeed begat buried recollections. "Repressed memories," Lutzker countered, "are not only important, they are the cornerstone of most psychotherapies. The fact is that the more awful the experience, the more likely it is to be repressed!"

Ofshe responded that there was "no evidence" so support such "nonsense."

Grimacing with disbelief, Lutzker said that Ofshe wouldn't make such outrageous comments if he bothered to pick up "any basic textbook on psychotherapy."

"Your making it up!" Ofshe spat. Lutzker stared at him in disbelief.

But the crowning contradiction to Ofshe's "expert" opinions appeared in a September 1994 *L.A. Weekly* article on alien abductions (another phenomenon said by the Foundation to breed "false memories").

"There are a lot of not particularly well-certified people out there," Dr. Ofshe told Dave Gardetta, "using very powerful techniques on people. Visualizing this kind of stuff under hypnosis—abduction, Satan cults, sexual abuse—is the closest thing that anyone can experience short of the experience itself. That's why it's so traumatic to the individuals undergoing hypno-therapy, and why the hypno-therapist today can be seen as a new form of *sexual predator.*"

But one morning, shortly thereafter, Gardetta awoke to find a triangular rash on the palm of his left hand.

"It didn't surprise me," Gardetta wrote. "Things around the house—which sits on a hilltop in a semi-rural area—had been getting weird. A jet-wash noise buzzed some afternoons around the house, its origin impossible to discern. Lights were turning themselves on, and the alarm system's motion sensor was tripping itself every morning between 5 and 6. One early evening, small footsteps crossed the roof. I ran outside to find the electrical wires leading to a nearby telephone pole swaying in the windless dusk."

The mysterious federal mind control fraternity had struck again, leaving behind more memories to be denounced by the "skeptics" of the FMS Foundation—the CIA's answer to the Flat Earth Society.

Chapter Four

Ray Buckey's Press Corps & the Tunnels of McMartin

A fusillade of press reports, OpEd Columns and television documentaries have dismissed the McMartin case as a "witch hunt" born of mass hysteria, coercive therapy, false memories and greed. Yet all seven jurors attending a press conference after the second trial raised their hands when asked who among them believed children had been abused at the preschool. So why the call to public denial from the press?

After the initial flurry of press coverage of the McMartin Preschool molestation case, a number of sympathetic reporters and psychiatrists publicly exonerated Ray Buckey and his co-defendants. This observer's gallery of "skeptics" also deny that ritual abuse is a social problem.

The argument consistently leads to the lament that the McMartin allegations were incited by mass hysteria, an ambitious district attorney and an incompetent child therapist. The hysteria thesis, promoted by a small group of pedophile defense psychologists, mostly, has appeared in publications of stature including the *Los Angeles Times, San Francisco Chronicle, Wall Street Journal, Village Voice, Harper's, New Yorker* and *Newsweek.* The McMartin case was the subject of an Oliver Stone cable feature.

Media boosters of the defense neglect to acknowledge the most damning evidence in the McMartin case. Instead, they explain away superficial, carefully-sifted pieces of the case. In preparation for the trial, 389 toddlers were interviewed—nearly all of them described abuse at the preschool, and do to this day. Some 80 percent had physical symptoms, including blunt force trauma of sexual areas, scarring, rectal bleeding and sexual diseases.

Interestingly enough, skeptics of ritual abuse in the public print often have dubious bona fides themselves. Some even participate secretly in the pedophile and occult undergrounds, most notably a couple of Los

Angeles writers who have written the only two book available on McMartin, taking mental health professionals, police, the press and prosecutors to task for pursuing false allegations of abuse.

The Politics of Child Abuse, by Paul and Shirley Eberle, purports to be something of a definitive investigation. A blurb for the book exults: "This has got to be one of the most devastating political detective stories of all time. The authors smashed open the child abuse witch-hunt so everyone can see it for what it is—the way it really happened, and why. Here is the amazing story, starting with the first spectacular accusations, the marathon pre-trial hearing, the endless series of false accusations."

Since the Eberles' first McMartin book appeared in 1986, they have achieved national status as child abuse experts. In courts of law their work is frequently cited, and they lecture widely to receptive audiences. The Eberles once appeared as featured speakers at a conference held by Victims of Child Abuse Laws (VOCAL), an organization that feted *The Politics of Child Abuse* as positively revelatory.

But Paul and Shirley Eberle can hardly be considered credible reporters. Blurbs in their own pornographic tabloid, *L.A. Star,* failed to mention that in the 1970s the authors once ran an underground tabloid for pedophiles in Los Angeles, *Finger,* which delved heavily into sadomasochistic sex, sex with children and sex acts involving human excrement. *Finger* contained sexual drawings by children and pedophile erotica, including "My First Rape," "She was Only Thirteen," "Sexpot at Five," and "What Happens when Niggers Adopt White Children." One issue featured a cover photo of two naked adults reclining amid a pile of inflated dolls. A letter to *Finger* declaimed: "I'm a pedophile and I think it's great a man is having sex with his daughter.... Would like to see pics of nude girls making it with their daddy, but realize it's too risky to print."

The book's publisher, Carole Stuart of Lyle Stuart & Co., told *Ms.* magazine that the Eberles have been "friends of the family for years."

In *The Politics of Child Abuse,* the Eberles claimed that since the McMartin arrests, "we have been barraged with hundreds of sexual abuse cases, in which many people have been sent to prison for staggeringly long terms on little or no evidence." That the Eberles themselves remain at large would seem to contradict the notion that child abuse laws are stringently over-enforced.

The Eberles attempt to portray *every* abuser as a victim of the justice system:

> We believe that every molestation case in which there has been a conviction should be reopened and reviewed. There is convincing evidence that innocent people have been imprisoned, that naive juries and judges were unable to believe the defendants would be brought to trial if no crime had occurred,

and defense attorneys have not been allowed to bring all the pertinent facts before the public.

Los Angeles attorney Sally Dichter, in a book review, argued that the Eberles have "nothing to offer to any discipline." The book, she lamented, "is an attempt to vindicate every individual who has been convicted of child abuse." Considering their credentials as child pornographers, of course the Eberles, as Dichter discovered, believe "every molestation case in which there has been a conviction should be reopened and reviewed." Dichter found this point of view unbelievable: "The Eberles seem intent on convincing the reader that child abuse *never* occurs."

The authors' "skepticism" of ritual child abuse is shared by Gerald Larue, professor emeritus of Biblical history and archeology at the University of Southern California. Larue is one of the principals behind the Noah's Ark hoax, which culminated in February 1993 with a two-hour CBS prime-time special, "The Incredible Discovery of Noah's Ark," billed by CBS as a documentary. Scholars immediately denounced it. The network refused to retract.

Satanism in America, a book that Larue co-wrote, attributed the McMartin case to a "satanic panic" incited by wild-eyed "religious fanatics, opportunists and emotionally unstable survivors whose stories simply are not to be believed"—an agonizing irony given Larue's instigation of the Noah's Ark hoax. He argues that the "child abuse hysteria sweeping the country is being fueled by people for whom facts have no meaning. They invent 'facts.'"

Langley Connections and the Rise of the Child Abuse Backlash

Another "expert" who has dismissed McMartin as a classic witch-hunt is Dr. Douglas Besherov, once the director of the National Center on Child Abuse and Neglect. He is also a director of the rabidly right-wing American Enterprise Institute, a Washington D.C. think tank.

To supplement his weighty credentials, Besherov writes for academic social and political quarterlies with long histories of collaborating with the CIA for propaganda purposes. He is a coeval of Irving Kristol, a veteran CIA psychological warfare specialist. In 1976, the Congressional Church Committee hearings revealed that the CIA is deeply entrenched in the American press. Some 400 journalists, it emerged at the hearings, had collaborated with the Agency at least once. CIA propagandists like Besherov and Kristol provide others in the field with a scholastic support base, and mold opinion on campus with such CIA-anchored academic journals as *Encounter* and *The Public Interest,* both edited by neo-con Kristol.

In 1986, *Public Interest* published a monograph by Dr. Besherov entitled "Unfounded Allegations—A New Child Abuse Problem." Besherov opens with the observation of legal scholar Sanford Katz that "the maltreatment of children is as old as recorded history. Infanticide, ritual sacrifice, exposure, mutilation, abandonment, brutal discipline and the near slavery of child labor have existed in all cultures."

Dr. Besherov, left dry-eyed by such conditions, blamed the media and mandatory reporting laws for dragging child abuse out of the closet (where he seems to prefer it) and blowing the severity of the problem out of proportion.

Besherov's influential follow-up article, "Doing Something About Child Abuse: The Need to Narrow the Grounds for State Intervention," was published in 1985 by Irving Kristol and the American Enterprise Institute. In it, Besherov argues that most allegations of child abuse are statistically unfounded. His slipshod use of statistics drove the Child Welfare League of America (CWLA) to publicly find him responsible for leading the public "to believe that child abuse is leveling off or that, as reports increase, the level of substantiation decreases." The CWLA notes that its survey results indicate a "substantial increase in reports," and "a stable rate of confirmation," directly contradicting Besherov's statistical red herring.

Turning to the children removed from their homes by social workers, Besherov states flatly: "According to data collected by the federal government, it appears that up to half of these children were in no immediate danger at home and could have been safely left there."

The government "data" cited by Besherov derive from a study conducted by the National Center on Child Abuse and Neglect. The authors of the study told *New York Times* reporter David Hechler that "the information is not there" to support Besherov's assertion that half of all abused children left in the custody of their parents are in "no immediate danger."

"He has used our statistics in this case to prove a point when (he) simply can't do it," a Center researcher told Hechler. When asked for his response, the AEI scholar refused to comment.

By fabricating statistics, Besherov reveals himself to be a propagandist.

Have unfounded allegations led to a national McCarthyite frenzy, as Besherov contends? "I'm sure there are false allegations," concedes David Finkelhor, a sociologist specializing in child abuse. "I'm sure when people are caught up in false allegations it's terrible." But in criminal cases of all kinds, "there's always the possibility of false allegations, and I don't think they're more severe in the area of child abuse that they are in—I want to say something innocuous—people making false allegations about having had money stolen from them, or false allegations of embezzlement."

Besherov's work has given rise to such *hysteria-producing* diatribes as "False Accusations of Child Abuse: Could it Happen to You?" (*Women's Day,* July 8, 1986), and "Invasion of the Child Savers: No One is Safe in the War Against Abuse" (*Progressive,* September, 1985)—both are adventures in hyperbole, like Besherov's cooked statistics.

"Family abuse," by A.C. Carlson, another protégé of Irving Kristol. appeared in *Reason* magazine, a publication that frequently runs CIA disinformation. Hechler writes that Carlson has gone "even further than Besherov, inflating the unfounded rate beyond belief." Erroneously, in fact, Carlson laments that "the victims pile up," like corpses on a pyre, and commiserates needlessly with "the sky-rocketing number of parents and teachers falsely accused of child abuse."

Ritual abuse "skeptics" with CIA connections are covering up the latest phase in Agency-sponsored mind control experimentation. For thirty years Agency scientists have collaborated with cults (many of them founded by the government) to conceal the development of mind control technology. Jim Jones and the People's Temple were one product of the alliance. McMartin was another. Both episodes have been buried in disinformation. The campaign to mislead the public about ritual abuse is ambitious, rivaling the campaign to conceal the facts in the murder of John F. Kennedy.

The smokescreen is also explained in part by reports implicating the CIA in child prostitution for the purposes of political blackmail—a variation on the age-old sex trap. CIA agents have been directly involved in organized child sex rings. In *Enslaved* (1991), an investigation of the worldwide slavery underground, Gordon Thomas found Agency participation in the kidnap of Latin American children "flown across the border in light aircraft, and sold to child sex rings, or sold so their organs could be used in transplants." Some of the pilots, Thomas discovered, "made two or three flights a day. The more experienced used Beech 18s because of the aircraft's capacity and maneuverability. The majority of the fliers were mercenaries who had flown for the CIA."

Ray Buckey's father, Charles, worked for Hughes Aircraft. There is an old adage that holds "Hughes *is* the CIA." Charles Buckey built the McMartin Preschool. The tunnels unearthed beneath the preschool were dug in 1966—the year the school was built.

Buckey Sr. testified on the stand that there were no tunnels. The media have been completely silent on this score, which brings us to....

This arch was pounded through a concrete footing in the foundation beneath the McMartin Preschool. Best estimates date the digging of the tunnels to circa 1966, the year the preschool was built by Charles Buckey, father of the key defendant. Photo: Dr. Roland Summit

The Tunnel Cover-Up

El Paso reporter Debbie Nathan, utterly convinced of the defendants' innocence, entered the fray in *The Village Voice*, and has appeared in newspapers across the country, including *The L.A. Weekly, Sacramento Bee, San Francisco Chronicle,* and elsewhere. She has been honored with the Free Press Association's H. L. Mencken Award, and Northwestern University's Medill School of Journalism prize.

She is a leading proponent of the "mass hysteria" thesis, the notion that many child abuse allegations are "unfounded." Her cavalier dismissal is not supported by objective research. Dr. David Chadwick of San Diego's Childrens' Hospital, in the *Journal of the American Medical Association* (May 26, 1989), contends that 8% of all abuse allegations are unfounded, at most, and are "rather easily distinguishable in a careful review."

At times it is difficult to tell whether Nathan is a "skeptic" or an apologist of sexual abuse. "Most pedophilia," she contends, "consists of caressing and fondling. For most children, these experiences appear to be at best confusing, at worst traumatic. But others seem to willingly participate, and some adults recall that while still legally minors they accepted, even *welcomed,* sex with grown-ups."

Nathan doesn't condemn the abuser. After all, "compared to the abuses of a child protection movement gone mad, could incest be any worse?"

Alex Cockburn is a Nathan supporter, and has on occasion gotten caught up in her pro-pedophilic obfuscations, as in this diatribe from *The Nation* for March 8, 1993:

> As a Miami-based anthropologist, Rafael Martinez, consultant to the Dade County Medical Examiner's Office, told Nathan, in traditional Latin American cultures "kissing and hugging is common with children up to three or four years old." It is common for females to kiss children all over the place— including on the genitals.

The practice of kissing children on the genitals may be traditional in some cultures, but it is frowned upon by the Manhattan Beach preschool licensing board.

Alex Cockburn's skepticism toward ritual abuse was summed up in an editorial appearing in the February 8, 1990 *Wall Street Journal,* "The McMartin Case: Indict the Children, Jail the Parents." The son of a British spy, and a loquacious defender of the Warren Commission, Cockburn has such strong feelings about the McMartin case that he once publicly maligned an editor of the *L.A. Weekly* for refusing to print a recommendation that "the tots bearing false witness in the McMartin preschool case be jailed for perjury."

His primary source on the subject of child abuse, Debbie Nathan, is herself something of a false witness. In "What McMartin Started: The Ritual Abuse Hoax" (*Village Voice*, June 12, 1990), Ms. Nathan moaned that "children at McMartin told of being molested in tunnels under the school. None were ever found, but until recently parents were still digging."

In fact, 30 days before Nathan's article appeared, the tunnels were discovered beneath the preschool by scientists hired by the parents, confirming the testimony of the children. The project employed a team of archeologists from local universities, two geologists, a professional excavator, a carbon-dating specialist and a professional photographer to document the dig's progress and findings.

The longest tunnel was six feet beneath the preschool, running eastward 45 feet from the southwest wall, and ten feet along the north wall. The tunnel walls were held in place by support beams and a roof of plywood and tarpaper. A branch of the tunnel led to a nine-foot chamber (the "secret room" described by the children?). Another extended from the preschool to the triplex next door, surfacing beneath a roll-away bathtub. Forensic tests on thousands of objects found at the site—including two hundred animal bones—were conducted.

Until the tunnels were found, the *L.A. Times* covered the dig—with a smirk. The parents and scientists involved were portrayed as crack-pots until the existence of the tunnels was substantiated by experts, at which time the newspaper abruptly stopped reporting the story. The public was left with the false impression that the search had failed.

Critics of the excavation pointed out that District Attorney Ira Reiner had already searched for tunnels. At best, this is a half-truth. Reiner's team tore up a bit of floor tile, but did not even bother to remove the glue that held it in place. The D.A.'s team, as it happens, dug up the lot *next to the preschool,* not underneath.

"Actually," McMartin mother Jackie MacGauley, who supervised the excavation, notes, "we were the first to dig on the property." The search for the tunnels was undertaken with ground-penetrating radar to probe for inconsistencies in the soil. A bell-shaped area of disturbed earth was discovered along the foundation of the west wall.

The tunnel beneath the opposite wall was unearthed (precisely where the children said it would be found all along) beneath the foundation. A passage had been knocked through the concrete. "It was interesting," MacGauley told L.A.'s Pacifica Radio, "because a lot of the child development specialists, psychiatrists and therapists across the country thought that it was some psychological phenomenon that the kids would talk about tunnels. Somehow that idea got 'planted,' and they had all these theories as to why all the kids would talk about something like this. It

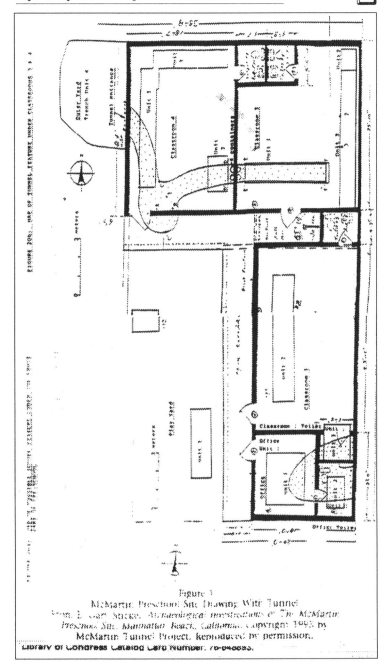

A blueprint of the McMartin Preschool with tunnels superimposed.

obviously couldn't be true. And the district attorney at the time just flatly did not believe it, and really didn't want to look."

Neither did the press.

A Cottage Industry of Child Abuse Debunkers

MODERN WITCH-HUNT—CHILD ABUSE CHARGES

bawled a *Wall Street Journal* editorial for February 22, 1993. But the tone of the column was dry and high-toned. Dr. Richard Gardner, professor of clinical psychiatry at Columbia University, cautioned that "a great wave of hysteria" had gripped the country.

In the early 90s, the mass hysteria premise was touted by big city newspapers and magazines of elite stature, all attempting to persuade— with evident bias and inflated "expert" opinion—that false child abuse charges were endemic. This school of disinformation coaxed public opinion with dire exhortations of a child abuse witch-hunt.

In his *Wall Street Journal* comments, Dr. Gardner warned of a great wave of hysteria, "by far the worst" in history, the most devastating "with regard to the number of lives that have been destroyed and families that have been disintegrated."

Gardner's basic argument is that allegations of child abuse are often fabricated by parents embroiled in custody disputes—another explanation not supported by statistics, the ones Gardner ignores. One study found that a mere two percent of all abuse accusations stem from visitation and custody disputes. (Other researchers have placed the percentage slightly higher.)

As for "mass hysteria," one of the earliest promoters of this thesis was Ralph Underwager, co-author with his wife, Hollida Wakefield, of *Accusations of Child Sexual Abuse.* "Few physicians will wish to invest the time and money ($70) to own or even read this book," complained a reviewer for the *Journal of the American Medical Association.* "It is of little value to those who work with abused children except as it may be important to be aware of all points of view. The book will be doubtless be useful to attorneys defending persons accused of sexual abuse of children. It appears to have been written particularly for that audience.... The authors cite over 700 references, but they do not really review this body of literature. When a given reference fails to support their viewpoint, they simply misstate the conclusion."

Since 1974, Dr. Underwager has been the director of the Institute for Psychological Therapies in Northfield, Minnesota. He has since been frequently called upon to provide expert testimony—in the late 80s he spent 60-70% of his professional life shuttling between courtrooms. He is the author of numerous articles debunking the credibility of ritual abuse victims. Dr. Underwager has frequently been cited by Debbie Nathan as a leading authority on the subject. Lisa Manshel, author of *Nap Time,* an account of the New Jersey ritual abuse case, found that "child sexual abuse was not his field of knowledge," but "it was his field of courtroom practice." He proliferated the opinion, 'No one knows how to tell accurately whether a child's been abused' throughout the nation's courts. He has testified in most states, and by satellite in foreign countries, before at least 200 juries.

Dr. Underwager once stated on the stand that he considered it "more desirable that a thousand children in abuse situations are not discovered than for one innocent person to be convicted wrongly."

Dr. Underwager, a founder of the False Memory Syndrome Foundation, is an ordained Lutheran minister. He believes, he once said in an interview appearing in an Amsterdam journal for pedophiles, that sex with children is not only acceptable, but "God's will."

> **Q:** Is choosing pedophilia for you a responsible choice for the individual?
>
> **Underwager:** *Certainly* it is responsible. What I have been struck by as I have come to know more about and understand people who choose pedophilia is that they let themselves be too much defined by other people. That is usually an essential negative definition. Pedophiles spend a lot of time and energy defending their choice. I don't think a pedophile needs to do that.

An outside entrance to the tunnels beneath the preschool partially filled in with soil foreign to the site.

Underwager insisted that pedophiles "should attack the concept, the image, the picture of the pedophile as an evil, wicked and reprehensible exploiter of children." Following the interview, Underwager was forced to resign as a founding member of the False Memory Syndrome Foundation (which is largely directed by CIA psychiatrists with backgrounds in mind control experimentation).

The *London Observer* for December 12, 1993 reported that Dr. Underwager denied ever condoning sex with children. He added, however, that "scientific evidence" had demonstrated that "60 percent of women sexually abused as children reported that the experience was good for them." He contended the same could be true for boys involved with pedophiles.

The Descent of Mann

In a five-part series that appeared after the hung jury verdict of Ray Buckey's first trial, *Los Angeles Times* reporter David Shaw found that the newspaper's research files explained little of "the crucial behind-the-scenes role played by screenwriter Abby Mann." Mann's writing staff and circle of disinformationists have shaped public opinion on the McMartin case.

Noel Greenwood, an *L.A. Times* editor, has described the wall of pro-Buckey PR thrown up by Mann and friends as "a *mean, malevolent campaign* conducted by people… whose motives are highly suspect and who have behaved in a basically dishonest… and dishonorable way."

Abby Mann, is an Oscar recipient for a film about the Nazi war crimes trial, *Judgment at Nuremburg* (an oxymoron, since there was precious little justice at Nuremburg, a carefully-managed show trial that culminated with the execution of a small clutch of Nazis, minor prison terms for some—and recruitment of thousands of others by the CIA.)

From the beginning, Mann was a vociferous advocate of the McMartin defendants. "We like to think we are different from Salem," Mann sniffed at the resolution of Ray Buckey's first trial. "I don't believe that anything happened at that school."

Abby Mann has worked diligently, largely back-stage, on behalf of The Buckeys. It was Mann who first interested *60 Minutes* in the McMartin case. The November 2, 1986 broadcast was decidedly biased in favor of Ray Buckey. Defense attorney Danny Davis characterized the segment as "wholly sympathetic to the defense point of view."

60 Minutes led off with the camera panning a long couch and five of the original defendants. Mike Wallace asked: "Do these women look like child molesters?"

New York Times reporter David Hechler noted "gaping holes in the story. Why were no police or D.A.'s investigators interviewed or even mentioned? And if Ira Reiner believed the case was so weak against the five defendants, why did he wait until the five-month preliminary hearing was completed before dropping the charges? These questions were never asked." The innocence of the defendants was assumed by Wallace and crew as a foregone conclusion, and the charges against them were framed as the aberrations of nattering lunatics.

Most of the *60 Minutes* segment on McMartin was taped in Abby Mann's living room.

But heavily-biased media coverage was only one of the strategies quietly enacted by Abby Mann. When Deputy District Attorney Glenn Stevens was caught leaking information on the prosecution's case to Mann, he was forced to resign. No charges were brought against him.

From the *Los Angeles Times:*

> Gaining the confidence of the McMartin defendants, the Manns were ultimately hired as "investigators" for the defense. That and their earlier alliance with former prosecutor Glenn Stevens sparked charges from parents of alleged child molestation victims of a conspiracy to obstruct justice for monetary gain.

After *Los Angeles Times* reporter Bob Williams met Abby Mann, he wrote a flurry of memos charging the coverage of Lois Timnick, the paper's reporter on the McMartin beat, with extreme bias favoring the prosecution. The accusation was investigated by Noel Greenwood, the regional news editor at the *Times.* Greenwood concluded that it was Williams who'd acted with extreme bias, not Timnick. Greenwood's memos state that Williams' memos were "reckless and irresponsible." Williams had "undermined a fellow reporter and seriously harmed the credibility and effectiveness of the *Times.*"

Williams was temporarily suspended without pay. Shortly thereafter, he went to work for Abby Mann.

Williams surfaced next as a consultant to Mary Fischer, whose "A Case of Dominoes" in *Los Angeles* magazine drew upon the argument (first postulated by the child pornographers Paul and Shirley Eberle), that former District Attorney Robert Philobosian initiated the McMartin prosecution for political gain.

Fischer once admitted to the late Wayne Satz, the KABC television reporter who broke the McMartin story, that she wrote the article under the direction of Abby Mann.

"There was never any case at all," Fischer wrote with absolute certainty. "At the very least, it is a blueprint for preying on public fears." Fischer has gone so far as to claim that therapists, parents and children attending McMartin masterminded a "conspiracy" to harass and imprison innocent people. When pressed on one occasion by Carole Hemingway, a Los Angeles talk show host, Fischer was unable to offer supporting evidence of conspiracy (as McMartin parents did), nor could she explain the motives of the conspirators.

Fischer did her utmost to dismiss the medical evidence that molestation took place at the preschool. In October, 1988 the *Los Angeles Times* reported that medical examiners of the original 13 children scheduled to testify found "scars, tears, enlarged body openings or other evidence indicating blunt force trauma consistent with the repeated sodomy and rape they described."

One of the children bled from the anus. Some contracted venereal infections.

Yet Fischer found relevant the findings of a Fresno pediatrician who refused to testify at the first McMartin trial. The 1987 study, summarized by Fischer, concluded that "any kind of irritation—not just sexual abuse—may damage children's genitals." This reader, at least, was left to ponder forms of "irritation" that might leave the McMartin children with chlamydia, confirmed by medical examinations and difficult to explain away.

Fischer's follow-up McMartin story in *Los Angeles* for October, 1993 opined that a "hysterical tone" in press reports on McMartin was established by Wayne Satz, who died of heart failure in 1992, "causing some to speculate it was karma," wrote Fischer, an ersatz and mean-spirited elegy.

"I still don't know how anyone could believe all that bull," Virginia McMartin told her. "Especially with a school as wide open as ours and people coming and going at all times. Or who could actually believe there were *tunnels.*" (The archeological team that led the excavation—ignored by Fischer—could have given her a guided tour.) "It shows the power of the media."

Apparently Abby Mann has a need for Ms. Fischer and the other writers in his employ. A best-selling Hollywood biographer (speaking on condition of anonymity) offers this insight into the career of Abby Mann. "He's incapable of writing scripts himself. It's true," he said, "he can't write. Abby keeps a fairly large stable of ghost writers to produce scripts in his name."

Who is Abby Mann? Mae Brussell, the late Carmel-based political researcher, speculated in a November, 1987 radio broadcast that Mann is a covert operator posing as a Hollywood progressive, plying extensive media connections to influence public opinion. Mann's behind-the-scenes manipulations, ghosts and an exhaustive supply of funds and press contacts support the hypothesis that Abby Mann is a media mole.

Indictment, yet another disinformation effort supposedly written by Abby and Myra Mann, premiered on May 20, 1995 on HBO. The movie was produced by Oliver Stone. As a political researcher, I had taken more than a passing interest in Stone's film *JFK,* and couldn't help but note that the media assault on Stone bore a resemblance to Mann's campaign to discredit the McMartin children. The day after an announcement of the "secret" project already underway appeared in *Variety*, I contacted Stone's office and spoke with Jean Marie Burke, a researcher for Ixtlan Productions, Stone's company in Santa Monica. I informed Ms. Burke that much of the information about McMartin in the corporate media was disingenuous, beginning with the Eberles. She brightened up. "Oh, the Eberles—I have their books right here!" She went silent when I told her that Paul and Shirley Eberle were child pornographers. I sent her a package of *accurate* information on the case by certified mail, then contacted her boss with a letter informing him simply that he had hold of a bad project, which had already been shot and was in the editing stage. Stone wrote back, asking me to clarify. My response follows:

Mr. Stone:

McMartin is poorly understood by most people because a disinformation gambit is afoot to discredit the childrens' testimony—a fusillade, in fact, similar to the one you were treated to after *JFK*. You asked me to clarify my objections.

Consider how difficult it was to sort through and communicate the multitude of facts relevant to the killing of John Kennedy. And then recall how a carefully-conceived film on the assassination can be explained away with a glib "no evidence" from an Edward Epstein or Dan Rather. This is the problem I'm up against with McMartin. There is a complex story behind the abuse—it involves CIA mind control experiments, and this is largely what the plants in the establishment press, and fronts like the False Memory Syndrome Foundation, are concealing. (Nine out of ten psychiatrists in both the U.S. and Great Britain from large samplings believe ritual abuse to be a very real social problem. But the media inevitably talks only to the one of ten who deny, and many of those are experimental scientists on the CIA payroll.) You now find yourself on the same side (of the McMartin argument) as Alex Cockburn, you recall the knock-down-drag-out *Nation* debate with a leading progressive who rejects key crimes of government (including the Kennedy assassination, for high-toned, but ultimately silly reasons), *Newsweek*, etc. That alone should make you uncomfortable in the extreme.

One of your researchers brightened up when I mentioned the only two books available on McMartin, both written by Paul and Shirley Eberle. She knew those books inside out. The problem is the Eberles published child pornography in the 1970s—garishly packaged in an underground rag called *Finger*—featuring adults having sex with children, children with excrement smeared on them, children in lewd positions and posing provocatively. This ludicrous pedophile sheet ran stories with such unsavory testimonials as "She was Only Thirteen," "What Happens when Niggers Adopt White Children," "My First Rape," and so on. Don't bother to read the McMartin books, if you haven't already. Each page is full of factual errors and conscious distortions. Your movie will perpetuate the Eberles' disinformation. But the *LA Times* will love it. (Buffy Chandler told a source of mine, in a moment of rage at her family, that her parents (the owners of the L.A. Times) funded weird genetic experiments years ago. This is no more bizarre than some of the things done in pre-schools around the country, and may explain the newspaper's change of attitude after the initial reporting.)

But Noel Greenwood, a *Times* editor, knew what he was talking about when he said there is a "mean-spirited campaign" in play to slant the truth about McMartin.

Abby Mann is a key proponent. His attorney threatened to sue if I didn't retract my comments when an early version of my research appeared several years ago. I did not retract. In fact, the newspaper, *Random Lengths* in Long Beach, backed me. Others appearing in the story threatened me. They did not sue. Why not? They made such a noise. Now they are the sources of your movie, still making noise about "innocence abused," and it's hollow.

They contend there is no evidence that children were abused at McMartin. On the contrary, there is an abundance of evidence. But the DA had no real intention of gathering it. Neither did the press. Same as *JFK,* eh?

The CIA connection to cults around the country began in 1963. The story was told by a Berkeley psychologist in a thesis entitled "The Penal Colony," which was presented at a psychiatric conference in San Francisco by Congressional aide Joe Holsinger after Leo Ryan was killed at Jonestown. The hybrid was conceived because people were asking questions about experiments at McGill, the University of Pennsylvania, John Hopkins, UCLA, Honeywell, and other haunts of the CIA's MKULTRA mind control fraternity. Jonestown was one product of the association. Another, more recent example was the Solar Temple killings in Switzerland. The British press reported that this cult was running arms to Australia and South America, and laundering the proceeds at BCCI. The American press couldn't find this information. What does this tell you?

Buckey Sr. testified that he did not have tunnels dug beneath the preschool. Why would anyone do that? Five scientists have put their reputations on the line to confirm that there are tunnels. One, a carbon-dating specialist, opined that the tunnels were excavated in 1966. That was the year the preschool was built. It was built by Charles Buckey. He lied on the stand. The kids gave fairly accurate descriptions of the tunnels. Did Abby?

Regards,
Alex Constantine

Despite this protest, and threats of a boycott of HBO from children's advocacy groups around the country, *Indictment* aired anyway. The movie simply reinforces the many misconceptions the public has been force-fed since Abby Mann became involved in the case.

The Most Hated Man at the L.A. Times

In January, 1990, after the anti-climactic, deadlocked verdict of the second trial, the *Los Angeles Times* ran a four-part series by media critic David Shaw, trashing the paper's own coverage of the McMartin case. Shaw described press coverage as a "media feeding frenzy" ranking with exposes of Gary Hart, Oliver North and Dan Quayle.

"More than most big stories," Shaw explained, "McMartin at times exposed basic flaws in the way the contemporary news organizations function. Pack journalism. Laziness. Superficiality." Daily newspaper coverage, he argued, was contaminated by "cozy relationships with prosecutors," and a competitive furor "that sends reporters off in a frantic search to be the first with the latest shocking alllegation."

Shaw's McMartin series won the *Times* its 18th Pulitzer, but few reporters attended the champagne party thrown in his honor. "Most people don't like him," *Times* staffer Lee Dye told a reporter for *Los Angeles* magazine. "He really is disliked at the *Times*," said restaurant critic Ruth Reichl. Bill Boyarsky, another staffer, says "everyone around me hates him."

The harshest opinion of Shaw came from the late Glenn Binford, the paper's late night editor at the city desk, who refers to Shaw as "an oily little prick." The nickname stuck. "Even the late Dial Torgerson," reported *Los Angeles*, "a droll, dry-witted newsman's newsman ... adopted the moniker, though it was uncharacteristic of Torgerson to disparage anyone."

Reporters for the "Metro" section particularly harbor a keen disdain for David Shaw.

Why is so much animosity directed his way? Most of Shaw's colleagues at the *Times* feel that he receives special treatment. He is contracted to write a mere four stories a year. He moonlights as the monthly

"Dining Out" columnist for *GQ* magazine. As the official ombudsman of the *Times,* one reporter complains, "Shaw plays favorites and purposefully ducks anything that may really irritate his superiors, tending instead to aim at those with no actual power."

Two of his primary targets were staff writer Lois Timnick and Cathleen Decker, whose McMartin coverage was hardly "frantic" or "superficial." Shaw's depiction of them as reportorial McCarthyites is not borne out by a review of the newspaper's McMartin coverage, and the air around Times Mirror Square has, since his series appeared, been thick with acrimony.

A week before Shaw received the Pultizer, Timnick (who has since stopped talking to him) threatened to organize an office "suicide party" if he won. When he did walk away with an award, the Pulitzer committee stated that it was given to Shaw not on the merits of his writing, but because the *Times* permitted him to criticize the paper's own coverage of a landmark trial.

Shaw was born on an Air Force base in Dayton, Ohio. He was educated at Pepperdine and UCLA. His career took off when, as a reporter for the *Long Beach Independent Press-Telegram,* he published a scalding investigative story on Max Rafferty, the Republican opponent of Alan Cranston for a Senate seat. Shaw's five-part series killed Rafferty's political prospects with allegations of draft dodging. Shaw received an award from the Los Angeles Press Club for the story and a job offer from the *Times.*

That was 19 years ago. He was informally assigned to "the sex beat." Shaw plied his investigative skills with titillating exposes of massage parlors and strip clubs. His piece on a nightspot featuring live sex with a dog threw the newsroom into turmoil—this is the same commentator who later dismissed most press coverage of McMartin as "sensational" and "superficial."

Shaw defines himself publicly as a "liberal," but he frequently expresses right-wing sentiments, and his writing can be fairly summed up as propagandistic. He chose to write on McMartin, *Los Angeles* magazine reported, "because he needed an excuse to stay in town. 'My wife was eight months pregnant, and I was looking for a story that would keep me in L.A. so I would be here for the birth.'"

"Experts" on the McMartin debacle—Shaw, the Eberles, Dr. Underwager, Abby Mann and others—have, in violation of their own admonitions, retried it in the press. Ray Buckey is supposed to be as innocent as Ceasar's wife. If so, why do Buckey's supporters ignore critical evidence? Why the statistical fabrications? Why lament repeatedly that the case took five years to try when dragging it out was a conscious defense strategy? Why ignore the tunnels and the bones?

And, most troubling off all, why has so much effort been put into propagating mass deception on Buckey's behalf?

Chapter Five

"What is that Odor?"

Mystery Fumes, the Poisoning of the Los Angeles County Commission for Women's Ritual Abuse Task Force & the Los Angeles Times

Introduction: Cults, Chemo-Terrorism and the CIA

After the deadly March 1995 subway gassing in Japan, 1200 police and military troops raided the "sixth santium" of Aum Shinri Kyo, one of the country's 17,000 religious cults, in the shadow of Mount Fuji. Sporting chemical gear, they cut their way into the Kamikuishiki warehouse with circular saws and oxyacetylene torches. On the first floor, police stumbled upon a "Perfect Salvation Initiation," a yogic ritual that employed electrical skull caps to deliver four-to ten-volt shocks to the novitiate in an attempt to open his chakras, the body's centers of spiritual energy. Among the healing rites practiced by the sect was the imbibing and vomiting of whole gallons of water, electric jolts and the "Christ Initiation," an arduous regimen of enemas and scalding hot baths.

Former members of the sect, according to a *Los Angeles Times* report, "paint a chilling picture of psychological indoctrination... sleep deprivation, mind control techniques and enforced isolation from the outside world. Access to family and friends—even newspapers and TV—is prohibited"[1] The cultists exhibited an alarming degree of mind control. Police freed a screaming woman from a stainless steel pod, and fifty cult members were found sprawled unconscious in a chapel on the second floor, six others in a drug-induced coma.[2]

Police announced that the stockpile of noxious chemicals discovered at the compound was the source of the nerve gas released in a Tokyo subway, killing ten people and injuring 5,000, with 70 in critical condition. Sadly enough, the neurotoxic effect of the gas is likely to be severe. Medical research has shown that acute exposure to toxic levels of sarin (a poison developed at chemical laboratories in Nazi Germany as a war gas) produces prolonged changes in brain function.[3] It was the first use of a chemical warfare agent on a large group of people by a non-military group[4] (though the apocalyptic sect is believed to have had a hand in an unexplained sarin "leak" in the Japanese Alps in 1994 that left eight dead and sickened 212.[5] "Birds dropped from the sky," one abashed correspondent wrote from Tokyo. "Dead dogs and cats lay in the gutters, and dead carp and yabbies floated to the surface of an ornamental pond"[6]).

It was not the first time that a cult has been accused of waging chemical warfare on unsuspecting civilians. In Los Angeles, for example, a series of mysterious attacks on members of the local County Commission for Women's Ritual Abuse Task Force in 1992 led to complaints of nausea, blurred vision, dizziness, headaches and elevated blood pressure. Eight of these cases had been independently confirmed by blood tests—yet, incredibly, *Los Angeles Times* coverage made light of the victims, blaming the outbreak of symptoms on the fertile imaginations of professional paranoiacs.[7] After all, allegations of abuse at McMartin Preschool in Manhattan Beach had been debunked. The expert opinions of "reputable" academics had shown that organized cult activity in southern California was non-existent, the zaniest of "urban legends." Hadn't they?

Surely the task force was laboring under another bout of cult "hysteria." The *Times* reassured the community that, once again, a few fevered brains had made monsters where none existed. The newspaper adhered to its position even when Dr. Catherine Gould, chairwoman of the Ritual Abuse Task Force, fired off a letter of rebuttal, pointing out that the allegations were backed up by blood-test reports verifying that members of the group had, contrary to the *Times* report, been exposed to organophosphate poisons.[8]

The *Times* did not print the letter. Dr. Gould, a licensed clinical child therapist, countered that she had found it shocking a major metropolitan newspaper would "deliberately bypass the available data in favor of a series of emotional charges which essentially amount to a chorus of 'it couldn't be true.'" She also bemoaned the newspaper's "pattern of biased and inaccurate reporting" on ritual child abuse, a tendency to side with perpetrators of Satanic Ritual Abuse (SRA) and promote the small minority of psychologists—only one out of ten, in fact—who deride recovered memory therapy and have largely succeeded at discrediting therapists who work with children abused by mind control cults.[9]

This small but highly "skeptical" school constitutes the pool of academic psychologists available to defense attorneys. They have received much play in the press, champions of the false memory theory of ritual abuse—though most are not licensed to practice child therapy. Ubiquitous in the media, this circle of academic psychologists includes Drs. Richard Ofshe, Margaret Singer and Elizabeth Loftus of the False Memory Syndrome Foundation, all of whom have made lucrative careers testifying on behalf of accused pedophiles. The therapists who actually *treat* the young victims are not sought out by reporters. This inequity, biased in favor of the False Memory Brigade, amounts to blanket censorship of all qualified professionals on the subject of ritual abuse. The press has thus become the sole domain of a small minority of defense psychologists.

Lopsided media coverage of ritual abuse amounts to a virulent form of disinformation. The perps and their hired guns in academia have a monopoly on the molding of public opinion. They are not representative, but they are quoted time and again by the press.

Their bona fides are often in CIA mind control experimentation. These include UCLA's Louis Jolyon West (LSD experiments) and Berkeley's Margaret Singer (brainwashing studies), both "experts" on cults. Dr. Ofshe, who turns up constantly in the newspapers to call recovered memory therapy a "quack" science, writes monographs on mind control strongly influenced by Dr. West's academic writing. Dr. Martin Orne, an original board member of the False Memory Syndrome Foundation, studied hypnotic persuasion at the University of Pennsylvania for CIA and Naval Intelligence paymasters.

What the *Los Angeles Times* neglected to tell its readership is that CIA behavior control scientists and the cults have formed an alliance.

The Agency uses the cults to further the techniques and technology of mind control.[10] In exchange, the CIA provides behind-the-scenes legal assistance and public relations. A perpetrator of ritual abuse, when nabbed, is often treated to friendly press coverage. In contrast, ritually abused children and their therapists have been targetted for harrassment because they threaten perps, cults and the Agency alike with exposure. Competent psychologists are, in the public print, made to appear greedy, incompetent opportunists practicing a medieval science based on quack theories of memory. Stories critical of those in the field of ritual abuse often bear an uncanny resemblance to a CIA disinformation campaign—and that, if the truth be known, is no accident.

Despite public pronouncements to the contrary, the CIA is still very actively engaged in mind control research. Communities around the world have been converted into laboratories. Cults in their midst are led by operatives practiced in the techniques and technology of behavior manipulation.

And media disinformation conceals the work of this mind control fraternity.

How the Times Suppressed the Medical Evidence

"In January of 1992," Dr. Gould recalled in her letter to the *Times,* "I became aware of a strange pattern of illnesses (affecting) both Los Angeles therapists treating ritual abuse patients, and individuals engaged in support and advocacy work on behalf of ritually abused children and adults." The afflicted complained not only of a general malaise that might be expected to accompany a demanding career, but also of such unusual symptoms as numbness in the face and extremities, blurred vision, muscle tremors and weakness, memory loss and even "incontinence."

The first to complain of symptoms saw a physician, who diagnosed her as suffering from diazinon poisoning. (Diazinon, like the sarin unleashed in Japan, is an organophosphate.[11]) Independently, another member of the task force had a blood test performed at Kaiser Hospital in Los Angeles, and was handed the same diagnosis. A third member of the group, an SRA survivor, was examined at the Glendale Adventist Medical Center and told that she had "organophosphate poisoning." Yet another member, a therapist suffering a constellation of toxic symptoms, bought a pesticide detection kit. She tested samples of food from the kitchen one evening when she discovered that her home had been broken and entered. A half dozen of the food samples proved positive for pesticide poisoning.

The therapist (requesting anonymity) claimed in a letter to the task force, "our home has been broken into several times, even during the day when witnesses were on the property. Neighbors inform us of continual nighttime surveillance. We have been followed several times by a variety of vehicles. On at least three occasions the interior of our home has been splattered with blood, and two birds have mysteriously died."[12]

Concerns were raised at the panel's March, 1992 meeting that some people engaged in helping ritual abuse survivors escape cult influence might be victims of pesticide poisoning. By that time, a number of therapists suffering from symptoms of organophosphate poisoning had contacted their physicians.

Satanic cult survivors on the task force also exhibited symptoms of toxification, including a young woman and incest survivor—referred to here as M—who received the following recorded message from her sister shortly after taking a blood test:

> I talked to mom this morning—she's very upset! She said she had a phone call yesterday about a meeting and that she wanted to tell you that any files, any medical reports that you go or that anyone else goes looking for will not be found, We know what you're up to and you're not going to get away with it. I repeat, anything you look for—medical files, reports—will not be found. Don't do this…. I'm telling you this to beware—you're

treading on thin ice—mom told me to tell you you'd better be careful. You'd better watch who you talk to. Watch what you say, because you're marked and you know that. We know what school (your child) goes to. You'd better be there for him. You'd better watch out for him. Anything can happen. Have a nice day!

Medical reports from clinics across the county vouch for members of the task force who reported toxic effects. Still, the *Los Angeles Times* took the position that they were suffering paranoid aberrations.

The adamant editors of the *Times* turned up their noses not only to the medical reports, but also to a number of letters from other therapists of ritually abused children in Los Angeles—they, too, exhibited symptoms of organophosphate poisoning.

One mother of two, after leaving a local cult, contacted Gould's task force in November, 1992 about the *Times* story: "I was alarmed, since I had all the symptoms last year, as had my children." Another mother wrote to say that in February, 1985 she'd discovered that her youngest daughter had been sexually abused in a day-care center in the San Fernando Valley. Her daughter's intense emotional trauma persisted, though she frequented a therapist for over a year.

Then the toxic siege began...

> In 1988 I started to experience physical problems. I was severely tired much of the time. It felt as if I had been drugged. Soon after that I started to have occurrences of tachycardia (rapid heart beat), headaches, shortness of breath, loss of memory, blurry vision, sweats, and at times I noticed a strange odor in my clothing, not to mention the female problems I was having. Doctors tested me every which way and yet every test was negative. They told me I was suffering from stress. I argued that I felt drugged, that I had some kind of chemical imbalance. They insisted it was stress, and I was referred to various stress programs, given tapes to listen to and forced to leave a very lucrative job. In July 1989, I was put on disability. Today I am considered permanently disabled. Early in 1992 it was suggested to me that I might be a victim of pesticide poisoning. Truth is I didn't believe it. I was afraid my doctor would think I was crazy. I eventually did go to him and asked his opinion. I was surprised at what he told me in a phone conversation the next day. He had consulted with two other doctors, and it was their opinion that I was suffering from chronic pesticide poisoning.[13]

Having amassed a bulky file of medical documentation to establish that members of the task force had been poisoned, Dr. Gould was still reluctant to contact the local press until she'd gathered enough evidence to convince even the most obstinate skeptic. In Los Angeles, the legal victory of Ray Buckey on molestation charges, after a five-year travail of public debate, had prompted a heated backlash against child therapists.

The task force was still collecting medical evidence and discussing possible courses of action when Stephanie Sheppard, a cult survivor, broke ranks and phoned the *Times* and a local television station to "blow the lid" off the group's "psychotic" belief they'd been poisoned.

Ms. Sheppard's admission was made to therapist David Neswald prior to a meeting of the panel. Dr. Neswald recalls that Sheppard "apparently mistook me for Dr. Papanek and called me out to the hallway to speak privately."[14] The agonizing irony in the confusion of identity is that Dr. Paul Papanek has long been a medical champion for the spraying of technical-grade malathion (an organophosphate and known neurotoxin) in densely-populated Southern California neighborhoods, a practice he commends as safe and effective to rid the region of periodic medfly infestation, despite growing evidence that the insecticide has adverse, often severe effects on human health.

A mother of two, referred to here as N.R., once sought advice from the task force when she suspected her two daughters had been abused. She struggled with an undiagnosed illness for a year before it occurred to her that the cause might be toxification. She phoned the task force office and was referred to Stephanie Sheppard, then acting as "contact person" on questions concerning poisons. Sheppard, the woman complained, "proceeded to question me at length," and gave several "lectures about how all of these symptoms I was having could be from other causes, including 'getting old' (I am forty)." N.R. became "very suspicious of her intentions and did not wish to talk to her again."[15]

After a routine blood test, Ms. R.'s doctor received not one, but three phone calls from Stephanie Sheppard. She asked how the tests had come out, and informed him that she seriously doubted anyone on the task force had been poisoned. When Stephanie rang N.R., "I told her that I had found out that she had called my doctor and that I was very angry. Her voice took on a tone that was obviously aimed at shaming me for questioning her. I told her in a strong voice not to call again and I hung up." Alarmed, she called the clinic, only to discover that Stephanie had called there repeatedly for a copy of the blood test results. (As it happens, the test proved negative. This means little, though, because Mrs. R. learned later that it was a test capable of detecting only high levels of toxicity from *recent* exposure.)

Ms. R. complained to the task force that her doctor had "no experience with ritual abuse. Now she certainly has a first-hand experience of cult attempts to sabotage all exposure of their violent harassment techniques. I am totally outraged." She characterized Stephanie Sheppard's intrusions as "a total red alert" to "infiltration."

But the quickest cuts, the harshest treacheries, were yet to come—from the *Los Angeles Times.*

British journalist Piers Brendon, in *The Life and Death of the Press Barons,* found in the course of researching the book in 1983 that "as an integral part of the country's power structure, the *Times* tends to overlook its public responsibilities."[16] But then, dodging responsibility is something of a tradition in the press, Brendon observed: "The First Amendment was drafted on the understanding that newspapers would be voices crying in the wilderness. It did not matter how raucous or even how deceitful they were."

The very paragon of this principle is the *Los Angeles Times.*

Catherine Gould is cautious of the press. She and other therapists working with ritual abuse victims have been repeatedly besmirched for shattering the spell of public denial woven by the media around any mention of ritual child abuse or cult mind control.

"We considered it too early to make any kind of definitive determination about the nature or extent of the poisonings," Dr. Gould says, "and had in no way thought to publicize our concerns at this time." She was still collecting medical reports when the *Times* came a-calling.

A cursory treatment of the story was written up by staff reporter Aaron Curtiss and appeared on December 1, 1992. It was founded solely on allegations, not hard evidence. Curtiss promised the group a follow-up story based on the medical data they'd collected. Gould agreed to give him the blood test results.

But the *Times* pulled a switch. Curtiss phoned Gould to say he'd been pulled off the story. It was instead assigned to John Johnson, the author of an earlier, heavily-biased pooh-poohing of ritual abuse that appeared in the *Times* on April 23, 1992.[17] Dr. Gould was still aching with resentment at the paper for printing Johnson's condescending denial of underground cult activity in Los Angeles. Gould told Curtiss that

Stephanie Sheppard

she saw no purpose in working with Johnson. Curtiss passed on Gould's concerns to his editor.

The next day Curtiss called to say that his editor had agreed that Gould could give the medical reports to the *Times* and expect fair treatment. He assured her that the information would be accurately reflected in the story written by Johnson. Thus assuaged, she turned over the medical reports.

Quite suddenly, without explanation, Curtiss went incommunicado. Gould phoned the *Times* repeatedly over the next ten days—Curtiss refused to either take or return her calls. Gould had a cold sensation in the pit of her stomach that the paper would cover up the poisonings.

"I was appalled," Gould later wrote to editors of the *Times,* "when the article appeared on the front page of the 'Metro' section with none of the available data included. The article represents a breach·of ethics on the part of John Johnson and the *Los Angeles Times,* and a breach of promise made by a staff member."

The *Times* story that appeared on December 13, 1992 glossed over the medical evidence entirely, depicting the task force as a collection of paranoiacs who "claimed they are slowly being poisoned by those who want to silence them." The paper noted that there were "43 reported victims of the alleged poisoning," but "so far, there is no proof that anyone was poi-

The first task force member to report toxic symptoms, a therapist, consulted her physician and discovered that she was suffering "Diazinon posioning (Insecticide)." Diazinon is classed as an organophosphate toxin. The doctor's notes mention a "long discussion regarding cults." The treatment, prescribed here, atropine, is used to counter the effects of chemical warfare agents.

soned and skeptics abound." Johnson cited as an example Paul J. Papanek, chief of the county's toxins epidemiological program and the most reviled public official in Los Angeles County—the very "authority" who has repeatedly sanctioned malathion spraying in Southern California despite overwhelming medical data, a multitude of case histories, and strident city hall testimony indicating that the pesticide is harmful to humans.

Dr. Papanek "attended a recent task force meeting and branded as 'outrageous' the poisoning claims." He sharply faulted the commission for not attending to "common sense rules of evidence." On the heels of this "controversy," nameless authorities had "begun an investigation into the activities of therapists and an acupuncturist linked to the poisoning claims by task force members."

Other "skeptics" were "turning up the heat for answers." Johnson reported, among them Tom O'Connor, executive director of the Board of Psychology. "Are they diagnosing diazinon poisoning?" O'Connor asked. "That's beyond the scope of their license. This sounds like some sort of mass hysteria."

Another categorical denial came from Stephanie Sheppard, who "said she checked out the claims of pesticide poisoning and found no facts to back up the allegations."

The *Times* had only to cite the medical reports supplied by Catherine Gould to silence these critics of the task force. The spurning of the blood tests reduced the story to a transparent smear, probably to discredit Gould and other therapists treating victims of ritual abuse. The deliberate distortions of most news reports on cult conditioning of children inspired San Francisco therapists Bruce and Dale McCulley, at the Seventh International Conference on Multiple Personality in Chicago in 1990, to object in a paper entitled "Disinformation, Media Manipulation & Public Perception" that "media misreporting of ritual abuse blurs public perception of the issue, and contributes to the continued vulnerability of children to this most heinous form of abuse.... If there is anything more bizarre than the atrocities revealed by ritual abuse victims, it is the ludicrous explanations advanced by the professional disinformationists."

More "Mass Hysteria"
& the Magical Mystery Fumes Molecule

The abysmal ethics of the *Times* in its handling of the task force poisonings extended to the paper's reports on a related story, the logic-defying "Mystery Fumes" case in Riverside, California. The half-dozen accounts of the case published by the newspaper were the exclusive domain of staff writer Tom Gorman.

In February, 1994 six emergency room attendants at Riverside

Hospital fainted after inhaling an "ammonia-like" odor discharged by the blood of Gloria Ramirez after drawing a sample with a syringe. "In the ensuing confusion," Gorman reported, "two people unaffected by the fumes tended to her as she went into full cardiac arrest. Within minutes, the 31-year-old woman—suffering from cervical cancer and weakened by nausea—died." State health officials and toxic specialists had no idea what prompted the incident, and Gorman reported that the Riverside Fire Department's hazardous materials squad found nothing peculiar in air samples taken from the emergency room.[18] (Five months later, however, Gorman reversed himself and reported that a chemical compound derived from ammonia *had* been found in the air samples.[19])

Dr. Huberto Ochoa, director of the emergency room staff, noticed white crystal spikes in the syringe used to draw blood from the dying Gloria Ramirez. "I'd never seen anything like it," he said. OSHA technicians detected an unidentified derivative of ammonia in Ramirez's body bag.[20] Nevertheless, one state hygienist blamed "stress" or "anxiety." This explanation, however, failed to account for the profound memory loss of Maureen Welch, a respiratory therapist. The strain of overwork seemed a lame explanation for the gangrenous knees of Dr. Julie Gorchynski after her blood had been contaminated, killing the supply of oxygen to her bones. She also suffered from breathing difficulties, muscle spasms and other symptoms reported two years earlier by members of the task force. In fact, the *New York Times* noted, medical professionals held that 'the toxic substance that felled the emergency room workers may have been an organophosphate, a chemical used in pesticides and military nerve gas."[21] (On the West Coast, the heirs of General Otis Chandler never once raised the possibility that Gloria Ramirez may have been exposed to organophosphates, quite possibly to avoid linking Dr. Gould's task force with the mystery fumes case in the minds of readers.)

"I had chemical burns in my throat and nose," Gorchynski told reporters, "lungs working at half capacity, biopsies showing dead knees, a drop of enzyme levels and crystals in my blood as well. It's all medically documented."[22] But the *Los Angeles Times*—which had ignored medical data in its reporting on the poisonings of ritual abuse task force members—also neglected to discuss Julie Gorchynski's medical examinations.

The *Times* wasn't the only local news outlet to spin a cloud of disinformation around the mystery fumes case. Dean Edell, a local talk show doctor for KFI, an AM radio station in Los Angeles, dismissed the incident as "mass hysteria."[23]

This diagnosis outraged Dr. Ross Kussman, Gorchynski's physician, who called in to explain that the hospital personnel displayed symptoms of toxicity.

"It doesn't fit the grounds for mass hysteria," Kussman said. "Julie became very ill from the toxin, developed pancreatitis and hepatitis, which are known to kill bone tissue." Dr. Edell scoffed, as though this diagnosis was the most preposterous abuse of medical science he'd ever heard. What poison could possibly account for Gorchynski's litany of symptoms, he asked.

"*Organophosphates* are well known to cause pancreatitis," Dr. Kussman offered. He explained that pancreatitis, in turn, is a known precursor of bone necrosis, the condition afflicting Dr. Gorchynski's knee. Edell asked why health authorities hadn't come to the same conclusion.

"Because," Kussman returned, "the county was uncooperative in helping us find out where it came from." (Gorchynski also claimed that county authorities were "stonewalling" her.)

"Trust me," Edell snorted with psychic confidence, "there ain't no fumes!"

This appeared to be the official position of the *Times* as well. Gorman parroted the statements of state health officials when, two weeks later, they too attributed the swooning at Riverside Hospital to "mass hysteria" (failing to point out, however, that this is formally considered to be a "diagnosis-by-exclusion"—meaning that if no other cause is detectable, mass hysterics could account for a spread of physical symptoms.[24])

At any rate, this explanation didn't wash well in the public print. But before the sighs died down another diagnosis was offered by Riverside County Coroner Scotty Hill. The coroner released a report from Lawrence Livermore labs—a few days before ballots were cast in Hill's run for reelection—concluding that the noxious fumes discharged by Gloria Ramirez were created internally from the bodily absorption of the pain remedy DMSO, chemically transformed by her unique bio-chemistry into dimethyl sulfate, a chemical warfare agent.[25]

But the DMSO theory had as many gaping holes in it as "mass hysteria." "DMSO is commonly used," Dr. Kussman pointed out, "and they're saying now that everyone who uses it emits a nerve gas?"

The Ramirez family denied that the patient had ever used DMSO. Besides, said Ron Schwartz, an attorney in the case, "the coroner's office is still saying that she died of cervical cancer, but now they're saying she created a chemical warfare agent that didn't hurt her. That doesn't make sense to me."

The *Los Angeles Times* neglected to report a second outbreak of mystery fumes that further decimated the DMSO hypothesis. After initial treatment at Riverside Hospital, two of the poisoned hospital employees were transferred to Parkview Hospital, according to a local television news report.[26] "What few people know," an excited reporter announced from Parkview, "is that four of the workers who treated them here were ill themselves. A poison expert examined the four new patients—he said the same symptoms at two different hospitals argues against a DMSO reaction, and points to an entirely different poison."

Lawrence Livermore chemists also overlooked an outbreak of mystery fumes in Bakersfield a week after the Riverside poisonings. The emergency room at Mercy Hospital was evacuated after doctors inserted a breathing tube in the trachea of a 44-year-old woman struggling with shortness of breath. As at Riverside, emergency room personnel noticed a gaseous cloud rising from the patient. They complained that a potent chemical odor originating with the patient's blood left them with burning eyes, nausea and headaches. [27]

The growing list of tenuous explanations contributed to suspicions of a cover-up. These were augmented by the announcement that the syringe used to draw blood from Gloria Ramirez had been thrown away.[28] And in the course of lawsuits filed by the Ramirez family, Dr. Gorchynski and nurse Sally Balderas, attorneys for Riverside County filed a court motion to destroy all of the evidence gathered from the contaminated emergency room. As it was, entire barrels of evidence had been kept secret from the Ramirez family. They and others filing suit therefore had no chance to have the contents of the barrels examined by toxicologists. An attorney for Sally Balderas complained that he had not been notified that the county wanted to destroy the evidence, or even that a hearing had been scheduled. Judge Richard Van Frank refused to give the county its way, ruling that interested parties work out a plan for the evidence before the hearing continue.[29]

Coverage of the mystery fumes case by the *Los Angeles Times* did not extend to the evidentiary hearing. The residents of L.A. were not told that the very "stonewalling" officials charged with investigating a case of mass poisoning wanted to burn every scrap of evidence to minimize "storage costs."

By suppressing significant details (medical evidence documenting a toxic assault on the ritual abuse task force, or symptoms of organophosphate poisoning in the mystery fumes case) the *Times* plays an insidious game. The newspaper has clearly distorted the chemo-terrorism of cults in the Southern California with a disinformation gambit that shields the culprits and defames victims (Gloria Ramirez?) for breaking out, talking to reporters, striking back or otherwise interfering with domestic CIA mind control operations.

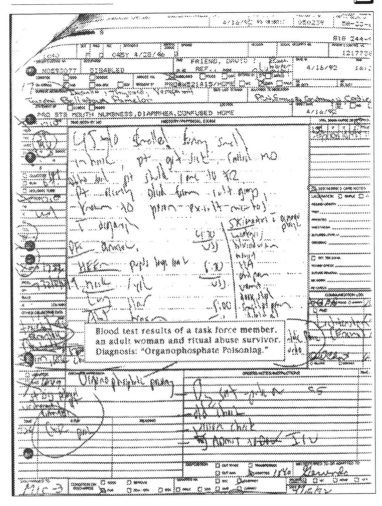

Blood test results of a task force member, an adult woman and ritual abuse survivor. Diagnosis: "Organophosphate Poisoning."

Footnotes

1. Teresa Watanabe and Carol J. Williams, "Japan Sect Uses Pain to Impel Faith," *Los Angeles Times,* March 25, 1995, p. A-1.
2. Jonathan Annells, "Temple of Doom," *London Times,* March 26, 1995, p. 1.
3. B. Boskovitch and R. Kusic, abstract to "Long-Term Effect of Acute Exposure to Nerve Gases upon Human Health," in *Mass Mind Control of the American People,* compiled and edited by Elizabeth Russell-Manning, published by Russell-Manning, San Francisco, 1992, p. 90.
4. There have been scores of military gassing incidents. In 1969, for instance, the accidental release of nerve gas in Okinawa hospitalized 25 Americans (see Sterling Seagrave, *Yellow Rain,* M. Evans, New York, 1981, p. 260-61). Non-military accidents are not all that uncommon. In 1976, the explosion of a factory owned by a subsidiary of Hoffman-LaRoche discharged a cloud of fumes that sickened and disfigured children of Seveso, Italy for life (see John G. Fuller, *The Poison that Fell from the Sky,* Random House, New York, 1977).
5. Annells.
6. Ben Hills, "Police, Scientists Still Baffled by Japan Nerve Gas Deaths," *The Age* (Australia), August 20, 1994.
7. John Johnson, "County Panel Scrutinized for Satanic Claims," *Los Angeles Times,* December 13, 1992, p. B-1.
8. Catherine Gould, letter with medical verification to the *Los Angeles Times,* December 17, 1992. Copies are available from Dr. Gould in Encino, California, or from the L.A. County Commission for Women's Ritual Abuse Task Force in Los Angeles.
9. Randy Noblitt, "Multiple Choice: Which of the Following is Most False: (A) The Memory, (B) The Syndrome. (C) The Foundation?" *Newsletter of the Society for the Investigation, Treatment and Prevention of Ritual and Cult Abuse,* vol. 1, no. 3, Fall/Winter 1993-94, pp. 3-5. The percentage of psychologists who believe recovered memory therapy to be effective is about 88%. The proportion is the same in Great Britain, according to one survey released last year. On January 1, 1995, the *Sunday London Times* reported that "the first expert investigation into 'recovered memory syndrome' in Britain reveals that nine out of ten psychologists believe the technique of searching for buried sexual trauma can produce accurate memories."
10. Jonathan Vankin, in *Conspiracies, Cover-Ups and Crimes* (1992), cites a lecture by Joe Holsinger, an aide to late Congressman Leo Ryan, at a psychology conference in Berkeley, noting: "the possibility is that Jonestown was a mass mind control experiment by the CIA." Holsinger offered as evidence "The Penal Colony," an essay written by a U.C. Berkeley psychologist. "The Berkeley author of the article... believes that rather than terminating MKULTRA (the Agency's mind control program), the CIA shifted its programs from public institutions to private cult groups, including the People's Temple" (p. 176).
11. Shirley Briggs, *Chemical Classes of Pesticides,* Hemisphere Publishing Co., 1972, Washington, D.C., p. 213. Immediate effects of organophosphate poisoning include behavioral disturbances, muscle twitching, headaches, nausea, dizziness, anxiety,

memory loss, weakness, tremor, abdominal cramps, blurred vision, slowed heart-beat and incontinence.

12. Anonymous attachment, Dr. Gould's letter to the *Los Angeles Times.*

13. Letter to Myra Riddell, then chairwoman of the L.A. County Commission for Women's Ritual Abuse Task Force, December 15, 1992. On file in the task force archives.

14. David W. Neswald, letter to Dr, Myra Riddell, task force chairwoman, December 10, 1992. Neswald found Ms. Sheppard's behavior "rather suspect."

15. N.R. in a letter to the task force, November 30, 1992.

16. Piers Brendon, *The Life and Death of the Press Barons*, Atheneum, New York, 1983, p. 232.

17. John Johnson, "Satanism: Skeptics Abound," *Los Angeles Times*, April 23, 1992, p. A-1.

18. Tom Gorman, "Family Claims Woman was Victim, Not Cause, of Fumes," *Los Angeles Times*, March 3, 1994, p. A-3.

19. Tom Gorman, "6-Month Probe Fails to Solve Mystery of Hospital Fumes," *Los Angeles Times*, August 16, 1994, p. A-21.

20. Tom Gorman, "Victims of Fumes Still Ill, and Still Seeking Answers," *Los Angeles Times*, April 14, 1994, p. A-1.

21. B. Drummond Ayres Jr., "Elaborate Precautions Taken for Autopsy in Mystery Fumes Case," *New York Times*, February 25, 1994, p. A-17.

22. Tom Gorman, "'Mystery Fumes' Doctor to File $6-Million Claim," *Los Angeles Times*, August 7, 1994, p. A-1.

23. Dean Adell program, KFI-AM, Los Angeles, August 8, 1994.

24. Kussman.

25. Tom Gorman, "Lab Suggests Mystery Fumes Answer," *Los Angeles Times*, November 4, 1994, p. A-1.

26. Mystery fumes update, late evening news broadcast, KNBC-TV, Los Angeles, November 26, 1994.

27. "Fumes Again Sicken People," *Los Angeles Times*, February 28, 1994, p. A-3.

28. Tom Gorman, "Syringe Used in Fumes Case Lost," *Los Angeles Times*, April 22, 1994, p. A-3.

29. Pat Murkland, "Bid to Destroy Fumes Evidence Lost," *Corona (Calif.) Press-Enterprise* , January 12, 1995, p. B-1.

Chapter Six

A Map of Hell

Devil Cult Mayhem—A Global Perspective

BRAZIL: In July 1992 a surly mob in Rio de Janeiro was dissuaded by state troopers with machine guns from lynching the wife of a small-town mayor accused of sacrificing a six year-old boy. The woman, her daughter and three male suspects who confessed to the killing were escorted from the police station under armed guard.

CANADA: As of 1977, Victoria had a black witchcraft population of about 1,000. Five of the cells were branches of the Canadian Church of Satan. Many of the witches were "prominent business people," according to a story in the *Victorian,* "and a substantial number (were) newspaper people."

In Montreal, a group known as the Continental Association of Satan's Hope (CASH) advises prospective members to "turn your fantasies into reality and discover for yourself the infernal power of mighty Satan."

ENGLAND: Newspapers in the UK insist that ritually abused children are suffering "false memories"—despite a survey by the British Psychological Society, published in January 1995, stating flatly that nine out of ten therapists believe that ritual abuse is real. The Society also found that the mental health community overwhelmingly endorsed recovered memory therapy. The prevalence of ritual abuse in Great Britain is difficult to pin down, but in June 1994 a research team at Manchester University released a study estimating that nearly 1,000 children were victims of organized sexual abuse over a four-year period. "Another 86 were allegedly subjected to ritual abuse," the *Daily Telegraph* reported, "in the same period up to 1991." The study encompassed every police force and child service organization in the country. Yet only a small minority of abusers were convicted.

Despite the assurances of Britain's False Memory Society, press accounts of cultic outrages appear at a regular pace. *The London Times* ran a news brief on June 26, 1993 reporting succinctly that "two men found dead in a fume-filled car surrounded with flowers at Fareham, Hampshire, were due to appear in court today." Both men had been "accused of offenses involving schoolboys and an animal."

In 1994 Princess Diana's brother, Earl Spencer, let on, in the House of Lords no less, that devil worshipers had been holding ceremonies on the estate where she was raised. "We have had everything from fences being pulled down and burned, animals killed, devil worship and motor-bike racing." Spencer claimed that "things" had been left behind by the devil worshippers. "It's just a diversion," he said, "I don't think it's serious."

In Leeds, the Sorcerer's Apprentice "magick" shop offers books on the occult, leather bullwhips, idols, spell-kits, pentacles, altar drapes, chalices and embalming fluid. Chris Bray, the shop's proprietor, boasts a clientele roster of some 300 self-avowed Satanists.

Mind control, torture and politics converged in the death of a Labor councilor in Manchester, a self-proclaimed sadomasochist and Satanist, who boasted of his involvement in the murder of several young men. The politician, Chris Rogers, was stabbed to death by cult leader Colin Henry, as reported in the *Guardian* for February 2, 1994. Dr. Gill, a psychiatrist, said that Henry feared his mentor, who he believed had "mental powers to manipulate him."

GERMANY: In *Magicians of the Golden Dawn,* Ellic Howe allows that "the belief in Crowley's authority survives even today in certain German and Swiss groups, notably at Stein near Zurich, where the Ecclesia Gnostica Catholica, a branch of the Order of the Templars of the Orient (OTO), still performs his Gnostic mass.

The Third Order of the Golden Dawn, vestiges of the original organization's inner order, is said to be highly political and still active in England, Switzerland and Germany.

GREECE: In December 1993 a pair of Greek military conscripts confessed to kidnapping, murder, rape, and the grisly murders of two women in Satanic rituals. Six others in the cult were charged with complicity in human sacrifices and black magic rites. On December 30, the *Daily Telegraph* reported, "the sect was discovered to have head-quarters on the northern outskirts of Athens after one of four women being readied for sacrifice at Christmas reported the rituals to police."

HONDURAS: The establishment of U.S. military bases in the 1980s gave rise to a high incidence of child prostitution. Newspaper articles from Honduras complained bitterly of the off-duty diversions of servicemen. *America* magazine ran a story in 1987 on a series of Satanic murders of children in the town of Comayagua, near the Palmerola military base. No arrests were made.

MALAYSIA: The dismembered corpse of Mazlan Idris, a Pahang legislator, was found in his country home in 1993, surrounded by black magic paraphenalia. In nearby fields, police found the remains of other victims.

THE NETHERLANDS: Unaccountable reports of child abuse in Oude Pekela, the proverbial sleepy village, population 8,000, near the German border, began to surface in May 1987 when two children, ages 4 and 5, exhibited physical symptoms of sexual assault including, in one case, persistent bleeding from the anus. The examining physicians reported "large-scale ritualistic abuse." Some fifty children may have been involved. The children disclosed "watching a videotape and seeing their friends on the screen" engaging in lewd acts, a tactic used to overcome the children's resistance and fear. Then parties were held, and the children were instructed to undress. They remembered sitting on the floor naked, being forced to lick the genitals and breasts of adults and walking around in circles with little leather belts tied around their penises. They also told of swimming in pools where their heads were dunked under water, of being washed with "colored shampoo."

Other substances given them included drugs, sometimes applied by injection or balloons placed over their mouths, and "feces rubbed on them." The children were ordered to hit a black child. This, they were instructed, was not a bad thing to do. Interviewers asked the children whether the victim of this moral exercise might have been a doll. They denied it, although some of them offered that they had played with decapitated dolls. When interviewed in groups, they often corrected each other and added significant details. One psychiatrist reported that many of the children discussed being abducted on several occasions. The children were approached by men and women on bicycles or in cars, dressed as clowns. The abductees were rendered compliant to the sexual abuse with drugged candy, ice cream and lemonade.

PANAMA: Jack Anderson's February 27, 1992 column reported, "U.S. military officials in Panama have uncovered a Satan-worshiping ring of about 20 American teenagers at an Air Force base there." The military attempted to contain the story, but Panamanian sources said "the cult was discovered by parents just in time to prevent a mass suicide the teenagers had planned. The teenagers were students at Corundu Junior High, a Defense Department school on Panama's Pacific coast. They ranged in age from 13 to 15, and most were children of military personnel at Howard Air Force Base."

SOUTH AFRICA: In Johannesburg, doctors contemplated sex-change surgery for a toddler with sex organs mutilated in a witchcraft ritual. The child was discovered in a Soweto field. His thumbs had been cut off and someone had attempted to gouge out his eyes.

UNITED STATES:
Alabama: In April 1986 cattle were mutilated by cultists in Gunterville and cattlemen were threatened.

Arizona: Confirmed cult activity near Tucson, and a long litany of cattle and goat sacrifices.

California: On December 19, 1987 in the town of Lancaster, Andra Reynolds stabbed her four year-old boy to death, then turned herself into the 700 Club hot line. "She had some problems," a neighbor told the *Los Angeles Herald*. The child suffered multiple stab wounds. Two open Bibles were found on either side of the body, which was sprawled on his mother's bed. Two full-grown dogs and three puppies had been drowned in the bathtub.

In February 1984, five residents of Newport Beach stole off with body parts from a mausoleum.

To curb the rise in animal sacrifices, the Los Angeles City Council approved an ordinance banning occult-style killings. A spokesman for the Department of Animal Regulation estimated that as many as 300 animal sacrifices had occurred in L.A. in the previous year, with reports coming in from every community in the city. Councilman Richard Alatorre said that he feared "these incidents are only the tip of the iceberg."

Connecticut: In Wilton, a satanic cult desecrated churches and threatened to murder young children.

Florida: In West Palm Beach, a gang of youths known as the Legion of Doom passed a death penalty on anyone who married outside the group. The Legion boasted 15 to 20 members who "played at Satanism," according to the *New York Times*. A search of the Legion HQ after the murder of 18 year-old Troy Collins produced a bloody chain, a baseball bat with hair on it and bloody clothing. Some play. The walls were decorated with Satanic inscriptions. Four adults were charged with the beating death of Mr. Collins.

Day-care center operator John Shaver of Fort Lauderdale was charged by police in 1990 with taking nude photographs of children in his care. As 14 of the children began medical and psychological exams, a hotel maid discovered him with his right wrist slashed. Child pornography was found in his home. Three of the children attending Shaver's day-care center were found to have gonorrhea.

In Stuart, Florida, Montessori school principal James Toward pleaded guilty to child abuse charges and received a 15-year sentence. His secretary, Brenda Williams, was convicted to six years.

Illinois: In 1980 a self-proclaimed witch in Chicago beat her roommate, who was left alone for six days to die. Four years later four Chicago area cultists were, according to police, believed to have been responsible for 18 murders. The victims were slashed, their body parts used in rituals.

Du Page County: In 1986 a series of murder trials of four men belonging to a Satanic cult was held. The prosecution charged that the men raped, killed and mutilated up to 18 young women, including Carole Pappas, wife of former Chicago Cubs pitcher Milt Pappas.

Also in 1986, a police officer was shot by hit men for the owner of "an unorthodox church." A *Chicago Tribune* article reported that the owner of the church was "a City Hall big shot." The hit men told police that they were on their way to Bridgeport to beat up a pastor when the officer intervened.

Maine: Desecration of churches a real problem.

Massachusetts: A cultist in Fall River ripped the head off of a prostitute with his bare hands in 1981. Cape Cod has been plagued by reports of repugnant cult activity since the early 1970s. The naked and mutilated bodies of four young women, their hearts cut out, were exhumed from shallow graves near the Cape in 1971.

In September 1984 parents in Malden worried about their daughter's inability to urinate. After a police investigation, a woman, her son and daughter were picked up on charges of child rape. Other children told of being forced to take part in animal sacrifices. Gerald "Tookey" Amirault was accused of dressing as a clown and abusing children in a "magic room." Amirault was sentenced to 30 to 40 years, and the women received terms of 20 years each.

In 1987 a Christmas creche was burned in Boston. A dead sparrow and a beef tongue were found nailed to the creche.

Missouri: In Carl Junction, the southwest corner of the state adjoining Arkansas and Kansas, several cults are said to be active. Favorite ceremonial sites are the dozens of abandoned lead and zinc mines scattered throughout the region. In December 1987 a boy was given 60 blows to the head. His body was found in a cistern. Three classmates arrested for the murder confessed that they'd been exposed to a local devil cult

Montana: Serial killer Stanley Baker confessed to eating the heart of one of his victims. He was recruited from a Wyoming campus by a cult based in California known as the "Four P" movement. The Four P's subscribe to a hybrid of Nazi beliefs and occultic lore. The cult has been known to sacrifice victims on an altar decorated with dragons. Baker, who has shown no remorse, formed his own cult of prison inmates.

New Jersey: Church and graveyard desecrations in several towns.

New York State: Police raided a Bronx apartment in 1980 and rescued 62 caged animals intended for sacrifice.

At West Point military academy, 58 children claimed to have been ritually abused by their preschool teachers, forced to play "Marry the Devil," swallow excrement, etc. The Army, parents alleged, launched an ambitious cover-up. Investigators insisted that abuse took place, but the case was plagued by a lack of material evidence and was dismissed. Some of the children contracted venereal diseases.

Jeanette Martin, an unlicensed day care operator in White Plains, was accused of molesting children and urinating on them. The defense claimed that child questioning techniques were tainted and charged that the children only gave "bizarre" accounts of abuse after coercion. Eighteen children testified in an 11-month trial. One perp was convicted on felony charges and received a 25-50 year sentence.

Ohio: In Cincinnati a loosely-organized circle of black magicians made their presence known in the late 1960s by leaving pierced sheep hearts in public parks—meant, white witches in Cincinnati feared, as a curse on the city.

Oregon: A nine year-old boy told friends that he wanted to grow up to be like his mother—a high priestess who "eats babies." The boy recruited 24 children into his cult of child witches.

In December 1987, in Roseburg, three Christian day-care centers were the source of allegations resulting in the sentencing of a minister, and his wife and son.

Rhode Island : Two boys were murdered within a week in late 1987. William Sarento, 21, was charged with the killings—ordered, he said, by Satan.

Texas: In Houston, a man was caught *in flagrante delecti* with an eight-year-old boy in the midst of a Satanic initiation ceremony in October 1980. An infant's body was discovered in a black box owned by a teenaged Devil devotee four years later.

In Fort Worth a babysitter received a 70-year prison sentence without probation for killing a two year-old child in her registered day-care center. The child was killed after the sitter repeatedly struck the baby's head against a blunt object.

Hard on the 1989 police raid on the Matamoros cult, the *Houston Post* reported that the name of a suspect in the case, Rick Block, had turned up in documents seized from the Southern Air Transport C-123K cargo plane downed by the Nicaraguan Sandinistas, kicking off the Iran-Contra revelations.

Near Austin, Daniel and Francis Keller, operators of a day-care center, were convicted in November 1992 for aggravated sexual abuse of a 3-year-old girl. Molestation aside, three children from the center alleged they'd had "giant germs" implanted in their bodies and been forced—at gunpoint—to participate in the making of pornographic movies.

Washington: Animal sacrifices and mutilations. Cult members were observed near ritual sites.

Chapter Seven

The "Fatal Vision" Murders & the Nomenclature of an American Death Squad

The Army's Body-Bag Heroin Connection and a Triple-Murder in Vietnam Era North Carolina

D r. Jeffrey MacDonald's prospects appeared far from grim. At 26, the Princeton graduate had attained the rank of captain in the Army Medical Corps at Fort Bragg, ten miles northwest of Fayetteville, North Carolina. He was a talented physician; his contributions to emergency medicine have been adopted by paramedic and trauma units across the country. Acquaintances maintain that he doted on his family. Colette, his wife, was pregnant with her third child when her life ended and his was coldly dismantled.

On February 17, 1970 Colette MacDonald and Kimberly, age 5, and Kristen, 2, were bludgeoned and stabbed to death. Military police responding to MacDonald's call for help found him unconscious with multiple stab wounds, one of which, examining physicians later testified, collapsed a lung. He was hospitalized for ten days. Despite the severity of his injuries, the government concluded they were "superficial" and "self-inflicted." MacDonald was charged, tried and acquitted in 1970 at an Army hearing. He was retried in the summer of 1979, found guilty, acquitted by an appellate court a year later, and sentenced yet again by Supreme Court decision in 1982. He is currently serving three life terms in a medium-security prison in Sheridan, Oregon.

The official account of the killings was packaged as a mass-market book, a critically-acclaimed popularization of the government's case against MacDonald. Before Joe McGinniss vilified Edward Kennedy in *The Last Brother,* which promptly backfired (one *Washington Post* reviewer described the biography as "shoddy, slimy and unrelievedly rotten"), he was the celebrated author of *Fatal Vision,* widely considered to be the authoritative account of the brutal triple homicide. *Fatal Vision,* MacDonald insists, was equally disingenuous, larded with long sections of imaginary dialogue and erroneous conjecture about his involvement in the killings. Unfortunately, the widespread critical condemnation of McGinniss for the Kennedy biography wasn't retroactive. The press asked no questions about the author's earlier production.

Did MacDonald, for example, really suffer "malignant narcissism" and acute "amphetamine psychosis"—two core premises of the book—rendering him capable of killing his own family? The drug theory, at least, is ruled out by periodic blood tests administered at the hospital where MacDonald worked. These proved negative, as did the blood test taken after the murders. His medical examination before surgery on the collapsed lung found no drugs or alcohol in his system.

MacDonald's defense attorney, Michael Malley, offers that "McGinniss simply made up this theory"—as he would later fabricate details about the life of Edward Kennedy.

In *Fatal Vision,* McGinniss promotes the government's unlikely revelation that MacDonald's knife wounds were self-inflicted, a false lead for the authorities to follow. Of course his 17 stab wounds—one life-threatening—could be viewed as confirmation that the family was, as MacDonald claimed, attacked by knife-wielding intruders.

Who is Joe McGinniss? It has not occurred to the press gang (which has done much to burnish his reputation) to ask. In the Kennedy book, the mass-market journalist admits, without explanation or detail, that his source was "FBI wiretaps" for the allegation that Ted's brother John defeated Hubert Humphrey for the Democratic nomination in West Virginia by promising to "bribe local sheriffs and other election officials" with funds from Chicago mobsters. Melinda Stephens, a friend of Jeffrey MacDonald and editor of a newsletter about the case, contends the author collaborated with the government's prosecutors "to present false statements about the evidence" in an attempt to mold public opinion. In both books, McGinniss gleans incriminating information from federal sources.

Fatal Vision is, like the Kennedy biography, a political hit piece. The small but vocal ranks of MacDonald supporters believe he is a surrogate for shadowy figures in the intelligence community with connections to public office and the Pentagon, imprisoned to obscure their crimes. The paperback indictment of MacDonald has reinforced the public perception of MacDonald's guilt, and kept dormant one of the most unconscionable scandals in American military history.

Three suspects in the murders have confessed. MacDonald's version of events has been confirmed by some 40 witnesses. *Fatal Vision* is myopic in its exclusion of any evidence that might clear MacDonald. McGinniss's claim to impartiality eroded completely in his flat refusal in

1980 even to look at the 1200-page report compiled by MacDonald's defense attorneys. This report, taken together with the sworn depositions of witnesses, press accounts and interviews with investigators, combine in a case sharply at odds with the government's.

Jerry Potter, co-author of a recent reinvestigation of the MacDonald case, *Fatal Justice* (Norton, 1995), contends "every piece of evidence that the government brought against Jeffrey MacDonald at trial can be destroyed by their own hidden documents. And every piece of evidence found at the crime scene that would have helped him was suppressed." Moreover, evidence that MacDonald was framed, as he has maintained consistently since his conviction, manifests the identities of the actual assailants of MacDonald's family, and their motive.

"Malignant narcissism," drugs and "rage at the female sex" aside, another perspective of the case begins with a young criminology student and police informant from Nashville, Tennessee—Helena Stoeckley.

In 1968 Stoeckley, whose information on the narcotics underground resulted in over 200 arrests in the Fort Bragg area (though she was ruled not credible by Judge DuPree, who presided over the MacDonald case), was transferred by her police contact, Lieutenant Rudy Studer, to the office of Detective Everette Beasley, a new cop on the narcotics squad. Beasley didn't know it, but Stoeckley had fallen in with a circle of Vietnam vets running heroin into the Fort Bragg area.

On one occasion, Stoeckly told Beasley, "drugs, primarily heroin, were being smuggled into this country in the body cavities of casualties returned by air from Vietnam. She named Ike Atkinson as the ring leader." Atkinson was assigned to Seymour-Johnson Air Force Base in Goldboro, North Carolina. He was "in the service," Stoeckley said, "but subsequently got out and continued his business in drugs with the same contacts."

In a 1985 deposition, Beasley stated that a shaken Helena Stoeckley contacted him after the murder of Jeffrey MacDonald's family. She told him that she had been in the MacDonald house in the early morning hours of February 17th. She also provided him with details about the drug operation. The recipients of the heroin, she said, had contacts in Vietnam who placed it in the bodies of war casualties. The bodies were re-stitched and shipped to Johnson Air Base and other installations around the country. When the bodies arrived in the U.S., they were met by a military contact and the heroin were removed. The bodies were then sent on to their final destinations.

"The person who met the bodies at the respective air bases knew which bodies to check, based on a predetermined code," Beasley says. "Helena told me that the people who handled the assignments in Vietnam, and those who met the planes in the United States, were military personnel."

She also told him that the couriers made their pick-ups at Fort Bragg. Distribution was handled by enlisted men, civilians, police officers. "Local attorneys and Army officers as high as generals were part of the operation. She stated that she would name and identify the people if given immunity by the U.S. government."

Beasley believes the workings of the drug operation were part of the "bomb-shell" she promised to drop at the trial of Jeffrey MacDonald. But the government would not offer her immunity. (Facing a conviction for participation in the killings, she admitted later, Stoeckley overdosed herself with drugs before appearing at MacDonald's trial. She was reeling under the influence when she recanted on the stand, and was dismissed as a witness.)

If granted immunity, Stoeckley's testimony would have surely drawn national attention to an obscure chapter of the war in Southeast Asia. Had she lived, Stoeckley might well have toppled an international drug empire.

During the war in Vietnam and after, small contingents of American soldiers settled in Thailand to enter the world heroin trade. Among the Yank opium gangs was a syndicate of G.I.'s known as the Black Masonic Club, led by Leslie "Ike" Atkinson, nicknamed "Sergeant Smack." They called Jack's American Style Bar in Bangkok, a favorite watering hole for Black G.I.s on furlough and a notorious drug dispensary, their home.

Atkinson was identified by Helena Stoeckley as the leader of the umbrella group linked to the MacDonald killings. Atkinson had no role in the killings, but a sub-group in Fayetteville reportedly did. One of this group, Cathy Perry, confessed to the FBI in 1984 that she took part in the killings. The word "cult" surfaced much earlier.

In December 1970, Perry confided to a friend that she had "killed several persons." She complained that "the Black Cult" had pressured her to do "things" against her will.

On the East Coast, said Stoeckley, the heroin was unloaded at Fort Bragg and Johnson-Seymour Air Force Base. The heroin was distributed along the eastern and southeastern states. According to a 1973 issue of *Time,* casualties of war were indeed used as couriers. The opiate was stuffed into coffins, body-bags and internal organs. The *Time* report described the scandal as "the most vicious case of war-profiteering" in American history.

Military police, looking into the black market in stolen supplies and narcotics, periodically snagged an enlisted man or petty officer. Pressured to plea bargain, they often named senior officials. One team of drug agents filed reports at military bases around the country. Eye-witnesses at Norton Air Force Base in California agreed to roll over under immunity and testify that incoming bodies, stuffed with as much as 50 pounds of heroin each, were surgically relieved of the contraband. *Wall Street*

Journal reporter Jonathan Kwitny reports in *The Crimes of Patriots*, published in 1987, that "corrupt U.S. and Vietnamese officials" arrested for complicity in the heroin pipeline turned evidence on "senior U.S. officers." "These reports checked out," Kwitny affirmed (leaving the identities of said officials a lingering mystery).

The Army acted quickly—not by rounding up the ring leaders, but by dismantling the investigative team and packing them off to combat duty in Vietnam. Skittish military officials, alleges Ted Gunderson, former agent-in-charge of the FBI's Los Angeles office and a long-time MacDonald supporter, only pursued low-level couriers in the drug transfers. "High-ranking Army officers," he says, "were in charge of this drug ring (and) have never been identified. Informants have advised that the Army investigation of the operation was controlled and manipulated to conceal its magnitude and the extent of (official) participation."

This gruesome successor to Air America began to fall apart in 1972 when federal agents were tipped off that 20 kilos of heroin could be found aboard a KC-135 bound for Delaware's Dover Air Force Base. The plane was ordered to land in Maryland, and the agents searched the transport. The search proved futile until one agent noticed that a body in the cargo-hold had been freshly stitched. The agents arrested Thomas Southerland, an Army veteran from North Carolina. His bail was set at $50,000. The jury was informed that Southerland was an operative in an international opium ring.

The DEA soon made the arrest of Ike Atkinson, currently serving a forty-year prison sentence. Federal authorities are convinced that he still has $85 million cabbaged away in offshore accounts. (Atkinson has since changed his name. He has told fellow prisoners that he was used in CIA mind control experiments. He was, apparently, a pawn, not a true Insider. Federal documents released under FOIA have since established that the Agency used the military as cover for experiments in behavior modification.) The stiff sentence is inconsistent with the fate of James Smedly, who directed the Thai end of the operation. Smedley spent two years in a Bangkok prison and was released to enter a guilty plea in a Raleigh, North Carolina courthouse. He walked away with a reprimand and parole. Jasper Myrick, a courier, did not fare so well—he was arrested in Bangkok and sentenced to 33 years in a maximum-security cell.

In Fayetteville, an accused drug dealer, Spider Newman, consented to turn state's evidence on his suppliers. The case was heard in federal court. During a break in the trial, Newman disappeared. His body was found in his car, behind his home. He'd been shot in the head. Police ruled the death a suicide.

But in 1970 the Atkinson syndicate was still operating undetected. Some of the local distributors feared and loathed one Dr. Jeffrey MacDonald. The primary aim of any murder investigation is the establishment of motive. The prosecution, and later McGinniss, smeared MacDonald by falsely attributing the murders to amphetamine abuse. Actually, according to testimony that surfaced in the 1970 military trial, addicts on base considered MacDonald a threat because he actively opposed drug use, and attempted to get to the bottom of the supply. As an Army drug counselor, he routinely treated soldiers who were down-and-strung-out at Fort Bragg, among them a boyfriend of Cathy Perry (whose murder confession has long been shunned by the prosecution's office) named Warmbrod. MacDonald couldn't help but notice the rising glut of hard narcotics at Fort Bragg. One study concluded there were 800 to 1,000 heroin addicts at the Fayetteville base alone. MacDonald pressured those in his treatment program to name sources of supply. Army Major Jim Williams, a drug counselor who worked closely with MacDonald, testified at the Article 32 hearing that his colleague had waded into perilous waters.

"I became very concerned not only for my health but for Dr. MacDonald's," he testified.

But MacDonald was increasingly disturbed by the prevalence of narcotics on the base. He persisted in his one-man crusade against the warnings of Major Williams. Major Williams's concern gave way to alarm. He felt that MacDonald was "way over his head."

Among the details that Stoeckley gave Beasley in 1970 were the names of police officers entangled in the body-bag operation. One of them was Lt. Rudy Studer, the informant's former contact. Shortly after the MacDonald murders, Studer was promoted to Captain, Chief of Detectives. The promotion was short-lived, however. Studer was soon forced to resign after "misappropriating" pornographic material seized in a police raid. Stoeckley said Studer supplied her with heroin for sale in Fayetteville. His partner in the drug trade was allegedly William Ivory of the Army's Criminal Investigations Division (CID).

This was a very pertinent bombshell because Ivory, the agent on duty the night of the murders, directed the search of MacDonald's home, and was placed in charge of the CID investigation—despite his age, 26, and the fact that he had absolutely no experience directing a murder probe. His immediate background was a stint as MP, investigating traffic mishaps and interrogating drug suspects. Ivory was clearly not qualified to head an investigation of this magnitude.

MacDonald's defense attorneys have probed Ivory's acquaintance with members of the Atkinson drug syndicate. In February 1991, MacDonald wrote in a letter to his attorney, Harvey Silverglate, that "Ivory perjured himself at the Article 32 trial over when his relationship began with Helena Stoeckley. We now know from recent informants in the CID that Ivory knew her pre-February 17th (prior to the murders), and secretly had her in a safehouse two days later for an 'interview.'"

In other words, the same military official who indicted MacDonald had an undefined working relationship with a confessed participant in the murders. Afterwards, an investigative turf war was waged between the FBI and CID. The Bureau was shut out. Ivory took over the investigation. Consistently, the same military personnel entangled in the body-bag connection figured prominently in the MacDonald killings, as Ivory did in the subsequent investigation.

Detective Studer's partner, Lt. Sonberg, disappeared immediately after the murders. It was bruited around the Fayetteville police department that he had double-crossed a ring of drug dealers. A police informant, Joseph Bullock, has stated to Fayetteville police that on more than one occasion he'd witnessed Studer and Ivory exchanging envelopes at a local Dunkin' Donuts shop. Shortly after talking to police, Bullock was ambushed in his home and, like Spider Newman, received a fatal bullet in the head.

City officials fingered by Stoeckley in the body-bag drug syndicate also had a direct role in the prosecution of Jeffrey MacDonald. "Helena once mentioned the name Proctor to me," Beasley recalled in a signed statement. James Proctor, a prosecuting attorney in the MacDonald case, was the former son-in-law of Judge DuPree, a certain conflict-of-interest in a case this sensitive

Alan Mazorelle, a drug courier named by Stoeckley, "was in the Army," stationed at Fort Bragg, and took part in the killings. She said Mazorelle was dealing drugs quite heavily by this time. He married, produced a daughter, but spent most of his time away on "military business," shuttling between military bases, mixing with smugglers and avoiding the MPs. Mazorelle once boasted to friends that he was assigned to the CID. Of all the underworld figures with whom she dealt, Stoeckley feared him most. "Mazorelle would kill you in a minute," she said.

Her dread was shared by Mazorelle's daughter, who alleges that he prided himself on homicides made to appear to be accidents. She told investigative reporter Ted Schwartz that her father was fascinated with mind control. He had learned hypnosis, and through it attempted to divide her into two distinct personalities. Schwartz's investigation of Mazorelle confirmed that he was active in cult activity. Beasley maintains that he compiled extensive intelligence files on all of Stoeckley's associates, "but this information has since disappeared from the Fayetteville police files," he said. Beasley discovered that the files had vanished in 1979. "During the MacDonald trial I was given a subpoena to bring these records to trial. It was then I discovered they were gone," he says.

Among them the file of Greg Mitchell, a G.I. placed by Stoeckley at the crime scene, one of several mysterious "Fatal Vision" casualties. His wife recalls that Mitchell once explained to her how drugs were smuggled into the country in the body cavities of soldiers killed in Vietnam. Mitchell was questioned by the FBI in 1982. Shortly thereafter he told friends he was leaving the country to evade arrest for "serious crimes," notably the murder of MacDonald's wife and children. Two reliable witnesses, Ann Sutton Cannady and Juanita Sisneros, found the words:

"I KILLED MACDONALD'S WIFE AND CHILDREN"

scrawled by Mitchell in red paint on a farmhouse wall. Unfortunately, Mitchell's travel plans were canceled by sclerosis of the liver. Sclerosis, normally a lingering illness, was *also* the instantaneous cause of Helena Stoeckley's death seven months later. Before she died, Stoeckley complained to friends that "two men in suits" were tailing her. Neighbors have since confirmed that a couple of well-dressed strangers parked for long periods in front of her apartment, according to Potter and Bost in *Fatal Justice*.

"Shockingly," Ted Gunderson gradually realized, as his own investigation for MacDonald's defense team led him from one witness to the next, "the group MacDonald described existed, was drug- and violence-oriented, was seen going to and coming from the house, was seen in bloody clothing, and fits his descriptions."

MacDonald passed a polygraph. He submitted to five independent forensic examinations. The government's own lab specimens link Fort Bragg's body-bag ring to the crime scene, including a long synthetic blonde strand corroborating MacDonald's contention that Stoeckley wore a blonde wig the night of the murders. A bloody syringe found in his home was "lost" by the prosecution.

In fact, Government files released since the trial verify that William Ivory, the CID investigator and alleged body-bag drug courier, misplaced or destroyed most of the evidence corroborating Dr. MacDonald's version of events. The defense team never knew that Stoeckley's bloody boots and clothing were turned over to the Army CID by a friend of Helena Stoeckley. Or that blood samples conforming to Greg Mitchell's type were taken from the MacDonald house, as were seven fingerprints of persons unknown—discarded because "they kept getting mixed up with the known prints." And federal prosecutors violated federal rules of evidence by bluntly refusing to provide MacDonald's attorneys with the addresses of witnesses required in preparation for trial. They were only given the list of addresses after the Fourth Circuit Court of Appeals ordered the prosecution to relinquish them.

Twenty-five years ago, MacDonald's life was turned upside down. All evidence that could reverse a conspicuous case of malicious prosecution is systematically rejected upon appeal—very comforting to the coterie of military officers and public officials connected by CID investigators, Stoeckley, Perry, Mitchell and others to the importation of heroin from Southeast Asia by casualty-courier to Fort Bragg.

But another motive was rough-sketched in 1987 by Melinda Stephens, a tenacious supporter of Jeffrey MacDonald, in *I Accuse: The Torturing of An America Hero*, a self-published debunking of the government's case. The suspects described by MacDonald "all existed," she observes, "all knew each other and all had a motive to kill… drugs. The Army had a motive for covering up their crimes, stemming from the fact that they were government informants involved in illegal LSD experiments at Fort Bragg." Her source of information was Major Jim Williams, MacDonald's colleague and the witness at the 1970 hearing who testified that he feared MacDonald had carried his investigation of drugs on the base too far, and had thereby exhorted disaster. Williams also stated on the record that the confessed "Fatal Vision" killers were "government informants."

As noted, Ike Atkinson has alleged that he was used in a CIA mind control operation involving brain telemetry.

All of this is consistent with CID Investigator William Ivory's recruitment of Dr. James A. Brussel, a mental health commissioner for the state of New York. Brussel has claimed to be an agent of the CIA and an adviser to the CID's counter-espionage division. He also, according to Potter and Bost, was "an innovative researcher into novel methods for controlling inmates in psychiatric institutions. Lamenting the frustrations of managing unruly patients and the cost of housing them in the late 1940s, Brussel and an associate instituted electric shock experiments on the brains of female inmates." Dr. Brussel's early ECT "treatments" were performed on 50 female mental patients, in some cases at the rate of 40-50 sessions per patient. Brussel also experimented with amphetamines and methedrine on depressed patients. He was recruited by Ivory in 1971 as a *secret* consultant to the government.

Yet another CIA mind control researcher brought into the MacDonald case was the infamous William Kroger, author of *Hypnosis and Behavior Modification* (1963), with a preface by MKULTRA's Martin Orne and H.J Eysenck. Kroger's work for the Agency involved hypnosis as an espionage tool. Of particular interest to Kroger was the development of a drug-assisted, hypnotic means of programming intelligence operatives to carry out an assignment and obscure any memory of it. Whether these mind control specialists had a direct role in the killings is not clear, but the confessions of Helena Stoeckley and Cathy Perry both mention dim recall of events of February 17, 1970, as if they'd dreamed the killings.

They have provided MacDonald's defense team with a wealth of details, confirming that the only "Fatal Vision" in the case is the government's own. McGinniss's version of events has had the effect of drawing attention from the body-bag connection and the CIA's attempts, in violation of repeated Congressional injunctions, to commandeer the mind. *Fatal Vision* is their cover story.

Chapter Eight

Family Ties

The Mephistophelian World of The Children of God

The fatal speedball seizure of River Phoenix on Halloween night, 1993, coincided in the media with the apocalyptic fire storm in Malibu and the death of Federico Fellini. In early September, newspapers in London and Buenos Aires headlined a story that directly concerned River Phoenix but, after the initial burst of coverage, was conspicuously absent from the American press—a raid on the Pilar, Argentina compound of the Family of Love, formerly the Children of God sect.

Police confiscated videos and magazines of children engaged in sex acts with adults. Also seized was a book for children, *The Life of Little David,* a Bible parody and tale of sexual initiation as told by "Sister Sarah." In one home video, naked young girls danced with silk scarves. Some 136 children were taken into protective custody, and 68 adults were detained for interrogation. The *London Times* reported that the children were "living in compartmented cells and answered questions like automatons. Whenever one of them tried to say something, another would look at him and he would fall silent, terrified." One cult house functioned strictly as a punishment facility, imprisoning some 50 adolescents.

Somos magazine reported on September 13, 1993 that the group's compound in Pilar is situated on "five kilometers of land hidden by high walls, constructed like a fortress off the Pan American highway." When Argentine authorities flew over the estate in a private plane, they discovered three observation posts on the roof. With binoculars, Police Commissioner Hugo Gabutti spotted three *rondina* units, or armed guards, on the roof. "They operated in a military fashion," Gabutti said, "looked and acted military. The security measures taken by the sect are incredible. They have received military training to protect themselves from outsiders."

Police in Buenos Aries were quickly inundated by "hundreds of telephone calls from the public requesting a special investigation,' according to the daily *Clarin.* After the raids, the *New York Times, Time, Espanol,* NBC and CNN all chimed in with prominently-placed features on the Family.

The investigation rapidly spread to Paraguay, Peru, Colombia and Venezuela. NBC's *Prime Time Live* interviewed disaffected Family members and flashed sexually-explicit videos: "We have had to edit them carefully," warned senior correspondent Fred Francis. The videos bore witness to intercourse with minors, "hooking for Jesus" and evangelical "sex orgies in rows of groaning bunk-beds." All over Latin America, *Clarin* reported on September 12, "Satanic and esoteric rites have been the subject of complaints concerning the sect." Silvina Cangaro, an interior decorator and former Family member, spoke to *Gente,* Argentina's answer to *People,* of her recruitment: "When I became a member, I immediately took part in Satanic rites. After I left the group and complained to the police, I received many death threats."

The *Times* of London reported on September 3 that video tapes seized by police—and broadcast on Argentina's nightly news—depicted "abhorrent Satanistic acts... in uncensored extracts of the videos after late-night news programs on Wednesday."

David "Moses" Berg, founder of Children of God, opened the door to esoteric religions and promiscuity in the 1970s, when in a letter to disciples he endorsed spiritism, witchcraft and astrology, according to W. Douglas Pritchett, who has compiled a book-length bibliography on the sect. Berg deified himself and proclaimed, "God is a pimp!" He claimed to have had sexual encounters with "goddesses," to have visited hell.

Ruth Gordon left the congregation in 1977, summing them up as a "pseudo-Christian" sect that dabbles in the occult. Other former disciples have described Berg as "Satanic," a charge first made by former members in 1973. Devil worshiper or not, he has long been a pugnacious anarchist, declaring "war" in 1968 "on the hypocritical old bottles of the religious system who were lined up on the back seat, and I cast in my lot with outlaws, drug addicts, maniacs, and the younger generation."

The allegations of former sect children were corroborated by the medical evidence—despite widespread and deceptive syndicated news stories like the one released by Reuters on September 5 claiming that "physical examinations carried out on the children turned up no signs of abuse." There followed a lull in the American press, a virtual news black-out.

Meanwhile, developments in the case continued to appear prominently in Latin American and European newspapers. On September 11 the *Manchester Guardian* reported that medical examinations of cult children *did* in fact find boys with "rectal bruises and excoriations," girls nine years old with "torn hymens and flayed vulvas": "Physical examination of children in Argentina's Family of Love sect has produced evidence of sexual injuries, according to a prosecutor in the case. "Those examinations, combined with psychological tests of the children and documents seized in the raids, are the basis for charges laid against the sect." Psychological profiles of the children detail characteristics of dementia and a trend of mental and psychological degeneration. Joyanne Treadwell Berg, 29, granddaughter of the sect's founder, told a magazine in Buenos Aires of her cousin Mene's sexual torment by leaders of the cult. "When my grandfather initiated her," Ms. Berg said, "he abused her sexually. She rebelled and endured all kinds of punishment. They used to hit her, tie her up in bed. They wrapped barbed wire around her body. They hit her so much—then they spread the news that she was mentally ill."

The Family fought back with denials that children had been harmed, accusing police of "religious persecution," of "stealing" and "torturing our children with physical examinations," as the Paraguayan branch of the sect maintained at a demonstration in Montevideo—itself under scrutiny for kidnapping and child abuse. Around the world, angry Children held outraged signs aloft:

> **"ARGENTINA ABUSES CHILDREN LIKE ME!"**
> **"THE GESTAPO STOLE OUR CHILDREN!"**

Gideon Scott, the "house shepherd" in Leicaster, England told reporters: "Nothing could be further from the truth than the wild allegations that our members abused or neglected their children. We do not promote or encourage sexual activity between adults and minors."

The group has long claimed to be the target of political oppression, especially when routed by police. Political martyrdom was a fundamental teaching of Moses Berg, the reclusive "prophet" who foretold the coming of the Anti-Christ in the form of a powerful dictator and the ascension of a One World Government. This, of course, is far-right religious programming—disseminated by Pat Robertson.

The cult's disavowals were echoed by Daniel Mujica, president of Argentina's Superior Council of Catholic Education, who said the allegations were inflated by the press. "The media are trying to make a big thing out of nothing," he said. "The sect isn't doing anything illegal." But his disavowals ran counter to the evidence: investigators in several countries have laid hands on a small library of photographic adventures in pedophilia printed by the Children. Most of the group's more lurid literary efforts were destroyed in 1987, including *The Davidito Letter,* written by Sara Davidito, a nurse in charge of group child care instruction. On October 10, 1993 the *Houston Chronicle* reported, "she writes of and is pictured having oral sex with the child. There are pictures of the child masturbating and being placed in a copulatory position with a small girl.

"The nurse writes of the boy sitting by while three couples, including his mother, have group sex. She describes giving him 'swigs of wine' so he would 'get happy,' then climbing into bed with him and asking if he was 'in the mood.'" Abigail Berry, a former member born inside the group, says she was coerced at age 13 into a carnal relationship with a minister. She can quote from *The Davidito Letter* by heart, and considers it "the child care manual for the Children of God."

The Family has a reputation as the ultimate in sackcloth-and-ashes millenarian cults, but sex with children has been a constant. A pamphlet written by Berg for his adherents twenty years ago, *My Little Fish,* had in it a photo of an unidentified adult stroking the penis of a boy of about three years in age. *Heaven's Girl,* an illustrated primer for teen-age girls, told the adventure of a young heroine who, while out flirty-fishing, is brutally gang-raped but perseveres to convert her attackers to Christianity.

Hooking for Jesus, sect leaders argue, was halted in 1987, when Berg instituted the great "Reformation and Revolution." They say that AIDS was a factor in the discarding of the Family's salacious sexual doctrine, provoking an argument from the *Houston Chronicle* on October 10, 1993. The "reformation" was extreme, though possibly not as complete as described by Family members. A January 1990 letter from Maria Berg's second-in-command ordered female members to require their "fish" to wear condoms. It also contained a section on "Which outsiders to still have sex with!" and advised them to restrict outside sexual activities to men in the "well-known" category.

Berg's disciples insist that the Argentine arrests are the latest instance of authoritarian jackboots tramping on their religious freedoms. Christie

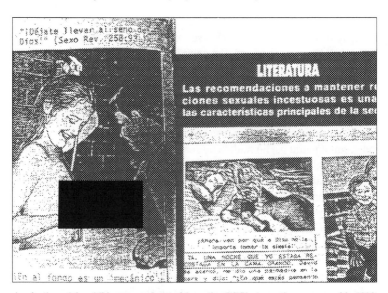

A selection of the child porn confiscated from the COG's Argentina compound in 1993.

Richards, a sect leader in Cleveland, Ohio maintains that "flirty-fishing" is "something we totally stopped." Ostensibly, Berg has proscribed sexual proselytizing, but former Children only shake their heads. Berg himself has, in a "Mo" letter to his congregation, warned that "sexual freedom must never be indulged in or practiced openly in the presence of visitors, strangers or uninitiated relatives or friends."

Julia Berg, his granddaughter, has quit the sect. She now lives in a mountain canyon two hours from Los Angeles, where she looks back with anger on her life in the COG. Women in the community, she says, "including pregnant girls, were ordered to do 'flirty-fishing' at night to bring in new members." She says that she learned by the "love of God" to conceal from outsiders the sexual teachings of Moses Berg.

Political Sugar-Daddies

The Children of God have gathered alms from powerful admirers. Chief Inspector Juan Carlos Rebello, who led police in the COG raids, said "we found evidence suggesting that the Family was funded by influential businessmen worldwide." One Argentine magazine found that some financial supporters of the cult were "well-known and powerful people," and pondered whether Berg's disturbed mental state "is being exploited by a network of powerful people to sexually control an army of children." Julia Berry, the prophet's own kin, has said that it was her "privilege" to be paired sexually with "very important men—men from the government." The Children of God, she said, "always had very powerful friends.... I met presidents from around the world. The children's chorus gave us an image of purity and innocence. It was a seduction."

According to the *Washington Post* for June 2, 1993, "the Family's leadership follows a policy of lying to outsiders, is steeped in a history of sexual deviance and has even meddled in Third World politics." Edward Probe, a Canadian who once edited Family publications, worked in the Philippines from 1986 to '88. He told the *Post* that "Family officials openly sympathized with right-wing military officers who tried to overthrow the government: What we were doing was supplying all the moral support." One former member from Costa Rica told Argentina's *Gente* magazine on September 9 about her life inside the cult: "My father used to have certain privileges inside the organization," she said. "He was considered a very important person for public relations. His paternal grandfather, the criminal lawyer, Guillermo Padilla, was a close friend of Chile's military dictator Pinochet, and Juan Carlos, the king of Spain." Pinochet and Carlos became financial and political benefactors of the cult.

The Family, according to David Hubert, a former member, contends that sexual evangelizing was used to curry political favor. "They would target special people," he told the *Washington Post,* "in the media, lawyers, in the government."

The guiding inner-circle of the Family is known as the Royal Family, and blue-bloods have in fact been sought out by Berg. In the 1970s, the prophet's "official representative" and second-in-command was Barbara Convair, the Italian duchess of Zoagli and Castelvari, rechristened Queen Rachel. Then in her twenties, the "ravishing, long-haired No. 2 leader" was rumored to have been a Berg consort. In 1973 she married Duke Emanuel Convair, a sect member, who invited the Family of Love to his estate, a wine-producing farm near Florence. The Duke graciously donated a vineyard to the cult. Germany's *Stern* reported in 1977 that a school on the estate trained women in the ancient art of religious prostitution. When *Time* asked her about the allegation, she denied it... but insisted: "There is nothing wrong with a sexy conversion. We believe sex is a human necessity, and in certain cases we may go to bed with someone to show people God's love."

In Bromley, south London, a recruit's millionaire father donated an abandoned factory, adapted as the Family's headquarters in England.

And they could not resist the call of the Holy Land, migrated to Egypt, and were expelled in November, 1985. Egyptian law, it seems, forbids the unorthodox sexual and religious practices of the cult. In 1977 the Children of God found a new messiah in Colonel Muommar Ghaddaffi, who offered them sanctuary from police investigations in California and New York. Louis Lefkowitz, the attorney general of New York, had charged them with kidnapping, brainwashing, imprisonment, enslavement, prostitution, incest and rape. But the U.S. Justice Department unexpectedly dropped the case, concluding, "'brainwashing' and 'mind control' do not constitute violations of federal law.... We have also concluded that the possibility of drafting effective federal criminal legislation in this area is unlikely." The New York attorney general's fraud division also lost interest in the case. "When it came time to prosecuting the group," reported the *Los Angeles Times,* then Atty. Gen. Lefkowitz sidestepped the issue with the claim that the Children "were protected by the First Amendment—a baffling rationale that later aroused suspicion the report was issued mainly to placate influential parents who had lost children to the sect. Lefkowitz, now retired, says he *doesn't recall* the matter."

The Justice Department probe hardly amounted to a bloody inquisition, but the Children cried religious persecution and fled the country. They left behind some nagging questions, foremost among them: Who murdered one of the Children in 1976, the body discovered with crushed internal organs at a medieval Belgium fortress? And who killed Berg's son, found in the same condition in Switzerland a few years earlier? Berg accused unnamed "enemies" of the Children for the murders. His critics blamed the sect. The public statements of some of Berg's followers fed their suspicions. In Canada, the Children declared on a national network that they were capable of lies, theft, murder, *anything* if so ordered by Berg. In 1972 a COG defector told NBC that she had been trained to commit criminal acts, including murder.

In Libya, Colonel Ghaddaffi was enamored with the cult. He provided them sanctuary, counsel, and even penned a song, addressed to "all industrial countries," performed at Children of God songfests around the world:

> *Do as I do.*
> *I pray to God.*
> *I'm very happy*
> *Because I found the road*
> *With Allah, Allah, Allah.*
>
> *You hate Negroes.*
> *You do not pray.*
> *You have lost your way.*
> *You're life is a falsehood*
> *Without Allah, Allah, Allah.*

The Children rechristened the budding psalmist "Godhaffi." Moses Berg enthused in *New Nation News,* a sect newsletter: "There has not been another worldly political leader in modern times as this young prophet of the seemingly impossible. There has hardly been such a godly world political leader since the days of his own prophet Mohammed... Jesus." Berg portrayed Ghaddaffi—now a deity—as "the savior who will ignite the young and rescue them from those twin forces of evil, godless Communism and American materialism."

Berg's politics were shared by messiah Ghaddaffi. Muommar Ghaddaffi was a product of the Libyan secret service, a branch of government assembled by Adolph Eichmann, Otto Skorzeny, Heinrich Muller and other engineers of the Final Solution who, like Berg, enjoyed the protection of totalitarian Middle Eastern despots. (Besides the Children of God, Ghaddaffi was also the patron of the infamous Paladins, a coterie of Nazi mercenaries from West Germany. Founded by Colonel Skorzeny, Hitler's commando chief, and the CIA, the Paladin group was responsible for a 1973 airport bombing in Rome that claimed thirty-two lives. They have linked up with death squads in Latin America and terrorists in Europe, South Africa and elsewhere.)

But the Libyan leader's fascination with the Children of God quite possibly ran through religion and politics to unconventional sex. His personal life is rarely discussed. He is said to be sexually eccentric, another trait he shares with Moses Berg.

Berg and his "prophet of the impossible" also found common ground in violent opposition to Israel. Reclusive, eccentric Moses David held a peculiar set of political beliefs for a demigod. One of his commentaries insisted that a small group of international Jews lurk behind a worldwide conspiracy. Berg assailed Jews again in a 1982 "Mo letter," and "their stooges, the Negroes... the curses of the world," the source "of everything that's evil." Berg claimed that his hatred of Jews and blacks sprang from a higher authority—"I'm a racist because GOD is!" he exulted in one of his delirious "Mo" letters.

In 1978 the COG changed its name to the Family of Love (and so continued to operate in Argentina after the Children were banned). By this time they boasted some 250,000 converts in 60 countries. The sect currently estimates that its ranks number about 300,000.

In the United States the political pull of the sect extended to the Bush administration. A chorale of Family children kicked off a Christmas show in 1992 for Barbara Bush in the East Room of the White House, for which they received certificates of appreciation signed by President Bush. The sect also sang for Bush after he toured the ravages of Hurricane Andrew in south Florida. (It wasn't the first time Bush's name arose in connection with a child prostitution cult. At the 1988 national Republican convention in New Orleans, Larry King of Omaha—a ranking GOP figure and convicted credit union rip-off artist—sang the National Anthem. In 1990, Nebraska state senator Schmit set out to investigate King and his circle of political operatives and business tycoons, alleged to have operated a national child prostitution network that catered to wealthy patrons. Shortly thereafter, Schmit received an anonymous phone call warning him off.)

The Family's political clout tends to put a damper on judicial investigations. Julia Berg recalls that adults in the Buenos Aries chapter "talked very openly about sex in front of children." At the age of 13, she alleges she was forced into a sexual relationship with a local pastor, and after leaving the Children attempted to press for his prosecution. But the judicial system, she says, flatly ignored her. After a police raid in 1989, Berry requested that a court-appointed physician examine her. The judge complied, but the doctor refused, explaining that he didn't want her "traumatized" by the examination—an ordeal, she says, incomparable to the trauma of molestation. "The doctor wouldn't accept my word that I wanted the examination." Family officials like to point out that "not once have we been found guilty of any kind of child abuse." This is true even in cases backed by solid evidence. The suggestion is that they are blameless, but another interpretation is that strings are pulled by well-heeled patrons to stifle public disclosure.

Police came away from the 1989 raid with cocaine, pornographic video tapes and childrens' books with condoms adhering to the pages. No Family members were prosecuted. Likewise, investigations in Brazil and Spain also fell apart. In May 1992 police in Australia swept into six Family communes, removing 142 youngsters. A key witness for the prosecution recanted his testimony and charges were suspended. Another case in Melbourne awaits trial. In June 1993 French authorities raided 12 of the sect's homes, but the court ultimately returned 40 children to their parents. Another raid in Spain also unraveled. Likewise, the September '93 raids in Argentina led nowhere. In December it was determined that a federal judge had no jurisdiction the case, and the sex abuse charges were dropped.

The Family is most assuredly not suffering religious persecution for their admittedly "controversial sexual beliefs," as the cult leadership often claims.

"Who Killed River Phoenix?"

The fatal overdose of River Phoenix on Halloween leaves hanging a host of questions concerning his death. Why is it, for instance, that three days later medical examiners announced that autopsy tests were inconclusive—but ruled out foul play? If the cause of death was unknown, how could the coroner possibly dismiss the possibility of murder? Toxicology tests revealed that the morphine levels of the cocaine and heroin ingested by Phoenix were respectively lethal. The day after he overdosed, the question reverberated on Hollywood streets: "Who killed River Phoenix?"

The conclusion that Phoenix died of an accidental overdose seems premature. No needle marks were found. The identity of his supplier is known. He is not some shadow melting back into narco-obscurity. Five witnesses, according to unconfirmed reports, accompanied Phoenix to a West Hollywood apartment at 10:40 p.m., on October 30, before departing for the Viper Room. One homosexual Los Angeles tabloid reported that the drug dealer who gave Phoenix the fatal dose "has been seen back in action at the club." If so, why wasn't he so much as questioned by police?

Media interest in the Family was eroded by false reports that Argentine prosecutors had been hamstrung by a lack of medical evidence. In fact, the death of River Phoenix coincided with investigations of the Family spreading across Latin America. The last thing the cult needed was a popular junkie film star shattering the news vacuum in the U.S. media by expanding, in some Hollywood fanzine, on his sexual initiation in a cult with notorious international political connections.

In fact, River Phoenix had a reputation for talking too much.

In the press, the Phoenix family has distanced itself from Berg's flock, emphasizing their separation from the Children of God. "We were flower children," John Phoenix told *People* magazine in September, 1987: "We were full of faith and loved everybody." John Phoenix was so deeply rooted in the cult that he was named "Archbishop of Venezuela" by the group. Rainbow Phoenix, River's sister, told *Life* in August, 1987 that she debuted as a performer at South American shopping plazas. "We used to sing and hand out pamphlets," she said. "But after two years in Venezuela, the family wanted out of the cult." Arlene Phoenix, River's mother, complained, "the guy running it got crazy. He sought to attract rich disciples through sex. No way."

The veneer of bohemian innocence was shattered in 1991 when, in *Details* magazine, River recalled his childhood in the cult. He admitted in this interview that he had intercourse at age four and sex with other children until the age of 10.

River Phoenix violated the cult's stricture of secrecy by discussing his early sexuality with reporters. Two years later, on All Hallow's Eve, at the most critical period in the Family's history, he was poisoned with a drug overdose. Had he lived, River Phoenix could have proven to be a dangerous liability to the cult, confirming reports of sexual abuse and child prostitution circulating throughout South America, but largely snubbed by the domestic press. Moses Berg's Family sleeps with powerful political allies.

Did one of them have reason to silence River Phoenix?

The Family Responds:

Note: The Family disputed many of the allegations made in the preceding story in *Paranioa* magazine Spring 1995. A point-counterpoint response to the cult by Alex Constantine follows the Family's comments.

My name is Phil and I've belonged to the organization, The Family, for over 20 years. I was in the former movement, too, known as the Children of God. I read your article with interest, and from what I understand of the "tone" of it, it is your intention to present an "alternative view" of the situation and circumstances surrounding the death of River Phoenix, which doesn't normally surface in mainstream media coverage. You seem to view River's death as being shrouded in mystery that might involve a type of "cover-up."

My reason for writing you is simply to ask: "How much do you really know about The Family?" My intention is to offer a better insight into our organization. We've opened our doors and had many visits to our communities by academics, sincere journalists, professionals, law enforcement officials, social workers, etc. who've wished to "see for themselves" what we are like. There's nothing we are trying to hide!

You present The Family as a dangerous "cult" and "sinister organization" with its tentacles sucking on politicians, powerful financial figures, and able to manipulate whomever it will. Is this your personal and professional opinion as well? Or is this an article that will "sell a copy" and fascinate its readers? If the case is the latter, let's hope that the readers will take it with a grain of salt and let it flow in one ear and out the other. As a Family member, I find it quite erroneous and I've counted 10 such gross misinterpretations of truth and/or wrongly quoted "out of context" statements. Speculations of The Family being "some sort of intelligence tool" and escaping criminal prosecution through the efforts of influential friends and backers" and, finally, "whether River Phoenix had been contacted by, or was going to be contacted by, the Argentine prosecutors investigating the Family." And If so, "did the cult want him silenced?" My response is: Would these speculations of yours hold any water in a court of law? The Family is not any sort of intelligence tool; nor is it secretly and clandestinely backed by political or financial figures; and we detest the notion that we as an organization would ever even conceive of "silencing someone" to escape the law or justice! Honestly, I can't find anything in The Family that would lend itself to such an allegation or even permit such intentions to exist.

The Family does not permit any substance abuse or abuse of its members and children. Such abuse is against our very basic tenets. We are opposed to any and all forms of violence—and these are not permitted in our communities.

As you also said: If only for the memory of River Phoenix, that cult's most famous abuse victim, it's time to ask "Why?" I, too, would like to ask you "why?" if any law enforcement agency, prosecutors, or whoever want to assert any type of action against The Family, we'd like to know why and based on what evidence or charges?

I've enclosed some material regarding The Family. I hope it [provides] a better or more conclusive view of our organization and its founder, as well as our true beliefs and practices:

OUR ORIGINS. The Family traces its origins to the Jesus Revolution of the late 1960s. Our founder, Father David, started a ministry of hippies in southern California, many of whom were subsequently delivered from drugs and chose to work with him to reach and help others. The group grew and was given the name The Children of God (COG) by the media. By 1978, the COG had become established in scores of countries. However, when reports of abuse of authority by some COG officials began to surface, Father David dissolved the COG and invited those interested to join him in a new fellowship, which over the years became known simply as The Family.

OUR BASIC BELIEFS. Our basic beliefs and doctrines are the same as those of millions of Christians the world over. We hold the Bible to be the divinely inspired Word of God, that Jesus is the only begotten Son of God, and that through His death on the cross redemption was brought to mankind. Salvation is a gift given freely by God to anyone who sincerely acknowledges their need for a savior and asks for Christ's forgiveness. We are persuaded by Scripture that we are living in the last generation prior to Christ's visible return to Earth.

Two of our beliefs which many mainline Christians do not agree with have fueled much of the controversy about out fellowship. We hold that Father David is a prophet of God for this generation, and that loving heterosexual relations between consenting adults is not a sin in the eyes of God, provided that it is with the agreement of all involved, and hurts no one.

Our children are safe from abuse. Although much has been made of our sexual beliefs and practices, our children have not been abused. We acknowledge that our sexual beliefs are controversial, but we emphasize that we do not promote nor condone any behavior that is unloving or perverted, let alone illegal. Sex is a very minor part of our lives. But rather than adopt the hypocritical double standard of much of today's secular society and even many professing Christians, we prefer to be honest and state our sincerely held religious convictions on the subject.

Our children are not permitted to engage in any sexual activity that is improper or illegal, and our teens are strongly encouraged to refrain from sexual relations until they are of legal age. If various American polls are to be believed, Family teens are much less active sexually than the average American teenager.

We cannot emphasize strongly enough that we do not tolerate any form of abuse of children within our communities. Sexual contact is prohibited between anyone over the age of 21 with anyone under 21. Offenders are expelled from our fellowship. In spite of the most determined efforts of our detractors to smear us with charges of child abuse, our members have always been completely exonerated by authorities who have examined our children and communities.

QUOTATIONS TAKEN OUT OF CONTEXT. Many of tbe quotations from letters written by Father David were taken out of context in these recent articles. Over a period of 23 years, 35,000 pages of Father David's writings have been published. As he is by nature an outspoken iconoclast, it is inevitable that some of his statements can be misconstrued....

Some articles have also quoted excerpts from a few of the more than 50,000 other pages of literature we have published throughout the years. Many of the controversial publications in question have long since been removed from our commumities, and in no way reflect the current practices of our membership.

The report about the discovery of 300 videocassettes in the La Herencia house does not coincide with the 251 video cassettes submitted. None [erotic videos] were found during the raids.

Another remarkable development is that after three months of having the phone lines of their multiple residences tapped, it was not possible to seriously associate any part of the conversations recorded with the exercise of the mentioned prostitution, nor were detected any possible rendezvous, encounters or invitations for the actual practice of the same.

At any rate, it is necessary to point out that the presence of the torn hymen is not sufficient to ascertain the concrete occurrence of the charge of the abuses claimed, especially considering these same young girls themselves stated that they in no way suffered abuse [as] hymen tears and damages may be the result of causes other than intercourse. There has not been the slightest shred of evidence to prove that any of the corruptive acts described above have actually occurred to any of the minors named in this proceeding.

> The Ruling: All Charges Revoked, All Detained Adults Freed, All Children Returned to their Parents, All Family Properties Restored.
> —from the San Martin (Buonos Aires) Court of
> Appeals, December 13, 1993 ruling on The Family

> I'm real impressed with the children, particularly. They strike me as being among the most emotionally well-grounded of any group of young people that I've ever been around.
> —Bart Cox, Assistant Attorney General of Texas

> The Family teenagers... have the benefit of living in a drug-free environment and they've had the benefit of being given a fairly strong moral code, so that they have something to face life as an adult.
> —Rev. Dr. J. Gordan Melton, Institute for the
> Study of American Religion

> When you hear the word 'cult,' you have some preconceived ideas. But all I saw was a well-built home that was very well protected against fire and nicely decorated.
> —Gary Looman, North York (Canada)
> fire prevention captain

We must remember the past. History shows us the struggle for freedom has always been between memory and forgetting, remembering the past, but working for the future. We permitted the demonization of the Branch Davidians. The reason people won't fund an independent investigative panel on Waco, is because this was a "cult"! People say, "There was evil there, sin. A threat to our religion, a threat to our established institutions, to our government, to our way of life." Everything that I work in, in terms of fundamental human rights and freedoms and peace, is terribly infected by the capacity for demonization in modern society.

We speak constantly in terms of "cults," but once the word "cult" is pronounced, most people can't think beyond that; the religious group becomes something inherently evil. The well has been poisoned and you can't drink out of it. As concerns The Family, it's absolutely appalling to observe what is happening to them around the world. It's clear beyond question that it involves inter-governmental coordination and communication, and the cooperation and participation of groups that call themselves "anti-cult" groups, who want to protect, as they see it, the population worldwide. Organizations like C.A.N., the Cult Awareness Network—which I've observed in several contexts now—have close relationships with law enforcement.

The Family is a very small, highly integrated group, numbering in a handful of thousands, spread all over the world. Since 1990, the attacks on them have been constant in Spain, Argentina, Australia, France and Peru. Argentina is perhaps the most flagrant case, with [over a] hundred children taken from their families, and scores of adults imprisoned. All of these cases have finally totally dissipated. There are some still in progress, but there is not a single case in which a single court or government agency has established a single incident of child abuse. All of these cases have ended—the ones that have ended—not only with a vindication of the church conduct, the parental conduct and the condition of the children, but with criticism or condemnation of government action as being ideologically based rather than factually based, reflecting inadequacy in investigation.

The trauma is something not talked about—the trauma of those children! Hundreds and hundreds of children all over the world were taken away from their parents. I think of those little kids in Waco, you know what the trauma on them was—they're dead! Suppose a little child had lived, might not that episode consciously and inescapably have been a dominant factor for the remainder of his life, affecting his perception of society and his interrelationships?

> The government of the United States, including the State Department, has shown awareness, international presence and suspicion regarding The Family. Interpol has involved itself with several Family members, in response to police input. The religious community must address this phenomena of the capacity of governments to brutalize small, unpopular religious groups who can be demonized when called "cults," and then action is taken against them without evidence. If a conventional crime is committed, it should be addressed, without calling a whole group a "cult" and condemning it and arresting all the adults, taking away all the children, keeping them in institutions, while they wonder where their mommies and daddies are.
>
> —Former U.S. Attorney General Ramsey Clark,
> in an address given to the Committee for
> Religious Liberty of the National Council of
> Churches, June 10, 1994.

Family Values—Alex Constantine's Rebuttal

In *Paranoia* 6, a spokesman for the Family, Phil Edwards, rebuts recent news stories written by "self-styled" critics of the cult, "without the interest of journalism or news reporting where investigative reporting, gathering of facts and analysis go into producing a written article." *Sic!* As a matter of fact, in preparation for a 1994 article on the cult for *Hustler* magazine, I collected every scrap of information I could find, primarily from European and South American newspapers. I went so far as to have publications from across Latin America translated after the Argentine raid on Family compounds, and culled all the information available from the UCLA research library's 11 million holdings. The claim that critics of the Family are making things up is as humorous as it is facile. He is relying on public naivete to promote an image of the group, a mere "handful of thousands" (elsewhere Edwards boasts of 9,000 members) as blushing innocents with a fierce devotion to gospel and "controversial" but widely-misunderstood "sexual beliefs."

The cult has a long history of lying its way out of tight situations, and Edwards is simply following this protocol for dealing with the press. River Phoenix himself publicly acknowledged that he'd been initiated to the cult's "sexual beliefs" at the age of four. Yet Edwards insists the cult does not "promote or condone any behavior that is unloving or perverted, let alone illegal." Perhaps he has not been informed that the Family's "sexual beliefs," as detailed in the cult's own publications, are proscribed by law in every civilized country on earth. What Edwards means to say is that the Family does not *openly* promote sex with children—he would undoubtedly argue that children's books with condoms stuck to the pages, seized in a raid on a Family compound in 1990, were planted there by disingenuous heathens from the press.

Edwards doesn't much care for the word "cult" to describe the Family. I'd prefer "doomsday sect" or "criminal syndicate" myself, so at least on this score we agree. On every other major point that Edwards makes, it is demonstrable from a thorough gathering of facts that he is relying on traditional, tried-and-true cult tactics for dealing with critics in the press—flagrant disinformation and smears.

To illustrate: The group has long claimed to be the target of political repression, especially when routed by police. Political martyrdom was a fundamental teaching of cult founder David Berg, the reclusive "prophet" who foretold the coming of the Anti-Christ and the rise of a "One World Government." This, of course, is far-right religious programming, the same dogma (excuse me, gospel) disseminated by the 700 Club.

But the Family is decidedly not suffering religious persecution for their "controversial sexual beliefs." On the contrary, if the group was harried by authorities—as were, say, the Black Panthers, Angela Davis, Allard Lowenstein or Danny Casalaro—the group could not boast that "our members have always been completely exonerated by authorities."

Exoneration even comes when there is solid evidence of wrong-doing. Last year, litigation concerning the Family in Australia was aborted after a *secret* Cabinet decision was made to overrule Dr. John Patterson, the Secretary of the Department of Health. Newspapers in Australia reported that preempting the secret judicial proceeding—in which Dr. Patterson had been "gagged"—was a "political" decision. Patterson was dumbfounded because his department had considered the evidence of child abuse strong enough to make a case for imposing legal measures to protect the 86 children it represented.

Phil Edwards, in his capsule history of the cult, misrepresented the cult's reasons for changing its name. "When reports of abuse of authority by some COG officials began to surface, Father David dissolved the COG and invited those interested to join him in a new fellowship, which over the years became known simply as The Family." The true story points up how tolerant even the most repressive political regimes have been of the cult's excesses. Years ago, Argentine authorities outlawed the Children of God. The cult simply changed its name to the Family and was therefore permitted, by some sort of oblique political reasoning, to remain in Argentina. Some crackdown.

Even the 1994 raid on 10 Family houses in the elite northern district of Buenos Aires came only after police had been swamped by complaints from the public over a three-year period of stubborn inaction.

Somos magazine reported on September 13, 1993 that the group's compound in Pilar is situated on "five kilometers of land hidden by high walls, constructed like a fortress off the Pan American highway." When Argentine authorities flew over the estate in a private plane, they discovered three observation posts on the roof. With binoculars, Commissioner Hugo Gabutti spotted three contingents of *rondinas,* or armed guards. "They operated in military fashion," Gabutti said, "looked and acted military. The security measures taken by the sect are incredible."

Appended is some of the child pornography seized in the Argentine police raid—including photographs of young children engaged in sex with adults. The kiddy porn should put to rest the ersatz claim made by Edwards that "we do not tolerate any form of abuse of children." Nonsense. When the police entered Family homes in well-heeled Buenos Aries suburbs, they discovered children who "seemed like Martians, autistic," according to the *London Times* for September 5, 1993. "They were living in compartmented cells and answered questions like automatons." The police came away with "videos showing the children, some of whom had been separated from their parents at age 12, performing various sexual acts with adults and each other." One cult house functioned strictly as a punishment facility to imprison some 50 adolescents.

Yet Edwards, in his transparent apologia, maintains that the cult's detractors "smear us with charges of child abuse." T'ain't so. It is because members incriminate themselves so thoroughly that the Family has fallen into disrepute.

The group's spokesman argues falsely that the only evidence of molestation found in the Argentina raid was a single torn hymen. This, Edwards claims, "is not sufficient to ascertain the concrete occurrence of the charge." I would agree—if it was only a matter of one rent hymen. But on September 11, 1993, the *Guardian* reported that medical examinations turned up "boys with anal wounds and girls as young as nine and 11 with torn hymens and flayed vulvas." The physical evidence was backed by psychological evaluations and documents seized in the raids, including freshly-printed birth certificates for children kidnapped by the group in Peru. Yet, as usual, the cult "denied all the charges, and claimed it is being subjected to religious persecution." In Montevideo, Berg's followers assembled at the Argentine consulate to wave banners declaring "Police Stole Our Children Like the Gestapo." One Family leader accused the justice system of "torturing our children with physical examinations."

Another criticism hotly denied by the group is its affiliation with influential patrons. The Argentine journal *Gente* reported shortly after the arrests that "many well-known personalities around the world were involved as main figures of political and financial support of the sect. Among them is Libya leader Muommar Kaddafi, and the Chilean dictator Augusto Pinochet."

Such connections led the magazine to ponder whether Berg was being "exploited by a network of powerful people to sexually control an army of children." Another of the cult's patrons is King Juan Carlos of Spain— adored by Franco as the son he never had—whose sexual appetite is legendary. In Italy, the Duke of Castelvari permitted the cult to use his estate, according to *Time* magazine, to train "good-looking disciples in the arts of seduction." Joyanne Berg, the granddaughter of the cult's prophet, claims "it was my 'privilege' to sleep with important men. I met many presidents from around the world." George Bush had the Family to the White House for a Christmas celebration, so I have to wince when Edwards bemoans "the capacity of governments to brutalize small, unpopular religious groups," and denies political connections.

(The nagging irony is, as a dissident political researcher, I have, on many occasions, been brutalized by the government and its hired guns. I have often been followed, harassed, beaten and even tortured. Why? Because I write, among other things, about CIA connections to the mind control cults. So who should write to complain about my research but the Family—with a Pennsylvania Avenue return address, no less.)

This fine, upstanding religious organization argues that many of Father David Berg's more outrageous comments have been quoted "out of context" and "misconstrued" by such heathens as myself. This is the same Berg who in 1982 published a book that described his preschool stepson engaging in sex with a nanny, interspersed with quotes from the prophet himself about how God expects children to enjoy intercourse with adults. (*The Age,* an Australian newspaper, reported on April 30, 1994 that a raid there found explicit literature on cult premises warning children that "they would be taken away if they revealed their sexual practices to outsiders.") Berg once, when accused of harboring anti-Semitic feelings, opined boldly that "God himself is anti-Semitic." Berg's belief system was clearly pedophilic *and* fascistic. Out of context or not, his own published statements damn him more than any critic of the cult, and such expressions of perversion and race hatred are impossible to misconstrue.

Even more disturbing are reports from around the world that the cult's leadership engages in Satanism, which frequently fronts for CIA mind control activity. Scholar Douglas Pritchett compiled an exhaustive, book-length bibliography on the Family in 1985, noting that "Mo" Berg has advocated witchcraft and claimed to have slept with goddesses. He once boasted that he had copulated with an incubus. The raids in Argentina were followed by reports from around the world that Family children had been drawn into Satanic rites. The charges in Buenos Aries included "sexual abuse, deprivation of liberty," and the use of children in "abhorrent Satanistic acts."

The *London Times* story reported there was evidence "the Family was funded by businessmen worldwide and that children were kidnapped in one place and taken to another so that they would be difficult to trace." Mind control cults with a religious facade often operate at this level of disregard for human rights—and are allowed to get away with it.

Phil Edwards is a slippery religious huckster straight from the pages of Flannery O'Connor. His rebuttal to press reports on the Family is a weak attempt to convince the public that his sect is a victim of the establishment, when in fact it is a behavior-modified, morally-diseased appendage of it.

That cults are dangerous has been proven time and again. That they are often fronts for intelligence activity is indisputable (as anyone who has dug into researching CIA mind control experimentation knows full well). Edwards has made a sentimental appeal for sympathy with a lot of pious talk about political martyrdom. Pathetic. I have watched in horror time and again as otherwise intelligent people have fallen for the whining of cult leaders and the CIA's hired guns in academia and the media, and it is a painful thing to observe.

But it is infinitely more painful for the true victims, particularly children, who are traumatized for life by the sadistic intrusions of mind control, and forced by public denial to swallow their rage at the transparent deceptions of cult apologists like Mr. Edwards.

Chapter Nine

A Sordid Tale of Two Cities:

The Conspiratorial Republican Elites of Omaha, Nebraska and Wilmington, North Carolina

Few newspapers reported it, but Omaha had become a hotbed of scandal. In October of 1989, Police Chief Robert Wadman, his shirt-sleeves still smoldering, cleared out of town. He left behind a growing awareness of his entanglement in a clique of well-heeled conservatives led by Lawrence E. King, an upper-tier Republican and the disgraced director of the looted Franklin Credit Union. Larry King, a name once tossed around freely at the White House, kicked off both the 1984 and '88 GOP conventions with his rousing basso rendition of the National Anthem. He nurtured Washington connections until the day Franklin was raided by federal agents.

The credit union was closed in 1988 after it was discovered that King had spirited away $39 million. The state legislature launched a probe, and the Franklin Committee soon found itself immersed in a nightmare of political corruption that trailed off to the Reagan-Bush White House, Republican political circles, the CIA and a national child prostitution network.

A February, 1989 report released by the committee relates a conversation between James Flanery, a reporter for the *Omaha World-Herald* assigned to the Franklin story, and Carol Stitt, director of the Foster Care Review Board, that took place shortly after the raid on King's credit union. Flanery complained that the FBI stopped cooperating with him after it was discovered that King was shipping guns and currency to Nicaragua for the CIA. Flanery considered resigning due to "the possibility of a White House connection," and King's ties to "a number of big people." Flanery told Stitt that he was edgy talking on the phone. "His editor was distressed," Stitt said. He had "edited" Flanery's copy, expunging political connections.

Among King's co-conspirators in Washington was the infamous Craig

Spence, a former ABC reporter and the proprietor of a call-boy service in Washington, D.C. The *Washington Times* ran a series on Spence in June, 1989, reporting that he had established a sexual blackmail operation on behalf of the Central Intelligence Agency. His lavish parties were attended by such luminaries as William Casey, Ted Koppel and Eric Severeid. Paul Balach, a ranking adviser to Labor Secretary Elizabeth Dole, immediately resigned under a cloud, admitting that he had received blackmail threats from one of Spence's male prostitutes. Five months after the series appeared, Spence was found dead in a Boston hotel room, an apparent suicide.

The King scandal might well have blackened scores of political reputations if not for the body count. Spence's suicide was soon followed by the plane-crash deaths of Gary Caradori, chief investigator for the Franklin Committee, and his son in July, 1990. A National Transportation Safety Board brief reported that Caradori radioed that the cockpit compass had swung erratically. His transmission was cut short by an in-flight break-up that scattered the wreckage of his Piper PA-32R across a wide swath of Ashton, Illinois. The Transportation Board ruled that a damaged wing stabilizer had failed and separated from the aircraft.

Other bizarre fatalities soon followed: two important material witnesses "died in their sleep." Four others were shot dead. One was strangled, another dropped from a window. Harmon Tucker, school superintendent and a suspected molester, was found dead in Georgia, his cadaver bearing ritual marks.

At the center of the carnage stood Lawrence King, Jr. In March of 1990 a federal magistrate ruled that the powerful conservative Republican was mentally incompetent, an opinion founded on the report of Dr. Dorsey Dysart, chief psychiatrist of the Federal Medical Center in Springfield, Missouri. Dr. Dorsey diagnosed King as a delusional paranoiac of a "grandiose type." The doctor held that in his condition, "the intellectual system of grandiosity leads to disorganization of thought processes." King was therefore ruled too delicate to withstand a lengthy trial, and a growing political scandal withered from public view.

The prosecution of Lawrence King culminated in a sentence totaling 15 years for the looting of Franklin Credit Union, but he is permitted to serve his sentences *concurrently,* a very liberal sentence considering the magnitude of the crime.

The conviction handed down by Judge Van Pelt, a political team-player, applied solely to gross financial misconduct. His grand jury "found probable cause to believe that King... used money or items of value to 'entice, inveigle, persuade, encourage or procure' men in their late teens or early twenties to engage in acts of prostitution." But the grand jury's "belief" was never addressed in the courtroom. By suppressing the male prostitution charges, Van Pelt re-enacted a role familiar to him. In 1984, for instance, Van Pelt was accused by 43 residents of Cairo, Nebraska of covering up the murder of political activist Arthur Kirk by a state police SWAT team.

Among the melange of well-off Nebraskans linked to King was multi-millionaire Warren Buffett, a ranking shareholder in the *Washington Post* and Cap Cities/ABC, not to mention the financial leviathans American Express, Wells Fargo and Salomon Brothers. All told, his wealth has been appraised at an excess of $4 billion. Buffett hosted Larry and Alice King's tenth wedding anniversary party, and Buffett's wife was a volunteer at Franklin Credit Union. Buffett has tried to distance himself from the scandal, but he couldn't hide the fact that King sponsored a fund-raiser for Buffett's son in his run for commissioner of Douglas County, Nebraska..

John DeCamp, a former CIA operative and Nebraska state senator, alleges in *The Franklin Cover-Up,* the fullest account·of the case to date, that Oliver North cavorted with King and his circle of rich Republicans. The connection to North was publicized by the *New York Times,* which noted that King contributed $25,000 to Citizens for America. The CFA booked speaking engagements for North. "King was a founding member and one of its largest contributors," DeCamp notes. He contends that King, as Franklin's director, laundered cocaine cash for the Nicaraguan counter-revolution at the behest of CIA operatives. In fact, King hob-nobbed so frequently in Washington that he rented a second home off Embassy Row for $55,000 a month.

Another notable link to King was Ronald Roskens, the former chan-cellor of the University of Nebraska. The notes of deceased Franklin Committee investigator Caradori report that Roskens was "terminated by the state because of sexual activities reported to the regents and verified by them." A year later, Roskens was appointed by President Bush to direct the Agency for International Development, a major CIA cover. By 1992 the House Operations Committee chaired by Rep. John Conyers, Jr. (D-Michigan), called for the dismissal of Roskens. A 107-page staff report alleged that Roskens' "abuse of the public trust during his crucial first year in office had gone unchecked" until AID's inspector general and Congressional oversight "forced a change in his pattern of behavior." The report also noted that AID had "more high-ranking employees convicted of federal crimes during the past two years than any other agency or department of the federal government."

The twice-disgraced Roskens quit his post in November, 1992 to promote the foreign policy proposals of the Interaction Council (a group that includes Gerald R. Ford, Mikhail Gorbachev and former French leader Valéry Giscard d'Estaing).

George Bush surfaced once again in connection with King's syndicate of eminent satyrs, specifically Harold Andersen, former publisher of the *Omaha World-Herald.*

According to DeCamp, "Harold Andersen moves in the upper circles of the U.S. intelligence community." When Andersen's reputation began to suffer as a result of his friendship with King, "his friends at the Nebraska Society of D.C. staged an awards dinner in Washington to polish his image." Bush sent a testimonial memo in praise of the adviser to the U.S. State Department.

Omaha's upper-crust is a small, tightly-knit cast of characters overlapping a small, tightly-knit cast of characters in Washington, D.C. According to *Birmingham Post-Herald* reporter Andrew Kilpatrick, Harold Andersen is "an old friend of Buffett's." The multi-billionnaire has also linked up with Bush, rather conspicuously, when they withdrew from a formal ceremony on November 28, 1990 for a private conversation. "We may never get the details," Kilpatrick writes. "But the discussion was about business, not politics."

Of Andersen's Beltway alliances, the most revealing is Robert Keith Gray. "Said to be Harold Andersen's 'closest friend in Washington,'" according to DeCamp, "Gray is also reportedly a specialist in homosexual blackmail operations for the CIA." The blackmail ring was, a vice squad official told DeCamp, established by Roy Cohn, the skulking ultra-conservative homosexual pimp. "Cohn's job was to run the little boys," the official told DeCamp.

Gray is one of Washington's most notorious Republican operatives, a fierce insider and public relations tycoon. The child prostitution charge against him gained credibility when Gray's name surfaced in the internal inquiry of the short-lived Congressional page-boy scandal. The probe was abruptly killed when a lobby of Washington homosexuals clamored its opposition. Susan B. Trento, Gray's biographer, reported that Congress was "discouraged from pursuing any further investigations in these areas in general." Lucky Robert Keith Gray.

In 1992 the Franklin Committee released a 91-page final report, stating that the investigation changed course when Gary Caradori produced for the committee a video-taped statement from Alisha Owen, who claimed to have been a witness and victim of sexual abuse. "She named persons of prominence in Omaha... involved in the abuse." She alleged that Chief Wadman had fathered her child.

And she offered to prove it, signing a voluntary agreement in January 1990 to submit to a lie detector test. The FBI refused to administer it. An independent agency did. She passed. Two other juvenile witnesses passed as well. Wadman countered by repeatedly telling the press that DNA tests proved his innocence. But an Omaha reporter who has followed the case from the start advises: "Forget about the DNA-blood tests... they never happened."

This powder-keg was dropped on the table of the committee, which was soon "haunted" by the possibility of a backlash of the sort that followed the McMartin preschool molestation case.. Would the public support Owen? Would there be attacks on her and the witnesses who stepped forward to confirm the allegations? Would Chief Wadman and his co-defendants apply pressure to bury the investigation?

Given the sensitivity of the probe, the committee decided to conduct it as quietly as possible, at least until indictments were handed around. But before witnesses could be induced to testify, bootleg copies of the Owen tapes were leaked to the press. State Senator Loran Schmit and his colleagues on the panel found themselves in the eye of a whirlwind fed by heated public speculation and gossip.

Michael McKnight, a reporter for Omaha's WOW-TV, later told Owen that the station purchased the video tape from agents of the FBI. The station had also purchased Caradori's taped interviews with witnesses Troy Boner and Dan King from the FBI. The tapes had been given to the Bureau by members of Schmit's committee.

From the Franklin Committee's final report:

> The act of broadcasting the tapes was exceeded in arrogance and irresponsibility only by the news media efforts to convene impromptu panels of self-proclaimed experts to talk about whether the stories in the tapes were 'believable' or not. We were bewildered as to how the investigation was furthered, or the public interest served, by such circus events. Did it not occur to anyone in authority within the news media that none of these "experts" had first-hand knowledge of anything.... They had nothing to offer except meaningless opinions. It occurred to us that these so-called "expert opinions about whether a story was true or not were just that, opinions.... A public debate of this nature is counterproductive... and polarizes the community.... Media hosts interviewed "experts" who had seen the tapes, and who criticized Caradori's questioning techniques. In fact, the investigation turned toward Caradori with charges that he unnecessarily led or coached the witnesses, or perhaps induced them to lie, or coordinated their stories for some undisclosed gain, perhaps book or movie rights.

The committee began to feel a force beyond their control running away with the case, moving it silently toward a predetermined end. Somehow, King had the wisdom to remove pornographic material from his home and office. He cabbaged it away in the trunk of his car. The FBI, however, confiscated a pornographic video featuring "local children"— yet no attempt was made to locate them.

Somehow or other, the invisible hand always bested the committee. A raid on the home of *World-Herald* columnist Peter Citron produced "a vast quantity of pornographic material." Citron pled no contest before a grand jury convened in March, 1990. The prosecution failed to introduce evidence against his cohort Alan Baer because it vanished, as did computer disks seized by police listing the names and addresses of every child he'd photographed.

The thieving wraith of the evidence room struck again after the legislative committee subpeonaed video-taped interviews of Alisha Owen and other witnesses from the FBI and Nebraska State Patrol. The FBI synopsis of the tapes, prepared for the attorney general, contained testimony that never appeared in the tapes. Owen complained that Troy Boner's deposition had been shed of corroborating details. "In one instance," the Franklin Committee's final report noted, "there was no break in the tape yet Boner's shirt was different from the previous one."

The evidence-devouring ghost had an ally in Owen's first legal counselor, Pam Vuchevich. When the abuse revelations surfaced into public view, Alisha Owen was serving a prison sentence for passing bad checks. On March 9, 1990 the FBI and state patrol searched her cell and removed evidence she'd assembled to support her grand jury testimony. The FBI drew up an inventory, but when the articles were returned some were missing. They had been scratched off the list. Ms. Vuchetich was dismissed, and charged with two counts of abusing attorney-client privileges. Two weeks later however an FBI agent appealed to the Omaha Bar Association on behalf of Ms. Vuchetich, and the charges were tossed out of court.

To judge by the 177 phone calls she made to the FBI in early 1990, Vuchetich betrayed more than a client's confidence. In April, 1990 she prodded Alisha Owen to lie that she conspired with Mike Casey, an Omaha reporter, to fabricated the sex scandal as raw grist for a TV movie. Owen refused.

Meanwhile, Paul Bonacci, one of some 80 child witnesses, recalled for Frances Mendenhall, a reporter at the *Nebraska Observer,* his descent into Omaha's sexual underground. In 1979 Bonacci met a man named Walter Carlson at an Independence Day picnic. Carlson took the boy home, where they watched cartoons, pornographic videos and eventually had sex. Bonacci was eleven years old.

He met Citron, the *World-Herald* gadfly, at a public park. Bonacci says that he was flown to California, Colorado, New York, Minnesota and elsewhere at the behest of the mercurial Larry King, and prostituted to politicians and wealthy businessmen.

Like other children drawn into King's circle, Bonacci tells a grim story:

> **Mendenhall:** Did you believe that they would kill somebody?
> **Bonacci:** They did.

Mendenhall: Who did they kill?

Bonacci: It was in California.... We picked up Nicholas who went out with us and when we got there, I don't know where we landed at or where we were at, they had me tied and drugged up. They took us out to a place and all I can remember is that there was a Kern River or something that went by, there was a bridge that had a name on it. It was near there that we would wait. And they had this little boy that was in a cage.... First they told us we better do what they told us. They told us we'd better do what they wanted or they'd kill us too. So we did everything they told us.

The children were used like sexual "rag dolls," Bonacci said, by a group of adults, among them Larry King. The incident took place in Bakersfield. Bonacci claimed that the orgy was attended by local cultists.

In a complaint filed with the U.S. District Court of Nebraska, Bonacci describes how, at twelve years-old, he was forced to attend "sexual parties" and "sadistic rituals" attended by influential citizens of Omaha. He was beaten on February 13, 1981 "for refusing to participate in a sadistic ritual." He was, according to the complaint, "burned with cigarettes during sadistic orgies." With no exit from his predicament, and shaken by the suicide of another child participant in these functions, Bonacci too tried to kill himself. He told Alan Baer, an official of J.L. Brandeis & Sons, a local department store, that he wanted out. In July, 1983, says Bonacci, Baer ordered a drive-by shooting to eliminate the possibility of exposure.

Bonacci estimates that he participated in 25-30 group sex rituals between 1979 and 1984.

Taped testimony from both Owen and Bonacci deals at length with former Omaha Police Chief Robert Wadman, whose beating heart kept time with the pulse of a secret Omaha. Chief Wadman mixed well with King's melange of Promethean tycoons, CIA procurers and Beltway politicians. In 1962 he began his law enforcement career, his father's vocation, with the San Diego Police Department. He was 21. Wadman left the force in 1968 for a stint at Utah's Brigham Young University. He turned up next in San Luis, Arizona, assigned to the DEA, according to his resume.

In 1976 he he was selected as chief of police in Utah, and two years later state deputy commissioner of public safety—an ironic position considering his part in the 1979 slaying of an unarmed civilian. Jerry Springer, whose only offense was a refusal to enroll his children in a public school, had been lured outside his home by Wadman and two sidekicks posing as reporters. Springer ran, the officers shot him in the back. Springer's widow sued, retaining Gerald Spence as her legal counsel, and received an undisclosed settlement. Wadman resigned and was asked to leave the state.

The Springer episode dogged him in Omaha. For two years the police union fought his appointment as chief. He met Alisha Owen, then 15, at a party in August, 1983. Also present were Larry King, Alan Baer and Harold Andersen. En route to the party, a friend promised cocaine and alcohol. When Owen arrived, King's guests were watching a pornographic video. "She observed a young boy... sitting on Harold Andersen's lap," according to Caradori's notes.

A month later, she attended another of King's parties, where she says she was forced into a sexual encounter with Chief Wadman, ala Caradori:

> He [Wadman] indicated to Alisha that he knew she wasn't a virgin and he felt her breasts. He told her that she had nice breasts. He felt her genitals and un-zipped the zipper of the jumpsuit she was wearing. She asked him to stop and he grabbed her wrist very tightly and twisted her wrist. He then removed her clothing and asked her if she knew what fellatio was. He said that he would show her what it was. He then instructed her to perform oral sex. Robert Wadman's pants and underwear were down.

Owen began to cry. She told Caradori that she went to the bathroom and vomited. Paul Bonacci was not called to testify that he had witnessed Wadman and Owen engaging in sex. Troy Boner recanted his testimony, but later admitted that FBI agents had threatened to kill members of his family if he testified against Wadman.

From *A Carefully-Crafted Hoax,* a book written by Owen's sympathizers in Omaha:

> Alisha Owen's perjury trial began on May 17. Judge Raymond Case of Plattsmouth was brought out of retirement to preside over the trial in the Douglas County District Court.... The prosecution spent the majority of its time in painting Owen as a promiscuous tramp. But the charges against her were for perjury.... The outcome of the trial should not have been in doubt. Before it even began, Judge Case ruled against several of the defense's pretrial motions and consistently refused to allow important items to be introduced as evidence (for example the tapes of Boner and King). There was much in the way of evidence the jury was not allowed to see.

Owen was sentenced to 9–15 years in prison for alleging that Chief Wadman was the father of her child. Before the sentence was overturned on appeal for retrial, she served more time in solitary confinement than any other woman in the history of Nebraska.

Wadman, not one to let a prime opportunity drift by, filed a $4,000 suit against Amanda, Alisha's *five year-old daughter,* supposedly to recoup the expense of a blood test. Wadman's itemized expenses include a first-class flight to Chicago and four days of missed work. But a charge of filing false paperwork was filed by Owen's attorney. Chief Wadman, it seems, had actually been on vacation in Arizona, and his counter-suit was thrown out of court. He paid $25 in court costs.

But by this time Wadman had resigned and moved to Aurora, Illinois. Aurora's Mayor Pierce selected Wadman for chief in September 1989. The local *Beacon-News* reported on June 6, 1991 that he was selected after "a lengthy national talent search conducted by the International Association of Chiefs of Police." Wadman once again reigned as top cop, but announced his resignation nineteen months later. He repeatedly declined to comment on his reason for stepping down, but Aurora Mayor David Pierce cited the Omaha scandal as a decisive influence. Wadman told the *Beacon-News* that the "false allegations" of Alisha Owen had undermined his authority. The paper reported falsely that "genetic testing has shown that Wadman was not the child's father."

One Aurora cop told the *Beacon-News:* "I'm not sorry to see him go. My only regret is that he's not going today."

Meanwhile, the pornographic photos and tapes seized in the Citron raid began to prove an embarrassment to some of Omaha's most prominent citizens. At first, the police department denied having the child pornography until one officer admitted it at Citron's 1993 federal trial. In the photos are the faces of King, Wadman, Andersen, Baer and others engaged in criminal acts, according to the Nebraska Leadership Conference, a non-profit citizens' group supportive of the children in the case. The police, caught suppressing the photos, refused to make them public, then decided to destroy them. Lawyers and investigators flew to Omaha, and a federal judge ordered the police to hand over the evidence. Citron was convicted. Andersen resigned as newspaper publisher. Alan Baer, the department store official, is rumored to be hiding somewhere in California.

Wadman surfaced next in North Carolina. Despite his record, Wadman was selected in 1991 above 200 other applicants for the position of police chief.

But it wasn't long before fallout from the Omaha case burned him once again.

In January 1993, Ron Lee Silver stepped off a train from Hollywood. Frustrated with his prospects as an actor, he moved to Wilmington, which boasted several newly-formed film companies. Coincidentally, he had passed the long rail ride from California reading John DeCamp's book on the Franklin affair, and was already aware of Wadman's notoriety.

Driven by a sense of outrage, Silver says, he appeared at a Wilmington City Council meeting on January 5, 1993 to argue for the recall of Chief Wadman. The *Wilmington Morning Star,* which is owned by the *New York*

Times, reported two days later that Ronald Silver "met a reception ranging from skeptical to hostile." But, as the paper noted, the aspiring actor was not the first to berate Wadman: "A growing faction of the Wilmington police department believes Mr. Silver's story might be true." Alas, "the resurrection of these allegations could bring internal discontent to levels Chief Wadman has not faced yet."

Silver asked that the city council conduct an investigation of past pedophilia and child prostitution charges.

Wilmington Mayor Don Betz had hired Wadman. He flew into a rage, blustering that he hadn't fought for two years in Vietnam, "in cold water eating cold food," to permit this blatant "abuse of free speech" to continue. Betz abruptly ended the meeting. The following day, Chief Wadman countered that the accusations were "a pack of lies" that could only affect his police work. "Every allegation has been made by people clearly identified as a supporter of Lyndon LaRouche," Wadman argued.

Silver's city council appearance made headlines, polarized public opinion. Supporters of the Chief claimed that Silver was a trouble-maker who had nothing better to do than pester "the Chief."

The local media rallied to Wadman's defense. A *Morning Star* editorial on January 8 attacked Silver, rejecting the charges against Wadman with a smirk:

PATHETIC FANTASIES AREN'T SO HARMLESS
Wilmington Police Chief Bob Wadman, who looks like a human being, is actually a seven-eyed alien from the planet Emmo. He has makeup done at the movie studio. "Mr. Wadman" (Zorgo is his real name) is high priest of an intergalactic cult whose goal is to seduce Earth's Christian children into unspeakable practices that will cause them to give birth to talking yams.

Public interest was stimulated by the headlines and the release of DeCamp's book in Wilmington. The *Star* reported that "local bookstores are selling copies as fast as they can get them," but assured readers that the book only "rehashes discredited testimony," and declared falsely that "followers of political extremist Lyndon LaRouche have been linked to the effort to discredit Mr. Wadman."

Silver was unprepared for the counter-charges and his sudden role as citizen-reformer. Disgruntled police officers began calling him with their own horror stories concerning the chief. There was talk that Wadman had been ham-stringing local police efforts to stem the flow of drugs into Wilmington.

So it seemed peculiar to Silver when the local media rushed to the Chief's defense.

Wadman claimed publicly that Silver had threatened his life.

Furthermore, he accused Investigator D.P. Pridgen of the Wilmington police force of plotting secretly with Silver to defame and "murder" members of his family. In a letter to Pridgen, the chief claimed that the "death threats" were a direct consequence of the loud city council session. In an internal WPD complaint filed on March 5, Pridgen noted that Wadman was "trying to gather enough information... to have Silver arrested." Further, Wadman "badgered, harassed and intimidated" Pridgen in a failed attempt to link Silver with a crime.

On a local radio talk show Silver emphatically denied the accusation he'd threatened Wadman. The hostess of the program repeated the charge that Silver was a "kooky," possibly dangerous conspiracy theorist bent on defaming an honorable city official:

> **Interviewer:** Hey there, good morning!
> **Silver:** I'm Ron Silver, the subject of your call-in show today....
> Let's talk about two undisputed facts. One, [Chief Wadman] has been punished for misconduct. And the other is that he claims I have threatened his family. It has even evolved into "a group of people" who threatened his family. When I heard that, I tried to get in touch with the police and cooperate since I was a "criminal suspect." I agreed to take a lie detector test. They wouldn't talk to me. The Chief has fabricated all of this. He bases his misconduct on fabrications and lies. No one has threatened his family that I know about, and I certainly haven't.

Silver denied that he had any connection whatsoever to Lyndon LaRouche, nor had anyone he knew. "Where are they, these fantasy LaRouchians coming out of the woodwork to haunt the poor chief?"

> **Interviewer:** Mister Silver, what is your vendetta against Chief Wadman?
> **Silver:** I have no "vendetta." I went before the council to exercise a political right. It was my duty as a citizen. I believe that he isn't qualified.

Silver's interrogator accused him next of "trying to make a quick buck." He said that he hadn't made a dime. Then why was he doing this? Silver replied that it was a matter of conscience. "Your chief has a history. The FBI synopsis lists him on no less than 40 pages in the Franklin investigation. It isn't over."

The morale of Wadman's foot soldiers struck bottom. This undercurrent of discontent at the station house swelled into a wave of insurrection.

Nobody knew who on the police force was behind The *Wadville Herald,* a raunchy newsletter parody with one subject: "Chief Bobby

Wad," and his loyalists, or "Wadsters." One issue featured lyrics to the tune of Jimmy Buffet's "Fins":

He came down from Illinois
It took him three days to get trained,
Lookin' for a piece who's quiet,
Can't get caught again.

Another song lyric crowed,

Well, my name is Bobby, but they call me The Wad.
Ask me what I want—I want a young kid's bod.
Don't want them too old, want them while they're still growin',
A cute young thing like Alisha Owen.

Under "The Meaning of Wad," the editor of the *Wadville Herald* supplied the following definitions: "common viper," "vermin," "evil pedophile," "an illusion or fraud," "abnormal animal," "pompous," "dull" and "ludicrous failure."

The title-page for a biography of Wadman, garnished with swastikas, entitled *Mein Wadman Kampf,* portrayed the chief as "a pedophilic, occultic dictator."

The Chief apparently did not inspire much loyalty in the rank-and-file.

Meanwhile, the Wilmington City Council was looking into Chief Wadman's past—and meeting secretly to discuss the Omaha powder-keg and the charges leveled at him. City Manager Bill Farris attempted to stop the secret discussions, and was summarily asked to resign. "The councilmen who wanted Mr. Farris to resign gave differing reasons," the *Star* reported on February 4, "ranging from differences over philosophy and financial policy to concerns about the police force." Beyond that, no specific explanation was given.

The Chief met the resistance head-on, applying talents honed in the Nebraska cover-up.

On February 2, Investigator Pridgen was ordered to Internal Affairs. He was interrogated by Lt. Pulley and Captain Thomas, both loyal to Chief Wadman. They asked Pridgen a few questions about his extracurricular contacts, then sent him back to work.

Shortly thereafter, Lt. Pulley entered Pridgen's office. "The Chief doesn't think you are answering the questions honestly," Pulley said.

"I did," Pridgen insisted. "Am I being accused of something?"

The lieutenant handed him a questionnaire to answer in written statements. The first: "Have you ever given any information to Ron Silver concerning any child sex abuse case?" Pridgen answered no. The remaining questions concerned any information he might have passed to Silver.

Since Pridgen had never met him, he felt the interrogation meaningless. He complained to Captain Thomas that "the people I associate with are Christian and respectable people," not "trouble-makers." But Chief Wadman was determined to find a conspiracy. The next day, Pridgen was ordered to Captain Thomas's office. "The Chief doesn't feel you are being honest," Thomas said.

"What part of NO did the Chief not understand?" Pridgen snapped. He was sent back to Internal Affairs. "I was told the Chief of Police Robert Wadman had filed a complaint against me. I asked for a copy of the complaint and was advised they were not required to give me a copy." Pridgen was charged with compromising the investigation of Ron Silver, who has not been charged with any criminal offense.

"I was harassed, falsely accused, intimidated with punishment and continued harassment," Pridgen wrote in his grievance. "When I was overseas in India and questioned by... radical anti-American communist rebels, I was treated with greater dignity." Wadman, he charged, had abused his authority and launched an "inquisition" based on fabricated charges. Information needed by Pridgen to defend himself was withheld in violation of departmental directives. "I have been refused, willfully, intentionally, deliberately, thoughtfully, maliciously, a copy of the allegations against me," Pridgen complained. He gradually awoke to the realization that Chief Wadman had "something to hide." "It is not a recognized method of investigation to continue to harass and intimidate and distort," Pridgen complained.

On March 5, the *Morning Star* reported that the Chief, concerned about "death threats," had launched an investigation of the whistle-blowers.

A newspaper OpEd piece backed Wadman: "CHIEF, NOT MALCON-TENTS, DESERVES CITY'S SUPPORT." The editorial applauded his performance, noting, "police foul-ups and cover-ups are down." Most dismaying, the editors sighed, was J.D. Causey, a city councilman who "seems to take seriously the loony accusations made against Mr. Wadman by people who have hounded him across the country." The "loony accusations" amounted to reading a book and discussing it openly, provoking a backlash as Wadman's reputation came home to roost.

When one city councilman tipped Silver that he was being followed, he packed his bags and moved to Nebraska to look more deeply into Wadman's past.

Back in Wilmington the tide of public opinion turned on Wadman when the Southern Christian Leadership Conference, the largest Christian organization in the country, sent lawyers to publicly retract support for him. The Police Benevolent Association did likewise, demanding that Wadman be indicted. On April 5, he was suspended for a week without pay for leaning on Pridgen and another officer. Silver appeared at the next council meeting to deny that he threatened Chief Wadman and offer to take a lie detector test. The council listened, but made no comments and adjourned silently.

Undeterred, the *Morning Star* again sided with the Chief in Wilmington's "police scandalette." The town was assured that Wadman's sins, distilled by one OpEd page minimalist from a closed hearing, were "relatively minor." After all, "the Chief says he and his family have been threatened. Understandably angry and worried about what his tormentors might do next, he apparently overreacted." After all, Wadman's indiscretions were "akin to neglecting to read a suspect his Miranda rights."

But the Wadman case continued to heat up, according to Silver. "The Chief is being investigated by the FBI for bribing a police officer," Silver says. "Several officers have stepped forward to say that I never threatened his family, that they did the investigation and the city attorney (Tom Pollard) had the information but covered it up."

Chief Wadman's turbulent career drew to an end, but the inevitable was postponed by the blindly jingoistic maneuvers of his cronies, operating with all the finesse of an Elizabethan secret society.

In July 1994 Wadman was yet again forced to turn in his badge and epaulets.

Section Three

The CIA's Black Budget & Domestic Operations

Section Three

The CIA's Black Budget & Domestic Operations

Chapter Ten

E. Howard Hunt's Death Squads

David Atlee Phillips, the underground government's savant of psychological operations, once claimed to have learned about Devil cults
from E. Howard Hunt and his CIA partner, William Peter Blatty of
Exorcist fame.[1]

Of his roots, Hunt writes in his memoirs, "Captain James Hunt served
in the Revolutionary Army and was a landholder of means in northern
Manhattan. It is after him that Hunt's Point, now New York's municipal
area, is named." E Howard's Victorian forebear, Leigh Hunt, the radical
political essayist, served two years in a British prison for his subversive
broadsides. Henry "The Orator" Hunt was a convict as well. He went on
to become a minister of Parliament.[2] Hunt's grandfather held a series of
political offices in New York State, including, consistently enough, commissioner of prisons.

"While I was myself a prisoner," Hunt once lamented, "I was often to
reflect on the irony of my fate."[3]

E. Howard's father was a 32nd-degree Freemason—that is, a "Sublime
Prince of the Royal Secret." Together with William Donovan of the Office
of Strategic Services (OSS), he was founder of the elite Buffalo Athletic
Club, a member of the Banker's Club, the Drug and Chemical Club and,
under Donovan's tutelage, founder of the New York chapter of the
American Legion.[4]

Hunt's deceased wife, Dorothy de Gautiere, was secretary to Averell
Harriman, the Skull & Bones ambassador, when the aristocratic pair met
in Paris. "She told me that she had spent the war years in Berne,
Switzerland," Hunt recalled later, "working for the Treasury
Department's Hidden Assets Division, the section that sought Nazi assets
abroad. At the end of the war, she was sent to Shanghai to open the
Treasury office there, and had served as technical adviser on a Dick
Powell film, *To the Ends of the Earth,* the story of Treasury's involvement
in international narcotics traffic."[5]

Their honeymoon was cut short by CIA orders to join Frank Wisner's Office of Policy Coordination (OPC). Early on, the OPC roll-call was made up almost entirely of Nazis recruited by the CIA, with a domestic power base that included John J. McCloy, Harriman, and James Forrestal. Hunt was assigned to the Political and Psychological Warfare staff to develop training courses on covert operations. He conferred often with the CIA's Dr. James Burnham, who once wrote an article for *Life* magazine praising rule by elites, and through him met William F. Buckley. The brainy and garrulous Buckley would be the first on Hunt's recruitment list when he opened the Agency's station in Mexico City.[6]

In the early fifties, Hunt trained Cuban exiles. They knew him as their cultivated patron, "Eduardo." His reputation within the CIA was less than resplendent, however.

"Listen to his music, not his words," Phillips once warned.[7]

Henrik Kruger, in *The Great Heroin Coup,* chronicled Hunt's forays into drug trafficking in collaboration with the Chinese Triads providing support to the Kuomingtang. In the far east he "served" with William Pawley, Lucien Conein, Mitch WerBell and Paul Helliwell, the same cabal of ultra-Rightists who founded the Latin American branch of the World Anti-Communist League.[8]

In Mexico, Hunt's job had been to sow anti-Communist fever. In his cleansed and self-serving memoirs, Hunt tells of disrupting Communist meetings with stink bombs and itching powder. More subtle PsyOps included the planting of a story in the Mexican press that falsely quoted a Leftist leader disparaging the "cultural inferiority" of Mexican peasants.[9]

In the 1950s the Pentagon transformed Guatemala into a counter-insurgency base to control the central parts of Latin America. The instrument of the decimation of democratic rule in Guatemala was a CIA operation called Operation Diablo—a blood purge directed by Hunt and David Atlee Phillips. E. Howard Hunt and Tracy Barnes, Allen Dulles's closest aide, ran newspaper commentaries claiming that Arbenz, the Guatemalan leader, was a closet Communist. To succeed Arbenz, Hunt freed the murderous Castillo Armas from prison. Frank Sturgis and Jack Youngblood took charge of training the death and destruction squads, and on June 18, 1954 the "Army of Liberation," led by Armas, crossed the border from Nicaragua into Guatemala. Unmarked CIA planes provided air cover. The CIA's proxies seized control of the government, and in August declared martial law. On cue, the military appropriated 800,000 acres of land from the peasants. Thousands of them were ruthlessly slaughtered. Hunt thus proved himself a capable handler of death squads, a talent that held him in good stead when Operation 40, a Cuban assassination team, was placed under his supervision in 1960.[10]

Hunt worked well with a menagerie of ogres. In May 1961 the dictator of the Dominican Republic was murdered. Political researcher Donald

Freed wrote: "Documents would indicate that President Kennedy learned of the plan to kill Trujillo only after the debacle of the Cuban invasion in April 1961." Kennedy's adviser Richard Goodwin ordered the CIA to not supply weapons for the dictator's assassination. Nonetheless, on May 30, 1961, Trujillo was ambushed and gunned down with carbines furnished by Langley. Among those on the CIA payroll and the death squad detail were Hunt and Sturgis.[11]

Hunt had extensive connections to organized crime, especially the national syndicate said to have been run by Seymour Weiss of the Standard Fruit Company (the sponsor of the Guatemalan coup) and Mafia kingpin Carlos Marcello. In 1958, Hunt organized an "anti-Communist" conference in Guatemala. The conference chairman was Antonio Valladores, Marcello's attorney in New Orleans. Also present at the meeting was Maurice Gatlin, whose office at 544 Camp Street was, in the CIA shell-game investigated by Jim Garrison, a base of operations for the Kennedy assassination.[12]

As might be expected, the Hunt cabal in the Nixon White House reeked of felony. Hunt was a close ally to Bernard Barker, a Bolivian bagman. The Cuban "Defense" Fund of Dr. Manuel Artime was a conduit for hush money to the Watergate burglars.[13] In the 1980s, Artime surfaced as the mentor of Ramon Milian Rodriquez, the money-laundering, "freedom-fighting" gallivant of Iran-Contra fame. Another of Hunt's allies in Nixon's Plumbers unit was Robert Mardian, a fierce neo-fascist Armenian and assistant attorney general in charge of the security division of the Justice Department under John Mitchell. J. Edgar Hoover once referred to Mardian as "that Lebanese Jew."[14] Co-felon James McCord was once described by Hunt as "self-centered, devious and sanctimonious... a weakling determined to save himself at all costs."[15]

Hunt's chain of unholy alliances peaked with the covert operations of the Nixon administration. As Hunt told it, psychiatric care for his daughter Lisa—whose memory was mysteriously *wiped clean* in 1970—forced him to "retire" from the CIA. On recommendation from Richard Helms, Hunt took a job with Robert R. Mullen, a former press aide to Dwight D. Eisenhower. The Mullens public relations firm had established and operated the Free Cuba Committee. Hunt's fellow cold warriors included Douglas Caddy, a Young Americans for Freedom founder and an attorney for General Foods. Robert Bennett, a former Miami operative for the Permindex assassination team, handled the Hughes Tool Company account.[16]

The sort of public relations Hunt engaged in came to light when Louis Tackwood, a former LAPD provocateur, exposed Hunt's Squad 19 plan to incite a riot at the 1970 Republican convention in San Diego. Nobody was over Hunt, said Tackwood, "but the top dogs."

Tackwood: "He was in Dallas when they got Kennedy. He left out of there for the Caribbean." James McCord was "in on the concentration camp thing."[17]

The stamp of Howard Hunt's demonic imagination was most clear in the overthrow of Chile in 1973. David Phillips, Hunt's psychopathic protege, handled PsyOp chores, drawing on methods developed by the CIA in Vietnam: a campaign of highly-publicized atrocities (blamed on leftists) progressing in stages of psychological terrorism, culminating in mass beheadings and mutilations. Witnesses have described rivers clogged with headless corpses and piles of bodies set aflame.[18]

Hunt, we hardly knew ye.

Footnotes

1. Donald Freed and Dr. Fred Landis, *Death in Washington*, Lawrence and Hill, 1980, p. 90.
2. E. Howard Hunt, *Undercover*, Berkeley, 1974, pp. 7-8.
3. Ibid., p. 14.
4. Hunt, p. 9. The American Legion, according to George Seldes, was "a natural for fascist action. When Alvin Owsley was Legion commander he was prepared to seize Washington. 'The Fascisti in are to Italy what the American Legion is the the United States,' he said in 1922." Several Legion conventions, Seldes wrote, "invited Mussolini, honored him, sent him medals. And high-ranking Legion officials, including one of its founders, actually plotted to seize the government." In 1963, E. Howard and his CIA-Mafia clutch would, ironically enough, accomplish exactly that.
5. Hunt, p. 51.
6. Hunt, pp. 68-69.
7. Peter Wyden, *Bay of Pigs: The Untold Story*, Touchstone, p. 32.
8. Henrik Kruger, *The Great Heroin Coup*, South End Press, p. 16.
9. Raymond Bonner, *Waltzing with a Dictator*, Times Books, 1987, p. 37fn.
10. Freed and Landis, pp. 42-43.
11. Freed and Landis, p. 49.
12. Peter Dale Scott, *Crime and Cover-Up: The CIA, the Mafia, and the Dallas-Watergate Connection*, Westworks, 1977, p. 16. A number of those in attendance were operatives of the Information Council of the Americas, a front that drew support from large firms in New Orleans, including Standard Fruit.
13. Bernard Fensterwald, Jr., *The Assassination of JFK*, Zebra, 1977, p. 513.
14. Hunt, p. 161.
15. Hunt's caption to a picture of McCord.
16. Scott, p. 26. Hunt, p. 142.
17. Citizens Research and Investigation Committee, *The Glass House Tapes*, Avon, 1973, p. 172.
18. Freed and Landis, pp. 108-13.

Chapter Nine

The GOP's Pink Triangle & the CIA

The true story of gay Republican power-brokers and the CIA's Neil Livingstone, an influential covert operator who inhabits a grim nether-world of GOP pimps, kidnappers, cocaine, arms smuggling, blackmail, pedopile rings and Nazi collaborators.

In January 1993 a privately-commissioned squad of American and British mercenaries were arrested in Luxembourg, Germany for the bungled kidnap of two young American emigres. Donald Feeney, a veteran of Fort Bragg, North Carolina's "elite" Delta Force, and James Brian Grayson, the father of one of the kidnapped children (buffeted in a tempestuous custody dispute), were nabbed scrambling from the scene of the abductions. They were stopped by authorities in an attempt to return to the U.S. with the children, 10 year-old Elizabeth Pittman, and Anna Grayson, age 5.

They can expect certain history-book notoriety for a daring, if ultimately disgraceful covert operation masquerading as a Sylvester Stallone film production about Viking warriors.

The kidnap-for-hire team, trained by the CIA and mustered under the nondescript company banner of Corporate Training Unlimited (CTU), blew into Reykjavic, Iceland in a flurry of movie-industry posturing. Reykjavic police charged that the "crew," led by Don Feeney, drugged Erna Eyjolfsdottir and stole off with her children.

The cadre gained the mother's confidence by recruiting her to the bogus production company. Jacqueline Davis, managing director of CTU, posed as the party's location manager. She made the acquaintance of the girls' mother, and hired her as "Kim Bassinger's personal assistant." Don Feeney adopted the guise of "Mario Cassare," a flamboyant film director. Feeney's wife Judy and his partner James Canavan flew in to join Davis at the Hotel Holt posturing as Stallone's personal staff. Stationed at posh lodgings in Reykjavic, Feeney's "tug-of-love" operatives lavished a total of

$35,000 on hotel suites, overseas fax messages and telephone calls to Hollywood—a gaudy smokescreen for the kidnappings, complete with local front-page publicity.

But the plot crumbled when a local newspaper received a tip that the film project was fraudulent.

Davis sequestered the girls' mother at the Holt and slipped her a "painkiller." She fell asleep... and woke to discover that the "crew" had stolen off with her children. She phoned police. Feeney and Grayson were about to board a plane for London with Anna when they were detained by authorities and arrested.

Judy Feeney, Davis and Canavan made it to Luxembourg, and police there rounded them up. Both children were returned to their mother. Feeney and Grayson were held by Reykjavic police on two counts of kidnapping. They were tried and convicted to two years in an Icelandic prison.

The notion of training paramilitary mercenaries for custody-dispute kidnap operations was conceived in 1985, according to CTU "chronicler" Neil Livingstone in *Rescue My Child,* an in-house public relations effort, "after Don and four other ex-Delta Force operatives polished off a case of Budweiser."

Four accounts of Corporate Training's "daring overseas rescues" are detailed in Livingstone's book, which appeared in 1992. It has been translated into eight languages. One of the company's kidnaps inspired an NBC movie-of-the-week, *Desperate Rescue,* starring Muriel Hemingway, and the network has announced plans to produce nine sequels. In eight years, Corporate Training has conducted seven successful snatch-back operations in Tunisia, Jordan, Ecuador and elsewhere around the world.

CTU bills itself as one of the nation's premier "boutique-sized security firms." The company's paramilitary training camp in North Carolina offers a variety of programs to corporate clients, police and federal agencies. Corporate "security" training courses offered by CTU include "Terrorist Operations," "Hostage Survival," "Surveillance and Counter-Surveillance," and "Explosive Devices." According to the course outline, the "Safe Haven" class instructs one in "How to prepare your office, home and vehicle to act as a secure area in the event of a criminal/terrorist attack."

The curriculum, despite CTU's disinfected image, could conceivably be construed as training in covert and mercenary warfare.

Corporate Training is based in Fayetteville, North Carolina, home of the Green Berets, the 82nd Airborne and—behind spiraling towers of concertina wire—the secretive Delta Force, a compound that denies access to all but military initiates and visitors from the Pentagon.

But the company's inauspicious origins and paramilitary public relations obscure connections to a frightening underworld on the ultra-right fringe, summed up by a company motto:

"KEEP AMERICAN CHILDREN AMERICAN."

Company founder Don Feeney, a veteran of Fort Bragg's Special Forces A-Team, grew up in Red Hook, New York, a largely Italian district. He joined the Army at 17, earned his wings and a place in Delta Force. He was sent on the failed 1980 mission to free American hostages in Iran. Assignments in the Middle East included a stint in Beirut and the organization of a cadre to rescue five American missionaries held hostage in the Sudan.

Feeney and his "tug-of-love mercenaries" trained for half a year at the CIA training camp known as "The Farm," in the wooded outskirts of Williamsburg, Virginia. "Their movements were restricted," Livingstone writes in *Rescue My Child,* "and they were allowed to venture outside only when a Soviet satellite wasn't making a pass overhead" Perhaps his training prepared Feeney to survive "Operation Eagle Claw," the doomed April, 1980 Desert One raid on Teheran.

Feeney also took part in the Richmond Prison sortie in the October, 1983 Grenada invasion, led by H. Norman Schwarzkopf. Media hype notwithstanding, Granada was one of the most ill-fated rescues in military history. One internal Pentagon document, published in *Defense Week,* found the mission "fraught with confusion... critical failures of military communication and faulty tactics." Intelligence officers Richard Gabriel and Paul Savage submitted a report describing Grenada as "a case study in military incompetence."

Republican power broker and CIA operative Robert Keith Gray was co-chairman of Reagan's gaudy inaugural ball, a recollection of imperial pageantry (and vapid megalomania).

Feeney's Blackhawk copter was blasted out of the sky. He survived—
only to be thrown out of Delta Force a year later for refusing disciplinary
action after an audit turned up financial irregularities in his Middle East
assignment. He was stripped of his pension. Feeney organized CTU to
keep a hand in the soldier-of-fortune set, and staffed the company with
Deltoid soldiers of ill-fortune.

His closest partner was Dave Chatelier, a retired CIA agent with a 20-
year background on the "dark side of the house" (covert operations in
Eastern Europe). In 1975, Chatelier was transferred to Fort Bragg and
assigned to the creation of an Army anti-terrorist team. Ultimately, the
team came to be known as Delta Force.

Chatelier's contribution to CTU was a 60-acre farm, which was trans-
formed into a mercenary training camp offering courses in "Explosive
Devices," "SWAT (Special Weapons and Tactics)" and "Introduction to
Terrorism."

CTU spokesman Neil Livingstone participated in the planning of the
Reykjavic disaster. The kidnap may have been a dismal failure, but
Livingstone isn't. He is an ominous by-product of the CIA, one of the most
powerful intelligence operatives in the country, a designate to corrupt
foreign leaders and international arms dealers. And he inhabits a criminal world of male prostitution involving minors, rendering dubious the
company blurb: "Fortunately for a few mothers there is a court of last
resort: the ex-Delta Force commandos of CTU."

Livingstone, an "expert" on international terrorism, is a frequent
expert guest on television news programs, in which capacity he once publicly defended the CIA's assassination manual.

The research departments at the network news bureaus can't be
accused of digging too deeply into Neil Livingstone's past. He entered the
grim world of espionage as a foot soldier in the Agency's heroin-infested
proprietary, Air America. Livingstone was recruited by James
Cunningham, founder of the airline—and a key figure in Edwin Wilson's
treasonous off-the-shelf arms sales to Muammar Ghaddaffi. One biographer referred to Wilson, currently serving a life sentence for his black
market escapades, as "an aberration of modern intelligence."

So is Neil Livingstone.

As a junior executive at Gray & Co., a Washington, D.C. public relations firm largely manned by right-wing CIA and military intelligence personnel, he climbed the corporate ladder instantly by interfering in a
Congressional investigation into a homosexual sex and drug ring. The
enterprise was operated by Robert Keith Gray, CEO of the firm, whose
client roster has included Charles Keating, BCCI, Adnan Khashoggi,
Richard Berendzen and Duvalier's Haiti. Gray was also a member of
Reagan's first presidential campaign team, and a suspect in the missing
Carter briefing books affair.

Livingstone was brought into the firm by Charles Crawford, head of Gray & Co.'s international division. Crawford is a politically hard-right product of the Army Counter-Intelligence Corps (CIC) and the national security operatives of the Reagan-Bush period. Under Crawford, the International Division served as a branch office of the National Security Council and Oliver North's "Enterprise." He has a long and sordid history in covert ops: as a CIC agent, Crawford assisted the escape of "special refugees" (fugitive, Nazi-collaborating Ustashi agents) from the U.S.-occupied zone of Germany along the Vatican's Nazi ratline escape routes.

At Gray & Co., Livingstone entered a hidden pocket of Washington politics. Reporter Susan B. Trento discovered that "Gray's button-down world of Republican politics, conservative business clients, and high society events turned into weekend sex parties with young men where drug use was common."

This was the world that surfaced briefly in the Congressional page-boy scandal. Carl Shoffler, a retired D.C. police officer—he and four others arrested the Watergate burglars—and a witness in the investigation of the House cocaine and call-boy ring, wrote that Gray "has used and supplied narcotics... thrown wild sex orgies at Rehoboth Beach... was affiliated with the infamous Ed Wilson... was used by the CIA. As a result of his past connections in the aforementioned areas and his close association with Ronald Reagan, his conduct has to be suspect in light of the fact that he ended up with the foremost lobbying firm presently operating in D.C."

When word filtered through the Beltway grapevine that the Ethics Subcommittee hearings, chaired by Congressman Stokes, would focus attention on a cocaine ring in the House using Congressional pages as couriers, Livingstone was called to testify. The probe revealed that the services of male prostitutes had been provided to leading politicians by the Diamond Shamrock Corp.—a client of Robert Keith Gray & Co. Diamond Shamrock—a major producer of Agent Orange during the Vietnam War—is chaired by a former official of the Immigration and Naturalization Service.

But the Congressional investigation of the page-boy scandal was quashed after Livingstone's stonewall testimony concerning Gray's involvement in homosexual prostitution.

The Stokes Committee found that backstair political intrigues were rife—unfortunately, House investigators were instructed to cease any further inquiry into the male prostitution and cocaine ring. In the end, two Congressmen received reprimands.

One Congressional investigator told John DeCamp, a former CIA operative and Nebraska state senator, that the call-boys were run by the CIA, and the hearings adjourned prematurely because the prostitution ring involved "kids."

In the wings of the Stokes probe, Carl Shoffler was questioned frantically by Neil Livingstone and an ally, Tom Fortuin, counsel to Robert Keith Gray and former law partner to Roy Cohn, the late ultra-right homosexual Red-baiter, to determine how much the police knew of Gray's circle of drug-dealing, gay CIA Republicans.

Like Livingstone, Gray had worked closely in Edwin Wilson's arms network in the 1970s. Their cover was a CIA proprietary called Consultants International. Frank Terpil, a partner of Wilson, told *Secret Agenda* author Jim Hougan that the three of them "directed sexual blackmailing operations" out of Tong Sun Park's George Town Club in Washington, D.C. Terpil stated in a letter to Hougan that one of Wilson's Agency jobs was to sexually compromise Congressmen to keep them under thumb. Some legislators, it seems, "could be coerced by living their sexual fantasies in the flesh (with) a remembrance of these occasions permanently recorded via selected cameras."

The CIA's role in the scandal was submerged in the headline-grabbing page-boy revelations. But the origins of the Washington sex-and-drug operation predate Wilson and Gray, according to DeCamp. He investigated the male prostitution ring in preparation for his book on the Omaha child abuse scandal, which implicated in organized child abuse a circle of affluent Republican Nebraskans with connections to Reagan and Bush, and turned up an interesting bit of history.

The call-boy ring was started by Roy Cohn, whose associate Tom Fortuin would run backstage interference with Livingstone to kill the congressional hearings. A District of Columbia vice squad official told DeCamp that "Cohn's job was to run the little boys. Say you had an admiral, a general, a congressman who did not go along with the program. Cohn's job was to set them up, then they would go along. Cohn told me that himself." (Confirmation that Roy Cohn was a pimp to homosexuals in high places came with the publication of Anthony Summer's colorful biography of J. Edgar Hoover, and the revelation that young male prostitutes were procured by Cohn for Bible reading, rubber-glove trysts with the late FBI director.)

Gray and Wilson inherited the homosexual sex-and-drug network during the Nixon era, and by then it had branched out and grown, amoeba-like. The page-boy scandal was a small part of the CIA's sexual blackmail apparatus. In fact, *60 Minutes* once reported that critics of Hill & Knowlton, then chaired by Robert Keith Gray, accused the Washington PR firm "of being an unelected shadow government." The male prostitution network presided over by Gray was featured in a 1982 article in *The Deep Backgrounder,* a newsletter edited by former CIA official Victor Marchetti, entitled "Reagan Inaugural Co-Chairman Powerful 'Closet Homosexual.'" Livingstone's loyalty to Gray is not the most propitious bona-fide for a "mercenary" in Corporate Training Unlimited's "tug-of-love" kidnap operation.

Nor were the death's head cufflinks Livingstone sported in Guatemala, where he was once employed as a registered agent of Dominga Moriera, an ultra-conservative presidential candidate. Gray's fixer in the Page-Boy scandal was rewarded for his stonewalling performance before the Stokes Committee by a promotion to senior vice president in charge of the International Division.

Livingstone's status in the country's most powerful PR firm allowed him to employ veteran CIA operators, including Rob Owen of Iran-Contra fame. Livingstone and Owen, in fact, collaborated on a public relations campaign for the Cuban-American Foundation. And it was Neil Livingstone who directed Owen to draw up a proposed contract with the Nicaraguan Contras on behalf of Oliver North.

Livingstone had long moved in intelligence circles. He had known former CIA Director Robert Gates since they were students at William and Mary College. Carter Clews, an international arms expert, worked with Livingstone at Gray & Co.—until a newspaper article in Spain exposed his role in the bribery of parliamentarians and undercover support to the fascist Popular Alliance Party, with its symbiotic ties to the Mussolini family. It also emerged that Gray & Co. had partaken in Iran-Contra by smuggling arms from Israel via Spain to Nicaragua. The company also engaged in secret contract negotiations for the defense firm of McDonnell Douglas.

The *Washington Post* followed up with a story denuding Gray and Livingstone as the brains behind the Spanish fiasco. Livingstone was forced to resign. But, in the shadow of Robert Keith Gray, he had blossomed into one of the most powerful intelligence operators in the country—a registered agent of Israel, one of the three trustees of Solidarity in Poland, an "expert" on terrorism at the conservative Center for Strategic and International Studies "and a leading light of Corporate Training Unlimited."

The revelations of Robert Keith Gray's involvement in sexual blackmail operations came with the publication of *Power House*, a biography by Susan B. Trento, in 1992. The book forced his resignation from Hill & Knowlton. Gray was succeeded as chairman by Howard Paster, a Democratic insider. Paster left the CIA-dominated company two months later to take the position of Bill Clinton's director of legislative affairs. But the CIA's male prostitution network survived the political pratfalls of Gray and Livingstone to surface periodically in the upper-tiers of the Republican Party.

Lawrence King, a 300-pound pedophile from Nebraska, Gray's home state, was alleged in 1984 to have operated a branch of the call-boy business in partnership with Harold Andersen, then publisher of the *Omaha World Herald*, and a close friend of Gray's. King, a baritone, sang the National Anthem at the 1984 and 1988 Republican conventions.

King enjoyed Republican society and took his conservative politics seriously. In 1987 he donated $25,350 to Citizens for America, an organization that arranged speaking tours around the country for Lt. Col. Oliver North.

In October 1988, King's Franklin Community Credit Union was raided by the FBI and IRS. A month later the Treasury Department filed suit to recover the $34 million that had disappeared from Franklin's vaults under King's management.

Before his arrest, King had commuted often to Washington, D.C. He was a business partner in a call-boy operation run by the late Craig Spence, whose antics were the subject of a week-long series published by the *Washington Times* in July 1989. The *Times* reported that Spence, a former ABC reporter, was said to have been running a CIA blackmail operation: Spence's Victorian Mansion on Wyoming Avenue, where he often threw parties for Washington's power elite, was "planted with electronic bugs and video recording equipment that, according to homosexual call-boys and others who routinely visited the house, was used to make incriminating tapes to blackmail guests." The parties were attended by the likes of William Casey, Ted Koppel, John Mitchell and Eric Severeid. A political tempest threatened when Spence's credit card receipts implicated Reagan and Bush appointees, but few names reached the public print.

Four months after the story broke, Spence was found dead at the Ritz-Carlton Hotel in Boston. Police ruled his death a suicide.

Another ramrod in the CIA's male prostitution network was Ronald Roskens, former chancellor of the University of Nebraska. Lawrence King had been one of his closest "advisers." Roskens was fired from the position in 1989 when his involvement in homosexual orgies was reported to the university's board of regents and verified by them. A year later, President George Bush called Roskens to Washington to head the Agency of International Development (AID), commonly utilized as a cover in CIA operations overseas. AID also disburses $7 billion in non-military foreign aid, and thus wields enormous geopolitical power.

In 1992 a 107-page congressional report was issued by Rep. John Conyers Jr., urging Bush to fire Roskens, who had "abused the public trust" for private gain until AID's inspector general "forced a change in his patterns of behavior." His "patterns," according to the *Washington Post* for October 2, 1992, included "taking thousands of dollars from outside organizations, including some that do business with AID."

This is the milieu in which Neil Livingstone travels. He has long nurtured a penchant to open a corporate intelligence front of his own, and in the child-snatching CTU he can flex his wings as a covert operator. Until his next misadventure blows up into another Washington scandal, Livingstone's will doubtless be a familiar face gracing the network news with his "expert" opinions on terrorism, and airing his para-military propaganda in CIA-backed publications like *Soldier of Fortune.*

Chapter Twelve

Funny Money—Johnny Carson, the CIA, and the S&L Crisis

Years before the public was made aware of the name Charles Keating, hints of impending financial disaster loomed in the back pages of the major dailies. In October 1982, the same month that President Reagan signed deregulation of the nation's thrift industry into law, the Commercial Bank of California in Beverly Hills announced a $2.5 million loan loss.

A founder of the bank, legendary NBC *Tonight Show* host Johnny Carson paid $1,950,000 for his shares of Commercial stock, and became the CEO. But the bank's financial troubles weren't all that preyed on Carson's mind. Tim Hoffman, an informant in the joint FBI/DEA investigation of John DeLorean, had informed agents that the auto maker had a partner in the cocaine trade—a certain well-known talk show host.

The alleged partnership was not as far-fetched as it might have seemed. Carson was a close friend of DeLorean. According to SEC registers, the comedian also owned 250,000 shares in DeLorean Motors, a $500,000 investment. Carson's assignee on the DeLorean board of directors was Carson's best friend and financial adviser, Henry Bushkin, a known mob associate.

After the arrest of John DeLorean in the ABSCAM sting, Howard Weitzman, DeLorean's attorney, told reporters that developments in the investigation had been closely followed by then U.S. Attorney General Edwin Meese III. Meese's cohort, J. Peter Grace, a leading light of Reagan's deregulation campaign, retained DeLorean on his payroll as a consultant, and was a director of DeLorean's company. Attorney General Meese, announced Weitzman, had made key decisions in building a case against DeLorean on charges of cocaine trafficking. DeLorean insisted that he'd been set up." He was, in fact, a cut-out, the designated fall guy, and the jury believed the cover story. But the Justice Department was desperate to staunch public exposure of others involved in the laundering operation.

Washington columnist Jack Anderson published a transcript of an audio tape after the arrest, in which De Lorean attempted to renege in a cocaine deal set up by the FBI. "When he tried to back out," Anderson wrote, "the FBI's undercover informant threatened to bash in his daughter's head."

The CIA's Bank of the Stars

The ABSCAM trap had originally been set for one William Morgan Hetrick, described by authorities as one of the foremost cocaine distributors on the west coast, and by his attorney as "a man who may border on genius." Hetrick was arrested with DeLorean on October 19, 1982. A pilot and operator of a private flying service in the desert community of Mojave, Hetrick had served four years in Vietnam, and went on to work with Nugan Hand Bank in Australia—the notorious CIA fiduciary with ties to the international mafia and third world dictators. The bank was looted by its CIA directors—foreshadowing the fate of the country's S&Ls—and collapsed after the lurid suicide of a founder, leaving a $50 million hole in the Australian economy. Although the bank was an independent business run by former CIA operatives, it provided cover for the Agency's underground arms/drugs network. (One of Nugan Hand's clients, Ferdinand Marcos, entered the American S&L scene by purchasing Redwood Savings in San Francisco. A Marcos cohort took over San Francisco's Oceanic Bank, and hired a former CIA Manila station chief to run it.)

DeLorean's intelligence connections were almost turned to his advantage in court. The *Los Angeles Times* reported: "The Drug Enforcement Administration, the CIA (and) the FBI were ordered to turn over documents to DeLorean in advance of the trial... for private inspection by the court." Also named in the judge's orders were Army intelligence, the National Security Council, the Internal Revenue Service, U.S. Customs, several departments within the Justice Department, the State Department, several field offices of the FBI, the Defense Intelligence Agency and the Pentagon.

Unfortunately for DeLorean's attorneys, when they asked to review documents concerning contacts between the U.S. and British goverments during the sting, the judge refused, insisting that "communications between sovereigns are meant to be confidential."

As a cover and base of operations for the DeLorean arrest, federal agents posed as crooked bankers for Eureka Federal Savings in the San Francisco Bay area. The president of Eureka was Kenneth Kidwell, a familiar face on the Nevada casino circuit, and a volatile eccentric in the stodgy California banking establishment. Kidwell was the protagonist in a series of bizarre events. One evening police spotted his car weaving on the road. They suspected he was drunk. The officers searched him and tumed up a .38 strapped to his leg and a .357 magnum. The pistols were loaded with armor-piercing, teflon-coated bullets. The police said that Kidwell had tried to talk his way out of the arrest by flashing a gold deputy sheriff's badge conferred upon him by a ranking offficial of the San Mateo Sheriff's Offfice. Some banker. The ultimate irony was that Eureka, the FBI's cover in the DeLorean sting, was saddled with some $32 million in delinquent loans—170 of them—to organized crime figures.

A key informant in the DeLorean sting was James Hoffman, who often boasted to his neighbors of daring covert exploits in Latin America, according to DeLorean biographer Hillel Levin. Hoffman proposed the cocaine deal to DeLorean and later turned evidence against him. Thus did DeLorean become the sacrificial cut-out.

Hoffman had, in turn, been fingered by Robert Durand, his partner in an Oregon airline used to smuggle cocaine from Bolivia into the U.S. The drug profits were laundered at Commercial Bank of Beverly Hills.

Commercial Bank began to flounder when the board's drug and organized crime connections caught the attention of federal regulators. FBI and DEA investigators refused to buy Hoffman's tip that Johnny Carson was involved in money laundering with DeLorean and the CIA, a charge that Carson publicly denied. But there was a surfeit of financial chicanery at Commercial, enough to prompt the FDIC to impose a $10 million lawsuit against bank officials, who had extended loans to clients "associated directly or indirectly with organized crime." In 1983, Carson's Beverly Hills thrift filed bankruptcy papers.

Among the dubious loans made by Carson financial adviser Henry Bushkin was $450,000 to Jack Catain of the Angelo Bruno crime family in Philadelphia. The FDIC couldn't help noticing that Bushkin was also an officer of Catain's TMX Marketing, a retail distributor of car alarms in Westwood, California. Catain eventually sold TMX to the North Ireland Development Angency, which subsidized the DeLorean Motors plant.

Shortly after DeLorean's arrest, several of the principals had a run of misfortune. Colin Chapman, DeLorean's partner in the car business, had a heart attack and died. Alan David Saxon, an officer of "Carson's Bank," apparently committed suicide. Saxon, who was known to travel frequently to places like Switzerland and Brazil, told friends that he feared he would be killed for his knowledge of the bank's business connections. Following Saxon's demise, investigators discovered that $60–80 million was "missing" from the coffers of Commercial Bank. The Los Angeles Police Department immediately cremated Saxon's body. Soon, two new directors of the bank reported that their lives had been threatened.

They took up shooting practice at the Beverly Hills Gun Club.

Chapter Thirteen

The Swirl and the Swastika:

NutraSweet & the Military-Medical-Industrial Complex

> *I recognized my two selves, a crusading idealist and a cold, granitic believer in the law of the jungle.*
>
> —Edgar Monsanto Queeny,
> Monsanto chairman, 1943–63,
> *The Spirit of Enterprise, 1934*

The FDA is ever mindful to refer to aspartame, widely known as NutraSweet, as a "food additive," never a "drug." A "drug" on the label of a Diet-Coke might discourage the consumer. And because aspartame is classified a food additive, adverse reactions are not reported to a federal agency, nor is continued safety monitoring required by law.[1] NutraSweet is a non-nutritive sweetener. The brand name is a misnomer. Try NonNutraSweet.

Food additives seldom cause brain lesions, headaches, mood alterations, skin polyps, blindness, brain tumors, insomnia and depression, or erode intelligence and short-term memory. Aspartame, according to some of the most capable scientists in the country, does. In 1991 the National Institutes of Health, a branch of the Department of Health and Human Services, published a bibliography, *Adverse Effects of Aspartame,* listing no less than 167 reasons to avoid it.[2]

Aspartame is an DNA derivative, a combination of two amino acids (long supplied by a pair of Maryland biotechnology firms: Genex Corp. of Rockville and Purification Engineering in Baltimore.[3]) The Pentagon once listed it in an inventory of prospective biochemical warfare weapons submitted to Congress.[4]

But instead of poisoning enemy populations, the "food additive" is currently marketed as a sweetening agent in some 1200 food products.

In light of the chemo-warfare implications, the pasts of G.D. Searle and aspartame are ominous. Established in 1888 on the north side of Chicago, G.D. Searle has long been a fixture of the medical establishment. The company manufactures everything from prescription drugs to nuclear imaging optical equipment.[5]

Directors of G.D. Searle include such geopolitical actuaries as Andre M. de Staercke, Reagan's ambassador to Belgium, and Reuben Richards, an executive vice president at Citibank. Also Arthur Wood, the retired CEO of Sears, Roebuck & Co., from the clan of General Robert E. Wood, wartime chairman of the America First Committee.[6] America Firsters, organized by native Nazis cloaked as isolationists, were quietly financed by the likes of Sullivan & Cromwell's Allen Dulles and Edwin Webster of Kidder, Peabody.[7]

Until the acquisition by Monsanto in 1985, the firm's chairman was William L. Searle, a Harvard graduate, Naval reservist and—a grim irony in view of aspartame's adverse effects—an officer in the Army Chemical Corps in the early 1950s, when the same division tested LSD on groups of human subjects in concert with the CIA.[8]

The chief of the chemical Warfare Division at this time was Dr. Laurence Laird Layton, whose son Larry was convicted for the murder of Congressman Leo Ryan at Jonestown ("Come to the pavilion! What a legacy!"). Jonestown, of course, bore a remarkable likeness to a concentration camp, and kept a full store of pharmaceutical drugs. (The Jonestown pharmacy was stocked with a variety of behavior control drugs: qualudes, valium, morphine, demerol and 11,000 doses of thorazine—a better supply, in fact, than the Guyanese government's own, not to mention a surfeit of cyanide.[9]

Dr. Layton was married to the daughter of Hugo Phillip, a German banker and stockbroker representing the likes of Siemens & Halske, the makers of cyanide for the Final Solution, and I.G. Farben, the manufacturer of a lethal nerve gas put to the same purpose.[10] Dr. Layton, a Quaker, developed a form of purified uranium used to set off the Manhattan Project's first self-sustaining chain reaction at the University of Chicago in 1942 by his wife's German-born uncle, Dr. James Franck. At Dugway Proving Ground in Utah, Dr. Layton concentrated his efforts, as did I.G. Farben, on the development of nerve gasses.[11]

Dr. Layton later defended his participation in the Army's chemical warfare section: "You can blow people to bits with bombs, you can shoot them with shells, you can atomize them with atomic bombs, but the same people think there's something terrible about poisoning the air and letting people breathe it. Anything having to do with gas warfare, chemical warfare, has this taint of horror on it, even if you only make people vomit."[12]

Nazis and chemical warfare are recurring themes in the aspartame story. Currently, the chief patent holder of the sweetener is the Monsanto

Co., based in St. Louis. In 1967 Monsanto entered into a joint venture with I.G. Farben-Fabriken, the aforementioned financial core of the Hitler regime and the key supplier of poison gas to the Nazi racial extermination program. After the Holocaust, the German chemical firm joined with American counterparts in the development of chemical warfare agents and founded the "Chemagrow Corporation" in Kansas City, Missouri, a front that employed German and American specialists on behalf of the U.S. Army Chemical Corps.[13]

Dr. Otto Bayer, I.G.'s research director, had a binding relationship with Monsanto chemists.[14] In the postwar period, Dr. Bayer developed and tested chemical warfare agents with Dr. Gerhard Schrader, the Nazi concocter of Tabun, the preferred nerve gas of the SS. Dr. Schrader was also an organophosphate pioneer, and tested the poison on populated areas of West Germany under the guise of killing insects.[15] (Schrader's experiments reek suspiciously of the ongoing aerial application of malathion—developed by Dr. Schrader, a recruit of the U.S. Chemical Warfare Service when Germany surrendered—in present-day Southern California.[16])

Another bridge to I.G. Farben was Monsanto's acquisition of American Viscose, long owned by the England's Courtauld family. As early as 1928, the U.S. Commerce Department issued a report critical of the Courtauld's ties to I.G. Farben and the Nazi party.[17]

Incredibly, George Courtauld was handed an appointment as director of personnel for England's Special Operations Executive, the wartime intelligence service, in 1940.[18] A year later, with the exhaustion of British military financial reserves, American Viscose, worth $120 million, was put on the block in New York. The desperate British treasury received less than half that amount from the sale, brokered by Siegmund Warburg, among others.[19] Monsanto acquired the company in 1949.[20]

The Nazi connection to Monsanto crops up again on the board of directors with John Reed, a former crony of "Putzi" Hanfstangl, a Harvard-bred emigre to Germany who talked Hitler out of committing suicide in 1924 and contributed to the financing of Mein Kampf.[21] Reed is also chairman of Citibank and long a confederate of the CIA. According to a lawsuit filed by San Francisco attorney Melvin Belli, Reed was an instigator, with Ronald Reagan, James Baker and Margaret Thatcher, of the "Purple Ink Document," a plan to finance CIA covert operations with wartime Japanese gold stolen from a buried Philippine hoard.[22]

Other covert warfare connections to Monsanto include Dr. Charles Allen Thomas, chairman of the Monsanto board, 1960–65. Dr. Thomas directed a group of scientists during WW II in the refinement of plutonium for use in the atomic bomb. In the postwar period Monsanto operated Tennessee's Oak Ridge National Laboratories for the Manhattan Project.[23] (Manhattan gestated with the Oak Ridge Institute for Nuclear

Studies, where lethal doses of radiation were tested on 200 unwary cancer patients, turned them into "nuclear calibration devices" gratis the AEC and NASA, until 1974.[24]) Nazi scientists and a 7,000-ton stockpile of uranium were delivered to the Project by its security and counterintelligence director, Col. Boris Pash, a G-2 designate to the CIA's Bloodstone program—and the eminence grise of PB/7, a clandestine Nazi unit that, according to State Department records, conducted a regimen of political assassinations and kidnappings in Europe and the Eastern bloc.[25]

Monsanto Director William Ruckelshaus was an acting director of the FBI under Richard Nixon, a period in the Bureau's history marred by COINTELPRO outrages, including political assassinations. Nixon subsequently appointed Ruckelshaus to the position of EPA director, a nagging irony given his ties to industry (he is a director of Browning-Ferris and Cummins Engine Co.). CIA counterintelligentsia on the Monsanto board include Stansfield Turner, a former Director of Central Intelligence, and Earle H. Harbison, an Agency information specialist for 19 years. Harbison is also a director of Merrill Lynch, and thus raises the spectre of CIA drug dealing. In 1984 President Ronald Reagan's Commission on Organized Crime concluded that Merrill Lynch employed couriers "observed transferring enormous amounts of cash through investment houses and banks in New York City to Italy and Switzerland. Tens of millions of dollars in heroin sales in this country were transferred overseas." Merrill Lynch invested the drug proceeds in the New York bullion market before making the offshore transfers.[26]

As might be expected in view of Monsanto's Nazi, chemical warfare and CIA ties, NutraSweet is a can of worms unprecedented in the American food industry. The history of the product is laden with flawed and fabricated research findings, and when necessary to further the product along, blatant lies—the basis of FDA approval and the incredulity of independent medical researchers. Senator Metzenbaum described the FDA as "the handmaiden" of the drug industry in 1985, but she comports under all regimes. In the Clinton administration, for example, Mike Taylor was graced with the position of deputy director of the FDA. Taylor is a cousin of Tipper Gore, Vice President Albert Gore's wife, and once an outside counsel to Monsanto. (Gore voted with Senate conservatives in 1985 against aspartame labeling.)

Under the tutelage of the Clinton administration, one Chicago reporter quipped, the FDA strictly enforces one "unwritten" violation of law"—failure to bribe.

Granitic Believers

G.D. Searle, the pharmaceutical firm that introduced NutraSweet, worked symbiotically with federal and Congressional officials, bribed investigators when violations of law were exposed, *anything* to move aspartame to market. As far back as 1969, an internal Searle "strategy memo" concluded the company must obtain FDA approval to outpace firms competing for the artificial sweetener market. Another memo in December 1970 urged that FDA officials were to be "brought into a sub-conscious spirit of participation" with Searle.[27] To that end, with enormous profits at stake, the pharmaceutical house set out on a long struggle to transform the Pentagon's biochemical warfare agent into "the taste Mother Nature intended."

The official story is that aspartame was discovered in 1966 by a scientist developing an ulcer drug (not a "food additive"). Supposedly he discovered, upon carelessly licking his fingers, that they tasted sweet. Thus was the chemicals industry blessed with a successor to saccharine, the coal-tar derivative that foundered eight years later under the pressure of cancer concerns. Aspartame found early opposition in consumer attorney James Turner, author of *The Chemical Feast* and a former Nader's Raider. At his own expense, Turner fought approval for ten years, basing his argument on aspartame's potential side effects, particularly on children. His concern was shared by Dr. John Olney, professor of neuropathology and psychiatry at Washington School of Medicine in St. Louis. Dr. Olney found that aspartame, combined with MSG seasoning, increased the odds of brain damage in children.[28]

Other studies have found that children are especially vulnerable to its toxic effects, a measure of the relation between consumption and body weight. The FDA determined in 1981, when the sweetener was approved, that the maximum projected intake of aspartame is 50 milligrams a day per kilogram of body weight. A child of 66 pounds would consume about 23 milligrams by imbibing four cans of Diet-Coke. The child might also conceivably down an aspartame-flavored snack or two, nearing the FDA's projected maximum daily intake.[29] Dr. William Partridge, a professor of neuroendocrine regulation at MIT, told *Common Cause* in August 1984 that it wouldn't be surprising if a child—"confronted with aspartame-containing iced tea, chocolate milk, milk shakes, chocolate pudding pie, Jello, ice cream and numerous other products"—consumed 50 milligrams in a day.

Internally, aspartame breaks down into its constituent amino acids and methanol, which degrades into formaldehyde. The FDA announced in 1984 that "no evidence" has been found to establish that the methanol by-product reaches toxic levels, claiming that "many fruit juices contain higher levels of the natural compound."[30] But *Medical World News* had already reported in 1978 that the methanol content of aspartame is 1,000 times greater than most foods under FDA control.[31]

NutraSweet, the "good stuff" of sentimental adverts, is a truly insidious product. According to independent trials, aspartame intake is shown by animal studies to alter brain chemicals affecting behavior. Aspartame's effects on the brain led Richard Wurtman, an MIT neuroscientist, to the discovery, as recorded in *The New England Journal of Medicine* (no. 309, 1983), that the sweetener defeats its purpose as a diet aid, since high doses may instill a craving for calorie-laden carbohydrates. One of his pilot studies found that the NutraSweet-carbohydrate combination increases the "sweetener's effect on brain composition." Searle officials denigrated Wurtman's findings, but the American Cancer Society has since confirmed the agonizing irony—after tracking 80,000 women for six years—that "among women who gained weight, artificial sweetener users gained more than those who didn't use the products," as reported in *Medical Self Care* (3–87). (Since his battle with G.D. Searle, Wurtman founded Interneuron Pharmaceuticals, Inc., the producer of a sports drink that enhances athletic performance, and a weight-loss drug marketed in over 40 countries. Wurtman's share of the company, established in 1989, was worth $10 million by 1992.[32])

Even more daunting are the findings of Dr. Paul Spiers, a neurophychologist at Boston's Beth Israel Hospital, that aspartame use can depress intelligence. For this reason, he selected experimental subjects with a history of consuming it but unaware that they might be suffering ill effects. The subjects were given NutraSweet in capsules of the FDA's allowable limit. Spiers was alarmed to discover that they developed "cognitive deficits." One of the tests required recall of square patterns and alphabetical sequences, becoming increasingly more difficult. The test is challenging, but most people improve as they learn how it is done. The aspartame users, however, did not improve. "Some frankly showed a reverse pattern," Spiers reported.[33]

Aspartame has been shown to erode short-term memory. At the May, 1985 hearings on NutraSweet, Louisiana Senator Russell Long related a bizarre anecdote:

> SENATOR LONG: I have received a letter recently from a person who is well known to me and whose word is impeccable, as far as I am concerned. This person told me that she had been dieting and she had been using diet drinks with aspartame. She said she found her memory was going. She seemed to be completely losing her memory. When she would meet people whom she knew intimately, she could not recall what their name was, or even who they were. She could not recall a good bit of that which was going on about her to the extent that she was afraid she was losing her mind.... In due course, someone suggested that it might be this NutraSweet, so she stopped using it and her memory came back and her mind was restored.

Senator Howard Metzenbaum replied that he had received "a number of letters from doctors reporting similar developments.... There have been hundreds of incidences of people who have suffered loss of memory, headaches, dizziness, and other neurological symptoms which they feel are related to aspartame."[34] Senator Orrin Hatch, a hidebound arch-conservative and NutraSweet advocate, downplayed criticism of the sugar substitute. "Some people have lost their memory after drinking a variety of things," he argued. "The bottom line is this: the studies supporting aspartame's approval have been examined and reexamined. More than enough sound, valid studies exist to demonstrate aspartame's safety."

Hatch of Utah, reports the *Wall Street Journal,* has "given his strong support of the pharmaceutical industries."[35] So have the "Hatchlings." David Kessler, FDA commissioner under presidents Bush and Clinton, was once an aide to Orrin Hatch. His former campaign manager and aide, C. McClain Haddow, was sentenced to prison for conflict-of-interest charges arising from his work as a Reagan administration health official. And Thomas Parry, Hatch's former chief of staff, has carved a sumptuous life for himself as a Republican fund-raiser and lobbyist with clients in the pharmaceutical industry. All told, Parry represents 30 clients, including Eli Lilly, Warner-Lambert, and Johnson & Johnson, not to mention ranking defense firms and the Bahamas government. Parry's pharmaceutical clients have enriched Senator Hatch's campaign coffers, and in turn Hatch lavishes his attentions on them.[36]

By the time Orrin Hatch was stumping for NutraSweet in the U.S. Senate, the Center for Disease Control in Atlanta had received 600 letters complaining of NutraSweet's adverse effects. The National Soft Drink Association (NSDA) had them too: "there have been hundreds of reports from around the country suggesting a possible relationship between their consumption of NutraSweet and subsequent symptoms including headaches, aberrational behavior, slurred speech, etc." FDA Commissioner Arthur Hull Hayes, appointed by Ronald Reagan in April 1981 (moving the *New York Times* to observe that "some industry officials consider Dr. Hayes more sympathetic to their viewpoints than past holders of the office"), considered such complaints "anecdotal."

Of course, like scores of other ultra-conservatives roaming the executive branch in the 1980s, the ethics of Arthur Hull Hayes were entirely malleable—not only did he approve a product based on studies that were "scientifically lacking in design and execution," according to a report issued by *Science Times* in February 1985, but upon leaving the FDA he took the post of senior medical consultant for Burson-Marsteller, the public relations firm retained by G.D. Searle.[37]

Burson-Marsteller, a huge public relations conglomerate, swelled in the 1980s by leveraging smaller competitors—including Black, Manafort, Stone & Kelley, a lobbying firm best known for influence-peddling along the Beltway—presently outsizing even the Hill & Knowlton empire. Typical in the aspartame story are Burson-Marsteller's links to the intelligence community and right-wing operatives of the GOP. Thomas Devereaux Bell, Jr., an executive officer of the firm, is the former chairman of the Center for Naval Analyses in Alexandria, Virginia. Bell was also the executive director of Ronald Reagan's Inaugural Ball Committee (ushering in the likes of Licio Gelli of Italy's notorious P-2 lodge). Bell's career in Washington began in 1971 as a deputy director of Richard Nixon's Committee to Re-Elect the President. He went on to serve as an administrative aide to Senator William Brock and the Reagan transition team.[38]

At the FDA, Hayes used aspartame as a political statement that the Reagan administration was embarking on a grand voyage of conservative "regulatory reform," sluicing through treasonous liberal constraints on "free enterprise." Despite what one FDA scientist described as 'very serious' questions concerning pivotal brain tumor tests, Hayes eagerly approved aspartame for use in dry foods in July 1981.[39]

Three FDA scientists advised against the approval of aspartame, citing G.D. Searle's own brain tumor tests, because there was no proof that "aspartame is safe for use as a food additive under its intended conditions of use."[40]

Hayes has since declined to answer any questions about his decision, which ignored the recommendations of the FDA's own board of inquiry. He relied instead on a study conducted by Japan's Ajinomoto, Inc.—a licensee of G.D. Searle. Hayes acknowledged in his 1981 decision that he had only consulted a preliminary report of the Japanese evaluation, and only skimmed it. More serious, Hayes violated federal law by basing approval on the Japanese test, as it had not been reviewed by the FDA board.[41]

Who is Arthur Hull Hayes? He was no disinterested bureaucrat. True to the biochemical theme of the aspartame story, Dr. Hayes served in the Army Medical Corps in the 1960s. According to the *Washington Post,* Hayes was assigned to Edgewood Arsenal at Fort Detrick, Maryland, the Army's chemical warfare base of operations, "one of a number of doctors who conducted drug tests for the Army on volunteers... to determine the effect of a mind-disorienting drug called CAR 301,060." According to a declassified 1976 report prepared by the Army Inspector General, Hayes had planned a research study to develop the mind-altering CAR 301,060 as a crowd-control agent. In 1972 Hayes left Edgewood Arsenal, and a new plan for the experiments was drawn up by Edgewood physicians. The 1976 report notes that similar tests had been conducted before Hayes took charge.[42]

Also at the center of the effort to land FDA approval of NutraSweet stood Donald Rumsfeld—"Rummy" to his friends—chairman of G.D. Searle upon leaving the Ford administration in 1977. Rumsfeld, the product of a wealthy Chicago suburb, was a Princeton graduate and a Navy pilot during the Korean conflict. He entered politics as a Congressional House aide attending night classes at Georgetown University Law School, which is closely aligned with the CIA.[43]

Rumsfeld campaigned ambitiously for Richard Nixon, who drafted him to direct the Office of Equal Opportunity on May 26, 1969. He quickly established an office to spy on his employees in a holy crusade to flush out "revolutionaries" said to be granting federal funds to politically subversive organizations — a throwback to McCarthy's tantrums.[44]

Rumsfeld also figured in Nixon's notorious Power Control Group, spearheaded by Charles Colson and John Ehrlichman.[45] Gerald Ford named Rumsfeld executive chief of staff upon the resignation of Al Haig.

In 1986 he was named chairman of the Institute for Contemporary Studies, a neo-conservative "think tank" (read propaganda mill) established in 1972 by Edwin Meese and Caspar Weinberger. ICS has sponsored such opinion-shaping projects as a study of expansions in "entitlement programs" and their erosive effects on the economy, and a book on the uses of coercion by Communist regimes.[46]

Rumsfeld, at 43, became the country's youngest secretary of defense. For many years he has been a vocal proponent of chemical weapons.[47] He is chairman of the Rand Corp.[48] In 1988 he dropped a presidential bid, and was named a v.p. of Westmark Systems, led by past CIA Director Bobby Ray Inman. Rumsfeld was one of Westmark's founding directors. He shared the board with Joseph Amato, a former vice president at TRW (and a colleague of Inman's at the National Security Agency), and Dale Frey, chairman of the General Electric Investment Corp.[49]

Rumsfeld, a veteran political operative, was an adept at the vulgar art of public relations. He was recruited by G.D. Searle because he had "a Boy Scout image," according to one company official.[50] A house politician was precisely what Searle needed to compensate for the damage done by independent researchers concerned about the toxic effects of aspartame. In March 1976 an FDA task force brought into question all of the company's testing procedures between 1967 and 1975. The task force described "serious deficiencies in Searle's operations and practices which undermine the basis for reliance on Searle's integrity." The final report of the FDA task force noted faulty and fraudulent product testing, knowingly misrepresented findings, and instances of "irrelevant or unproductive animal research where experiments have been poorly conceived, carelessly executed or inaccurately analyzed."[51]

Richard Merrill, the FDA's chief counsel, petitioned Samuel K. Skinner, U.S. attorney for the northern district of Illinois, for a grand jury investigation of Searle's "willful and knowing failure" to submit required test reports, and for "concealing material facts and making false statements" in reports on aspartame submitted to the agency.[52] Yet industry analysts, interviewed by the *Wall Street Journal* six months after Rumsfeld's appointment as chairman, noted a rapid turnabout in Searle's fortunes as a result of his direction.[53]

Searle denies that Chairman Rumsfeld ever had any contact with the FDA, or the Carter and Reagan administrations, to lobby for aspartame.[54] But the *Wall Street Journal* article reported in 1977 that Rumsfeld "keenly understands the importance of a public image. So he has been mending fences with the FDA by personally asking top agency officials what Searle should do to straighten out its reputation." Westley M. Dixon, Searle's vice chairman, told the *Journal* that without Rumsfeld "we wouldn't have gotten approval for Norpace," a drug investigated by the FDA in 1975.[55]

The grand jury investigation of Searle disintegrated in January, 1977 when the FDA formally requested that Samuel Skinner, U.S. attorney and a protege of Illinois Governor James Thompson, investigate the firm for falsifying and withholding aspartame test data. A month later, Skinner met with attorneys from Searle's Chicago law firm, Sidley & Austin. Jimmy Carter ascended to the presidency a few weeks later. He announced that Skinner would not be asked to remain in office, but the outgoing Republican wasn't found wanting for employment. He informed reporters that he had already "begun preliminary discussions" with Sidley & Austin.[56]

G.D. Searle and Sidley & Austin are Siamese Twins. They are financially and politically one. Edwin Austin, a senior partner in the law firm, was appointed to the Illinois Supreme Court in 1969. The Searle family drew upon his services extensively, and he taught Sunday school in Wilmette, a Chicago suburb, as did Dr. Claude Howard Searle, whose father co-founded the pharmaceutical house.

The firm is grafted to the beating heart of the Republican party. Morris Leibman of Sidley & Austin was for many years chairman of the American Bar Association's "Standing Committee on Law and National Security," a position that won him Reagan's Medal of Freedom in 1981.[57]

John E Robson, head of Sidley & Austin's Washington office, was appointed executive vice-president of Searle & Co. in 1977, the same year Skinner was named a partner in the law firm. Robson, too, was active in Republican politics. He was the first general counsel of the Department of Transportation, and at the behest of Gerald Ford in 1975 chairman of the Civil Aeronautics Board.[58]

He moved on to Searle, and stayed with the company until it was bought outright by Monsanto in 1985. Howard Trienens, a law clerk to the late Chief Justice Vinson in the early 1950s, was a G.D. Searle director and worked for Sidley & Austin since 1949.[59] Archconservative California Governor George Deukmejian joined Sidley & Austin's Los Angeles branch upon leaving office in 1991, and is reportedly making a "very comfortable" living. He has a keen "sense" for bringing in corporate clients, a partner in the firm told the *Los Angeles Times,* many of them past contributors to his campaign fund. Deukmejian's business connections have given him a reputation as a Sidley & Austin "rainmaker," but the L.A. city council has questioned his ethics in promoting a contract with Sumitomo Corp. on a metropolitan railway project.[60]

Searle aside, Sidley & Austin has served some of the most notorious special interests in the country. The firm lobbied overtime, for instance, on behalf of Charles Keating's Lincoln Savings & Loan, and provided counsel on tax issues and dealing with federal authorities. The firm assisted Keating when Lincoln was foundering, and curried political favor to keep the S&L operating despite massive debts. As a result, the firm was forced to settle with Lincoln depositors in 1991, agreeing to cover an excess of $40 million in claims.[61]

Sidley & Austin also represented the AMA when a group of drugstore chains sued seven drug makers—including Searle—for price-fixing and antitrust violations. The lawsuit, filed in October 1993, amounts to billions of dollars in compensation.[62]

Skinner recused himself from the Searle prosecution four months before leaving office—in a memo to subordinates asking that the matter be kept "confidential to avoid any undue embarrassment"—a stall that nearly allowed the statute of limitations to expire. William Conlon, a senior U.S. attorney, inherited the case. He eased off citing case load pressures and gave a deaf ear to complaints of delays from the Justice Department, which urged that a grand jury be convened to prosecute Searle for falsifying NutraSweet test data. In January, 1979 Conlon too joined Sidley & Austin.[63]

The 33-page letter from Merrill to Skinner charged Searle with criminal fraud in its animal rest results. In 1984 Common Cause asked Dan Reidy of the U.S. attorney's office how the investigation had stalled. Reidy replied that because it was a grand jury investigation, he was "bound by law to secrecy." A Searle spokesman exploited the demise of the grand jury to claim there was "no validity to the charges," that the company had been "exonerated." Philip Brodsky, an investigator for the FDA, expressed surprise that Searle hadn't been indicted. "I thought surely they would prosecute them," he said.[64]

Eleven years later, Senator Metzenbaum issued a press release charging Skinner with stalling the criminal investigation as he prepared to leave office. Metzenbaum and his staff demanded an FBI investigation of Skinner's mishandling of the case. In December, 1988 the conflict-of-interest bombshell blew up in the face of newly-elected George Bush, who was about to appoint Skinner to the position of transportation secretary.[65]

Like most of the Machiavellians in the NutraSwseet story, Samuel Knox Skinner kept company with hard-right Republicans. He entered Republican Party politics as a campaign volunteer for Barry Goldwater.[66]

In 1975 he was appointed by President Ford to the office of federal prosecutor in Chicago. Sidley & Austin promoted him to senior partner after only one year with the firm. Skinner was the director of George Bush's presidential campaign in Illinois. On occasion he was berated for his involvement with the state's Republican apparatus: in 1987, for instance, the *Chicago Sun-Times* linked him with a circle of lawyers close to Governor Thompson who were awarded lucrative assignments handling the financial affairs of financially-crippled insurance companies. Skinner was a leading light of the Illinois Fraud Prevention Commission—he targeted welfare cheats (as opposed to white-collar criminals in the drug industry) —and President Reagan's Commission on Organized Crime. In December 1991 he left Transportation to take the position of President Bush's chief of staff.[67]

"A Shocking Story"

Had Skinner pressed on with the investigation, aspartame's manufacturer would have been forced to explain a long history of fabricated laboratory tests and slippery dealings with federal regulators, not to mention the public. Dr. Alexander Schmidt, a former FDA commissioner, said of the original Aspartame Task Force investigation: "What was discovered was reprehensible... incredibly sloppy science." A 1980 public board of inquiry opined that the company's testing procedures were "bizarre."[68]

Searle's decision to market aspartame culminated with the falsification of test results to obtain FDA approval. In November 1969, officials of the firm hired Dr. Harry Waisman, a researcher for the University of Wisconsin, to test for brain damage in Rhesus monkeys. Seven monkeys were fed aspartame for periods up to one year. In the end, though, the evaluation flopped because the technicians failed to perform the intelligence tests and autopsies required to determine brain damage. When questioned about the false data by the FDA, Searle officials claimed to have had no direct control over the study. But the protocol for the study was written by a Searle pathologist *after* it had begun. And according to Dr. Gross, "frequent high-level communications took place between Searle executives and Dr. Waisman prior to and during the study."[69]

To make matters worse, Dr. Waisman died in March, 1971 in midstudy. Searle submitted the toxicity test to the FDA on October 12, 1972. It bore Dr. Waisman's name as coauthor. Richard Merrill noted: "Dr. Waisman was the expert in the field and his name would carry great weight," but complained to Skinner that Searle took "great literary license" in drafting the report, "which covers up the admitted inadequacy of the design, control and documentation of this study."[70]

Searle submitted some 150 test reports, yet Dr. Martha Freeman of the

FDA Bureau of Drugs noted in a 1973 memo, "the information provided is inadequate to permit an evaluation of the potential toxicity of aspartame."[71] The FDA task force set up by Dr. Schmidt in 1975 reviewed 25 studies on seven products manufactured by G.D. Searle, a total of 500 pages and 15,000 exhibits.[72] Searle was held to be the author of "reports that the FDA believes contain false information" and "concealed facts resulting from having drafted Dr. Waisman's 'pilot' monkey study so that it would appear to be a valid, thorough scientific study," and not a forgery.

In 1975 Searle submitted a battery of cancer test results entitled "The Willigan Report," which contained a statistical table that excluded four malignant mammary tumors detected by Dr. Willigan and incorporated in his data. The malignancies were made to appear benign. Searle dismissed the misrepresentation as a computer "programming error" undetected by supervising statisticians. Dr. Gross interviewed all concerned with the tests. He concluded in a statement to Metzenbaum's committee in August 1985 that "to accept the Searle explanation is to believe that the unfavorable mammary malignancy data were innocently omitted from the summary table four separate times by three different individuals."[73] The Waisman and Willigan Reports were prepared by Searle Labs, as were 88% of the safety evaluations conducted by 1981.[74]

They are typical of the shoddy documentation upon which FDA Commissioner Hayes based his decision that aspartame would not constitute a public health risk. Although two members of the 1975 task force considered the tests to be criminal frauds, Hayes and Searle declared the results valid. In an appeal to Hayes's decision, James Turner said: "the entire argument that since the studies are no longer considered fraudulent by FDA they are therefore scientifically valid is an example of a rhetorical shell game that, if successful, can only bring discredit and ridicule on the FDA."[75]

Dr. Gross, the chief scientist on the FDA task force, told the CBS *Nightly News* staff in January 1984 that Searle made "deliberate decisions" to cloak the toxic effects of aspartame. "They took great pains to camouflage the shortcomings of the study," Gross said, "as I say, filter and just present to the FDA what they wished the FDA to know. And they did other terrible things. For instance, animals would develop tumors while they were under study—well, G.D. Searle would remove these tumors from the animals," surgically masking the cancerous effects of aspartame.[76]

Yet one 1986 *New England Journal of Medicine* article claimed that non-compulsive aspartame intake has "no sinister effects." Dr. Woodrow Monte told CBS, "every time a truly impartial team of scientists have looked at NutraSweet, it has been turned down." Dr. Monte, director of the nutrition laboratory at Arizona State University, held that these studies "show *extreme* dangers over the long term."[77]

Dr. Monte was rewarded for his comments by a fusillade from the press. On February 23 Dan Dorfman, a business news reporter for WCBS in New York, broke a story that several CBS employees had invested in put options on NutraSweet that pay off if the stock price drops.[78] Dr. Monte and his attorney had purchased the options as well. It emerged that the CBS staffers had purchased them on the advice of stock market newsletters printed prior to the nightly news report. The investments were not illegal, nor did they reap a profit. Searle's stock was not affected by the publicity, and the investors took a loss. Nevertheless, the *Wall Street Journal* ran a front-page story condemning the "inside trading." Reed Irvine's Accuracy in Media picked up the cudgel against Dr. Monte and the CBS employees as if they'd committed a shocking Wall Street swindle.[79] Accuracy in Media, formed in 1969, is an intelligence operation abetted by the CIA. The rabidly right-wing organization was cofounded by Bernard Yoh, a counter-insurgency adviser under the notorious Edward Lansdale in Vietnam, and a fount of CIA funds to military intelligence units in the Delta region. Board member Elbridge Durbrow was once a foreign service "diplomat," and advised commanders of Maxwell Air Force Base in Alabama. Another AIM board member, Frank Trager, has conducted research for the Pentagon and CIA, and churns out pamphlets on international business and intelligence operations. Major financial contributors to AIM have included the late Richard Nixon, "Bebe" Rebozo, Edward Scripps, the wretched Dr. Edward Teller and former Treasury Secretary William E. Simon.[80]

Accuracy in Media is a strident advocate of the chemical industry, which provides it with generous funding. The media "watchdog" has long waged a campaign on behalf of dioxin, denouncing the "Agent Orange scare" as the creation of delirious, anti-business liberals. Among the leading manufacturers of Agent Orange for the Vietnam war effort was Monsanto, preparing—at the very moment AIM took aim at detractors of NutraSweet—to buy G.D. Searle.

The Good Stuff

Dr. Monte cautioned in 1987 that he didn't want to sound like a "conspiracy theory" hound, but the aspartame chronology clarifies its commercial emergence. The FDA board of inquiry advised against the sweetener on September 30, 1980. On January 21, 1981—the day after Reagan's inauguration—Searle submitted "ten new studies." Dr. Monte was skeptical. "It is impossible that they could have conducted those studies in four months," he said. "Obviously they'd previously done those studies but hadn't officially submitted them, although much of the information in those studies was informally presented to the board of inquiry." With the "new tests" in hand, Hayes dissembled as though critical, overriding evidence had proven the safety of aspartame.[81]

James Turner, representing the Community Nutrition Institute in Washington, D.C., said that Arthur Hull Hayes, to arrive at his decision that aspartame is safe, firewalked a path "through a mass of scientific mismanagement, improper procedures, wrong conclusions and general scientific inexactness." Two FDA officials declared in 1985 that Hayes was determined to clear all obstacles to NutraSweet approval. One FDA bureaucrat reported that "people at the top" were closed to questions concerning the quality of the tests submitted by Searle.[82]

In July, 1984 a broad investigation of NutraSweet's adverse effects was conducted by the FDA and the Centers for Disease Control. Federal health officials said at the outset that they believed no harm would emerge from the data to indict aspartame. Robert McQuate, Ph.D., science director of the National Soft Drink Association, predicted with mystical confidence that the study would "provide further evidence that aspartame is a safe ingredient."[83]

Dr. McQuate didn't fret the goring of his biochemical ox. In November the CDC announced that no "serious, widespread" side-effects had been found.[84] It was "unlikely," said CDC officials, that "complainers" could establish a link between NutraSweet and their maladies—the very same bromide once tossed to victims of radiation experiments. Reported side-effects of aspartame fell into two distinct categories: central nervous system (65%) and gastrointestinal disorders (24%).[85] Yet the CDC claimed erroneously that no consistent reaction pattern had been found.[86] Robert Shapiro, then president of NutraSweet, used the occasion to enthuse that the survey "clearly established the safety" of the sugar substitute.[87]

Nevertheless, the CDC recommended a new set of studies because aspartame users continued to complain of ill effects. Based on the ersatz assurances of the CDC report, PepsiCo announced that it would drop saccharin and begin sweetening its diet drinks entirely with aspartame.

The decision would have been approved by Wayne Calloway, then CEO of PepsiCo and a director of the multinationals Citicorp, General Electric and Exxon. In 1983 soda bottlers, organized around Pepsi, had petitioned the FDA for a delay in approval of NutraSweet for soft drinks until further evaluation verified its safety—interpreted by market analysts as a ploy to drive down the price of the sweetener. They soon abandoned the effort to block approval (and all health concerns they might have had). "We believe saccharin is safe," Pepsi USA President Roger Enrico lied, but "we wanted the taste improvement."

PepsiCo, already drawing on a tenth of Searle's 7.5-million pound annual production of aspartame, signed an agreement with G.D. Searle to boost purchases a whopping 500 percent.[88] (Like other corporate pushers of aspartame, Pepsi has long maintained ties to the intelligence community. One product of the relationship was a Pepsi plant in Vientiane, Laos with a laboratory outfitted for heroin production. Alfred McCoy, in *The*

Politics of Heroin in Southeast Asia, documents the efforts of Richard Nixon to promote the plant's construction in 1965, and the CIA's continuing subsidization of the plant. McCoy complained to Pepsi officials that the facilities were but a cover for the importation and refinement of morphine, but it continued to operate unhindered.)

Yet another report was filed by Reagan's General Accounting Office in July 1987, this one on the FDA's handling of NutraSweet. The GAO concluded that the agency had observed proper procedures and conducted valid studies. But the report noted that the FDA had followed guidelines for food—not drug—testing, despite the recommendation of the agency's own biologists favoring drug tests, which are considerably more stringent. This recommendation was overruled by FDA officials.[89]

Another blemish in the study was bared by Dr. Louis Elsas, director of medical genetics at Emory University in Atlanta. "They never asked the right questions about what it does to brain function in humans," he told the *Washington Post.* Half of the scientists polled expressed reservations about the safety of NutraSweet. One-fifth reported "major concerns." Monsanto quibbled in a press release that these critics had themselves never conducted aspartame safety research. A score of independent scientists have. They found side effects.

Senator Metzenbaum berated Searle's flawed and fabricated tests at the August 1, 1985 Senate hearings. "The FDA," he said, "is content to have the manufacturer of aspartame, G.D. Searle, conduct these studies. How absurd."

He also faulted the AMA: "*The Journal of the American Medical Association* recently published a report on aspartame which, with some significant disclaimers, stated it was safe for most people. I wish that this report could ease my concerns. It does not. It merely restates the FDA position which relies solely on the tests conducted by G.D. Searle. As I have indicated these tests are under a cloud. In addition, the concerns raised recently by the scientists... were not even included in the report." In defense of the tests, executives of G.D. Searle argued that the sweetener has been approved by foreign regulatory agencies and the World Health Organization. But H.J. Roberts, an internal medicine specialist in West Palm Beach, Florida, reviewed the foreign studies and found that "the vast majority of these agencies accepted company-sponsored research without ever having done independent confirmatory studies."[90]

Deficiencies in testing were aggravated by a lack of laboratory training at Searle. One of the pivotal safety studies involved fetal damage, but the FDA task force found that the medical researcher in charge was "inexperienced in conducting studies of this nature and yet given full responsibility." They were appalled to discover that his sole credential was a field study of the cottontail rabbit for the Illinois Wildlife Service, yet at Searle he'd been assigned to laboratory training and supervision. When asked about his curriculum vitae in fetal research, he replied that he'd once attended a seminar on the subject, and the company had provided him with a stack of reference works.[91] (Yet G.D. Searle, in its 1981 Annual Report, billed itself as "a research-based pharmaceutical company.")

Corporate control of NutraSweet testing continues at Monsanto, torturing the ethics of academic medicine. In August, 1987 the University of Illinois, a recipient of Monsanto's largesse, issued a study exonerating aspartame of causing seizures in laboratory animals. Dave Hattan, a safety regulator for the FDA, responded that the study only confirmed the need for testing on humans. At independent labs, he insisted, aspartame provoked seizures.[92]

Industrial support tends to contaminate test data. Dr. Elsas, in a 1988 letter to the *New England Journal of Medicine,* advocated unbiased review of clinical research. "The NutraSweet Co.," he said, "may have had an interest in protocols that would find that their product had no untoward effects."[93]

Monsanto reportedly granted one NutraSweet researcher a $1.3-million honorarium.[94] The same hired gun willing to manipulate lab results will have no qualms publicly defending a tainted pharmaceutical, like the diabetic specialist who objected that a Senate hearing on aspartame, which called him as a witness, might arouse "groundless" public anxiety.[95]

Victims and health activists have attempted in the courts to put a stop to the marketing of NutraSweet, to no avail. In 1985 a coalition of consumer groups were handed a ruling by the federal Circuit Court of Appeals for the District of Columbia that the FDA had followed proper procedures in approving aspartame for soft drinks. A year later the *Washington Post* reported that the Supreme Court refused to consider the case "despite critics' arguments that the product, sold under the brand name NutraSweet, may cause brain damage."[96]

Likewise, the medical establishment has thrown up an impenetrable wall to aspartame critics. Dr. Roberts, author of a brief study, "Aspartame-Associated Confusion and Memory Loss: A Possible Human Model for Early Alzheimer's Disease," found it impossible to publish the monograph in a peer review medical journal. This was peculiar, he thought, "considering the increasing magnitude of Alzheimer's disease, and the relevance of my observations to newer biochemical findings and avenues of research." He can "personally vouch for the enormous difficulty in getting published articles concerning reactions to aspartame products," a trend in censorship with "ominous overtones." The options, Dr. Roberts says, are "generally limited to 'burying' the findings in a small-circulation journal (such as the bulletin of a county medical society), reporting the results as a letter to the editor, or (unfortunately, most often) discarding the project."[97]

Silence surrounds the most odious conspiracies.

Footnotes

1. "Sweet Talk," Science and the Citizen column, *Scientific American,* July, 1987, p. 15.
2. "Adverse Effects of Aspartame—January '86 through December '90," Current Bibliography series, National Library of Medicine pamphlet, National Institutes of Health, U.S. Department of Health and Human Services, 1991.
3. "Pepsi Switches Sweeteners—Aspartame Winning Diet Cola Market," *Washington Post,* November 2, 1984, p. A-1.
4. Mae Brussell, World Watchers #842, KAZU-FM, Monterey, Calif., January 25, 1988.
5. *Moody's Industrial Manual,* 1975, p. 2606.
6. *G.D. Searle's 1981 Annual Report.* Also, Arnold Foster and Benjamin R. Epstein, *Cross-Currents,* Doubleday & Co. (New York: 1956), p. 153.
7. Nancy Lisagor and Frank Lipsius, *A Law Unto Itself: The Untold Story of the Law Firm of Sullivan & Cromwell,* William Morrow (New York: 1988), pp. 137-38, 163.
8. John Marks, *The Search for the Manchurian Candidate: The CIA and Mind Control,* Times Books (New York: 1979), pp. 58, 67 & 212. Marks writes that incapacitating "large numbers of people fell to the Army Chemical Corps, which also tested LSD and even stronger hallucinogens. The CIA concentrated on individuals."
9. John Peer Nugent, *White Night: The Untold Story of What Happened Before—and Beyond—Jonestown,* Rawson, Wade (New York: 1979), pp. 143 & 177.
10. Michael Meiers, *Was Jonestown a CIA Medical Experiment: A Review of the Evidence,* Mellen House (Lampeter, UK: 1988), p. 42.
11. Ibid., p. 43.
12. Ibid., pp. 42-43. For a sanitized account of Dr. Layton's career, see Min S. Yee and Thomas N. Layton, *In My Father's House: The Story of the Layton Family and the Reverend Jim Jones,* Holt, Rinehart and Winston (New York, 1981).
13. National Council of the National Front of Democratic Germany and the Committee of Anti-Fascist Resistance Fighters of the German Democratic Republic, *The Brown Book: War and Nazi Criminals in West Germany,* Verlag Zeit im Bild, 1965, pp. 33-34.
14. Dan J. Forrestal, *Faith, Hope & $5,000: The Story of Monsanto,* Simon and Schuster (New York: 1977), p. 159.
15. *Brown Book,* p. 34.
16. Tom Bower, *The Paperclip Conspiracy: The Hunt for the Nazi Scientists,* Little, Brown & Co. (Boston: 1987), pp. 93 & 95.
17. Howard W. Ambruster, *Treason's Peace: German Dyes and American Dupes,* Beechhurst Press (New York: 1947), p. 144.
18. Nigel West, *MI6: British Secret Intelligence Service Operations, 1909-1945,* Random House (New York: 1983), p. 92.
19. Jaques Attali, *A Man of Influence: The Extraordinary Career of S.G.Warburg,* Adler & Adler (Bethesda, Maryland: 1987), p. 167.
20. Forrestal, p. 121.
21. Anthony Cave Brown, *The Last Hero, Wild Bill Donovan,* Vintage (New York: 1982), pp. 210-211. Also, Ernst Hanfstangl, *Unheard Witness,* J.R. Lippincott (New York: 1957).

22. "Search for the Tiger's Treasure," *Las Vegas Sun,* December 26, 1993, p.1.

23. *Moody's Industrial Manual,* 1968, p. 4080.

24. "Radiation and the Guinea Pigs," *Guardian,* March 3, 1994, p. 3. Also see, "Nuclear Scientists Irradiated People in Secret Research," *New York Times,* December 17, 1993, p. A-1.

25. Christopher Simpson, *Blowback: America's Recruitment of Nazis and its Effect on the Cold War,* Wiedenfeld & Nicholson (New York: 1988), pp. 26, 152-53. Col. Pash, a former high school gym teacher from Hollywood, was an officer of the Office of Policy Coordination under Frank Wisner. His unit, Simpson writes, "known as PB/7, was given a written charter that read in part that 'PB/7 will be responsible for assassinations, kidnapping, and such other functions as from time to time may be given it... by higher authority.'" Pash was a member of the Russian Orthodox Church, a veteran of the Russian Civil War. Monsanto's Clinton Engineering Works in Oak Ridge became the Manhattan Project's headquarters in 1943, and was "manned almost entirely by experienced officers and agents of the CIC." See Ian Sayer and Douglas Botting, *America's Secret Army: The Untold Story of the Counter Intelligence Corps,* Franklin Watts (New York: 1989), pp. 71ff. & 346.

26. Robin Thomas Naylor, *Hot Money and the Politics of Debt,* Simon & Schuster (New York: 1987), p. 289.

27. "Statement from Adrian Gross, Former FDA Investigator and Scientist," *Congressional Record,* August 1, 1985, p. S10835.

28. Florence Graves, "How Safe is Your Diet Soft Drink?" *Common Cause,* July/August, 1984.

29. Ibid.

30. "FDA Finding on Aspartame," *New York Times,* January 14, 1984, p. 28.

31. Article in *Medical World News,* 1978, cited in I.N. Love, "NutraSweet Isn't that Sweet," *Gentle Strength Times,* October 1987, p. 3.

32. "Dick Wurtman's Ideas Aren't So Crazy After All," *Business Week,* December 14, 1992, p. 60.

33. "A Sour View of Aspartame," *San Francisco Chronicle,* August 25, 1987.

34. "Amendment No. 60" (debate), *Congressional Record,* May 7, 1985, p. S5516.

35. "Lobbyist's Cozy Ties with Ex-Boss Sen. Hatch Include Client Referrals, Political Fund-Raising," *Wall Street Journal,* February 18, 1993. Eli Lilly contributed $17,500 to Hatch's campaign chest between 1985 and 1988. Sen. Hatch filed a friend-of-the-court brief on behalf of Eli Lilly in a 1989 patent case. Other pharmaceutical houses enjoy his political favors. Lobbyist Thomas Parry remains a key adviser to Sen. Hatch: "Nobody gets better care than his former chief of staff," reported the *Journal.*

36. Ibid.

37. Jane E. Brody, "Sweetener Worries Some Scientists, "*Science Times,* February 5, 1985.

38. *Who's Who in Industry and Finance,* 97th ed., MacMillan (Wilmette, Il.: 1991), p. 583.

39. "Food and Drug Administration Food Additive Approval Process Followed for Aspartame," *GAO Report B-223552,* June 18, 1987.

40. "GAO Investigating NutraSweet Approval," UPI, reprinted in the *Congressional Record,* August 1, 1985, p. S10823.

41. Graves.

42. "Head of FDA Tested Drugs on Volunteers," *Washington Post,* June 26, 1983, p. A-4.

43. Austin H. Kiplinger, *Washington Now,* Harper & Row (New York: 1975), pp. 36-37.

44. Daniel Guttman and Barry Willner, *The Shadow Government: The Government's Multi-Billion-Dollar Giveaway of its Decision-Making Powers to Private Management Consultants, "Experts," and Think Tanks,* Pantheon, (New York: 1976), pp. 63-90.

45. Bruce Oudes, ed., *From: The President—Richard Nixon's Secret Files,* Harper & Row (New York: 1989), p. 173.

46. James A. Smith, *The Idea Brokers: Think Tanks and the Rise of the New Policy Elite,* Free Press (New York: 1991), p. 282.

47. Sterling Seagrave, *Yellow Rain: A Journey through the Terror of Chemical Warfare,* M. Evans and Co. (New York: 1981), p, 258: "After a meeting with President Nixon, Representative Gerald Ford attacks politicians who criticize the Pentagon CBW efforts, saying the critics seem to favor 'unilateral disarmament.'"

48. Christopher Palmeri, "Act Three," *Forbes,* October 26, 1992, p. 88.

49. "Westmark Systems Expands Board, Hires 3 New Vice Presidents," *Wall Street Journal,* February 11, 1988, p. 33.

50. Graves.

51. Graves.

52. "Hon. Samuel K. Skinner," *Congressional Record,* Congressional Printing Office, Washington, D.C., August 1, 1985, pp. S10827 & S10835.

53. Graves.

54. *Congressional Record,* August 1, 1985, p. S10823.

55. Graves.

56. "Critics Cause Bush Cabinet Search to Stumble," *Los Angeles Times,* December 22, 1988.

57. Herman Kogan, *Traditions and Challenges: The Story of Sidley & Austin,* R.R. Donnelley & Sons (Chicago: 1983), p. 266.

58. *Who's Who in America,* 48th ed., 1994.

59. Ibid.

60. "Deukmejian Thrives in Private Life, Law Work," *Los Angeles Times,* January 3, 1992, p. A-1.

61. "Chicago Law Firm Agrees to Pay Up to $34 Million in Lincoln S&L Case," *Los Angeles Times,* May 21, 1991, p. D-5; and "Sidley & Austin, RTC Said to Reach Pact," *Wall Street Journal,* October 31, 1991, p. B-4. The basis of the suit was a memo written on May 10, 1988 by Margery Waxman, a partner in Sidley & Austin's Washington office, to Charles Keating. In it, she said "pressure" had been applied to M. Danny Wall, then chairman of the Home Loan Bank Board, "to work toward meeting your demands and he has so instructed his staff."

62. "Suit Accuses 7 Drug Makers of Price-Fixing," *Los Angeles Times,* October 15, 1993, p. D-1. Other pharmaceutical houses accused of conspiring to fix prescription drug prices included Smith-Kline Beecham, Ciba-Geigy Corp., American Home Products, Schering-Plough and Glaxo.

63. Ida Honorof, "FDA Coverup of Hazards of NutraSweet," *Report to Consumers,* Vol. XVIII, No. 401, December, 1987. Also, "Two Ex-U.S. Prosecutors' Roles in Case

Against Searle are Questioned in Probe," *Wall Street Journal,* February 7, 1986, p. 4. Ironically enough, William Conlon won an appointment to the Illinois State Board of Ethics in 1982 (Kogan, p. 359).

64. Graves.
65. *Los Angeles Times,* December 12, 1988.
66. "Sam Skinner: A Pragmatist in a Storm," *Wall Street Journal,* December 6, 1991.
67. "Samuel Knox Skinner," *New York Times,* December 23, 1988.
68. Graves.
69. "Statement from Adrian Gross, Former FDA Investigator and Scientist," *Congressional Record,* August 1, 1985, p. S10835.
70. *Congressional Record,* August 1, 1985, p. S10831, and "Statements from Adrian Gross," p. S10838.
71. "FDA Handling of Research on NutraSweet is Defended," *New York Times,* July 18, 1987, p. 50.
72. H.J. Roberts, M.D., *Aspartame (NutraSweet): Is it Safe?,* Charles Press (Philadelphia: 1990), p. 10.
73. *Congressional Record,* August 1, 1985, p. S10828.
74. Ibid., p. S10834.
75. Graves.
76. "Sweet Suspicions," three-part *CBS Nightly News* series, January 1984. Transcript printed in the *Congressional Record,* August 1, 1985, p. S10826.
77. Ibid.
78. Raymond Bonner, "Searle Stock Query Held 'Smokescreen,'" *New York Times,* February 29, 1984, p. D-5.
79. William Safire, "Sweet and Sour," *New York Times,* June 1, 1984, p. A-31.
80. Louis Wolfe, "Accuracy in Media Rewrites the News and History," *Covert Action Information Bulletin,* Number 21 (Spring 1984), pp. 24-37.
81. I.N. Love, "NutraSweet Isn't that Sweet," in *Gentle Strength Times,* October 1987, p. 3.
82. Graves.
83. "Complaints on Aspartame Lead to Nationwide Investigation," *Los Angeles Times,* July 5, 1984, p. H-1.
84. "Federal Agency Sees Little Risk in Sweetener," *New York Times,* November 2, 1984, p. A-22.
85. *Los Angeles Times,* July 5, 1984.
86. *New York Times,* November 2, 1984.
87. "U.S. Study of Aspartame Finds no Serious Effects," *Washington Post,* November 2, 1984, p. A-18.
88. "Pepsi Switches Sweeteners," *Washington Post,* November 2, 1984, p. A-1.
89. "Most Scientists in Poll Doubt NutraSweet's Safety," *Washington Post,* August 17, 1987, p. A-23.
90. Roberts, p. 238.
91. *Congressional Report,* May 7, 1987, p. S5500.
92. "New Findings Back Use of Sweetener," *New York Times,* August 1987, p. 30. The *Times* showed a marked prediliction to slant news reports in favor of the

sweetener, to the point of distorting information.

93. "Researchers Differ Over Long-Range Effects of Sweetener," *Los Angeles Times,* November 3, 1988, p. H-1.

94. Roberts, p. 244.

95. Roberts, p. 248.

96. "High Court Rejects Sweetener Review," *Washington Post,* April 23, 1986, p. C-7.

97. Roberts, p. 246-47.

Chapter Fourteen

The Holocaust Gallery

How the CIA Stole Jewish Art Treasures Looted by the Nazis

By all accounts James Kronthal had the makings of a ranking CIA official. He had attended New York's prestigious Lincoln School with Nelson Rockefeller. At Yale, he rejected the advice of his father that he major in business and studied art history instead. He joined the rowing crew and Phi Beta Kappa. Upon earning his degree in 1934, he found employment at the prestigious Frankfurt, Germany banking house of Speyer & Co. (the Kronthal's were blood relations of the Speyer family). Shortly thereafter, he established a network of middlemen to market artwork confiscated by the Nazis from Jewish collections. Kronthal was an eager Quisling, an advisor to Himmler and Goebbels. In fact, their intervention once pried him loose from the Gestapo after he was snared on charges of pedophilia.

His favors to the Nazi Party enriched him, but he was increasingly troubled by Nazi brutality and returned to the States to pursue a graduate degree at Harvard. There he befriended James Jesus Angleton, then a Law School freshman and a decade later the CIA's highest ranking Soviet specialist. After the raid on Pearl Harbor, Kronthal and Angleton offered themselves to the Office of Strategic Services (OSS). Kronthal was assigned to Switzerland's Berne Station under Allen Dulles, whose family, like the Speyers, had conducted business with the Nazis as Hitler ascended to power.

After the war Kronthal was assigned to the recovery of art plundered by the Nazis. Millions of paintings and antiques had disappeared. Some of these had made their way to Switzerland and flooded the galleries, sold to finance the rearmament of Germany in the 1930s—with Kronthal's assistance—and the postwar ambitions of leading Nazis. By 1942 galleries of Zurich, Madrid, Laussanne, New York and elsewhere were glutted with plundered artwork, sold at a fraction of their true worth. .

Sol Chaneles, former chairman of the Department of Criminal Justice at Rutgers University, notes that "countless objects can probably be found today in the homes of friends and relatives of Nazi and Nazi authorized art dealers where they were stored 'temporarily.' But the Nazis kept precise, detailed records of their pillage. Incomplete though they are, the records that survive list some 12 million individual items." A postwar inventory by the U.S. Army's Monuments, Fine Arts and Archives Division (MFA&A) counted 16 million pieces, but to date a full inventory has not been attempted.

Following the Anschluss—Germany's annexation of Austria on March 13, 1938—Hitler oversaw the wholesale confiscation of Jewish property, including the great art collections of barons Louis and Alphonse de Rothschild, the priceless paintings and rare volumes of the library belonging to Baron Butmann, and many more. Hitler's invasion of Czechoslovakia in May, 1939 involved the seizure not only of Jewish-owned art, but also the library of Prague University, the holdings of the Czech National Museum, the palaces of the Schwartzenbergs and Collerdos, and the Lobkowicz collections, which included Flemish painter Brueghel's masterpiece, *Hay Harvest.* The best of this loot was shipped to Germany, as were the Habsburg crown regalia from Vienna and the Bohemian crown jewels from Prague.

Raping nations of their cultural heritage not only demoralized conquered states—the reflected glory of pillaged landmarks of civilization lent the Third Reich an aura of grandeur. Having promised the Austrian city of Linz, where he'd attended school, a museum, Hitler demonstrated in the Polish campaign of 1939 how highly the acquisition of precious art rated in his strategic military operations. SS units accompanying the invading Nazi troops, provided with detailed information about the location of dozens of works of art, captured the famous altar by Veit Stoss in Cracow, relocated by the Nazis to Berlin, and the legendary Czartoryski collections of coins and relics, Limoges enamels, and engravings by 15th-century artist Albrecht Durer.

An unknown number of invaluable European artifacts have been stored in American bank and Treasury Department vaults since the war, classified a "national security" secret by the CIA. Only 200,000 of the items on the MFA&A inventory have been returned as restitution, primarily to wealthy German families and countries crushed by the Nazis. The CIA kept its share. A rare exception were the Hungarian crown jewels, found in a German salt mine as WW II wound down, returned in 1978 by order of President Jimmy Carter.

Kronthal succeeded Allen Dulles as head of the Berne station in 1947 under the newly formed CIA, an extremely powerful position that put him in charge of most covert operations in Western Europe. (In the immediate postwar period, most of the CIA's recruits were staunch Nazis, among them Otto Skorzeny, Martin Bormann, Joseph Mengele and Klaus Barbie. In the moral vacuum of cold war realpolitik, they were employed in the importation of drugs, the instigation of foreign coups, the arming of terrorists and death squad training.) Kronthal was given nearly complete authority in the handling of the plundered cultural wealth of Europe.

Unfortunately, Kronthal's pedophilic urgings rendered him vulnerable to blackmail by the Soviet NKVD intelligence service under Lavrenti Beria, and comprehensive information on CIA activities in Europe soon flowed from Berne to Moscow Center. In 1952 Kronthal returned to Washington to assist in the reorganization of the Agency. A year later he met secretly with his former Berne handler, Allen Dulles, the newly appointed Director of Central Intelligence. The subject of discussion is not known. The next day, Kronthal's housekeeper entered his bedroom to find him dead, an apparent suicide.

"The death was quickly hushed up," according to late CIA operative William Corson. The Washington police force was called in "to cover up what the CIA wanted hidden.... A chemical analysis failed to determine the cause of death or the contents of the vial found next to Kronthal's body."

Among the secrets that Kronthal took with him were details of the network established by the nascent CIA for recovering art stolen from the Jews of Europe.

Another was the way the U.S. freely helped itself to the confiscated art. As early as 1941, the Treasury Department had laid claim to German assets. A cover story was circulated that the booty was intended as a buffer against inflation in postwar Europe and South America. Secretly, according to Christopher Simpson, author of *Blowback,* the early CIA (signed into existence by Truman in 1947) drew from Treasury's vaults of spoils to finance covert operations abroad.

The first transfer of "black currency" from the "Exchange Stabilization Fund" to the CIA was laundered through a miz-maze of bank accounts to influence Italian politics in 1947. The nexus in the handling of the loot was Cardinal Francis Spellman (the "Back Door to the Vatican" and a notorious pedophile), who claimed that the $10 million windfall was a donation to the Church's holy war on Communism. The profits of Jewish genocide thus ended up, Simpson wrote, with "clerics and other leaders who were themselves closely tied to Fascist rule."

In 1963 a newspaper in Graz, Italy caught wind of the transfers and reported that "valuables of gruesome origin, and worth millions, have vanished without a trace. Other millions of mysterious origin showed up in the possession of former leaders of the Nazi Party and the SS. Even more bloodstained money is now said to have been spent on an obscure rescue mission of which a high Vatican official was reputed to be the leader."

A rare instance of restitution occurred early in the war by spies of the

Special Liaison Unit, an Anglo-American group established in Bermuda. W.S. Zuill, editor of Bermuda's *Royal Gazette,* wrote in 1973 that the intelligence operation had been set up to intercept traffic between the U.S. and Europe. "Large numbers of experts and linguists moved into the Princess and Bermudiana hotels and their work exposed German spies already 'in place' in the United States," he reported. "Art treasures stolen by the Nazis in France and shipped through neutral ports to be sold in New York for Hitler's war machine were confiscated. In one case, the American Export Lines ship *Excalibur* carried valuable paintings in a sealed strong room. When the captain refused to open it, the British burned it like safecrackers, took the paintings and stored them in the Bank of Bermuda vaults until they could be returned to the Paris owner, who got all 270 of these Impressionist works back intact, to his own considerable astonishment."

Another caché of stolen paintings, rivaling any collection in the world, was discovered on April 7, 1945 by a contingent of officers of the Army's 90th Division, stored by the Nazis in a vault 2,100 feet underground. The vault lay at the bottom of Kaiseroda mine, near Merkers, Germany's geographical center. A huge hoard of treasure was discovered at the bottom of the mine, including gold valued at an excess of $238,000,000. About 400 tons of paintings and sculpture were found in a tunnel chiseled in the dry subterranean salt rock. The art had been looted from 15 German museums, including works by Rembrandt, Titian, Renoir and Durer. The art was priceless, but the most interesting piece discovered in the bowels of Kaiseroda was a 3,000 year old statuette of Nefertiti, the Egyptian queen, the most valuable work of art in all of Germany. Also found were the Goethe collection of Weimar and two million books confiscated in Berlin.

The art caché was sufficiently interesting to entice General Eisenhower, then the Supreme Commander of the Allied Expeditionary Forces, to Merkers, accompanied by General Omar Bradley and General Patton. Patton counted the stars on the uniforms of his companions as the elevator plummeted through the mineshaft. A half-mile beneath the surface, the party stepped into the gloom. Eisenhower was awed by the stacks of paintings lining the tunnel walls. But Patton, not exactly a connoisseur, was bored by the whole affair. Most of the paintings, he grumped in his memoirs, "were the type normally seen in bars."

The hoard was inventoried and loaded into 32 trucks for transfer to Munich for storage. The convoy was accompanied by five infantry and two machine gun platoons, ten anti-aircraft units and air cover. Yet a rumor has persisted for many years that one of the trucks managed to slip off in the night with a full load of gold or artwork.

Francis Taylor, wartime director of New York's Metropolitan Museum of Art, argued vehemently that "the contents of the Merkers mine should be treated as booty," and liberated by the U.S. Army. "The controversy over the Merkers' treasures raged," Chaneles wrote in *Art & Antiques* in

1987, "amidst persistent rumors that both senior U.S. officers and OSS personnel were involved in theft from the Munich repository. Thousands of ounces of gold are apparently missing along with hundreds of millions of dollars in cash and untold numbers of valuable works of art. All the records pertaining to the Merkers inventory and military intelligence reports concerning theft by U.S. Army officers and OSS personnel were later classified by the CIA, and so they remain to this day."

Patton died six months after his inspection of the Merkers mine, the cause of death an embolism resulting from a traffic accident. This was the same day he had informed General Hobart Gay that he wanted the "bastards" behind the theft turned over the the Criminal Investigation Division. "I don't want anybody ever to say that sonovabitch Patton had stolen any part of it," he told Gay. The share of the plunder that disappeared under guard of Patton's Third Army was worth $5 billion in today's currency. It has never been recovered.

At a salt mine in Alt Aussee, another 100,000 paintings, many by old masters, were discovered by the Allies. Also found were a fortune in prints, drawings, sculptures and books. About 7,000 of the paintings had been chosen by Hitler for transfer to the museum he planned on opening in Linz, Austria.

In June, 1990 some of the priceless works from the Alt Aussee mine surfaced in Whitewright, Texas, near the Oklahoma border. "It was one of the world's greatest art thefts," according to Florentina Mutherich, former deputy director of Munich's Institute for Art History. Joe Meador, an art lover and Army officer of the 87th Armored Field Artillery Division in 1945, was widely considered to be the culprit. The division had been ordered to guard the art, including a medieval manuscript, *The Four Gospels,* bound in gold and silver, which was among the disappearing works and "rare beyond belief," according to London art historian Richard Camber in the *New York Times.* Meador also absconded with the gold crucifixes of ostentatiously pious ninth and tenth century German emperors, and a small silver reliquary inlaid with gems. The pelf was recovered by West Germany's Cultural Foundation of the States, which paid a "finder's fee" of $3 million to an American dealer's attorney for the pieces, with a proviso that the American's name remain anonymous.

The loot has, like a multitude of bad pennies, surfaced in some unexpected places: the famed *Boy Blowing Bubbles* by Jean Baptiste Chardin, for instance, turned up in the possession of the Metropolitan Museum of Art. In 1987 at least five paintings hanging at the Met were identified as Nazi confiscations. Other paintings at the Metropolitan snatched from the Holocaust and European occupations, as reported by the *New York Times* on November 24, 1987, included *Man with a Bulbous Nose* by Adrian Brouwer, "Young Woman Reading" by Fragonard, and Eugene Delacroix's *Lion Attacking a Snake.*

The Metropolitan bought the paintings from Wildenstein & Company in New York, a Jewish art dealer. The history of the acquisitions was cleverly obscured: the museum neglected to mention the Delacroix in its catalog of holdings, and a historical account of the Fragonard glossed over seizure by the Nazis. However, one catalog entry did mention that Chardin's *Boy Blowing Bubbles* once hung in the "Fuhrer Museum" at Linz, and a forty year old museum publication reports that the painting still bore "the labels of the Einsatzstab Rosenberg, the German looting organization."

Officials of the Metropolitan have since claimed that the Chardin was legally purchased from the heirs of Fritz Mannheimer, a Jewish banker who fled Stuttgart when Hitler assumed power and settled in Amsterdam. (The Nazis destroyed Mannheimer's Dutch bank, whereupon he perished of a heart attack. From his creditors the SS purchased the collection at a fraction of its worth, threatening to confiscate it as enemy property if they refused the offer.)

Dr. Chaneles offers another explanation: "Leading art dealers and galleries in the occupied nations collaborated with the Nazi art experts. In Paris, Wildenstein's facilities served as a depository for objects eventually transferred to Hitler, Goering and Bormann. The company prospered immensely during the war."

Jeremy Epstein, an attorney for Wildenstein & Co., countered that allegations of Nazi collaboration were "ridiculous," since the family fled Europe before the war and lost scores of paintings to the Germans. He failed to mention, however, that before the Wildensteins decamped, Roger Dequoy, an employee, was entrusted with management of the gallery.

The Germans were given preference in the acquisition of paintings stored there. Martin Bormann, "Hitler's Mephistopheles," authorized the purchases, made in Hitler's name with stolen funds. Far from bullying the art dealers and cultural authorities of Paris, Hitler was uncharacteristically solicitous to assuage the resentment of the French people. Two weeks after the occupation, Field Marshal Wilhelm Keitel issued an order to safeguard the art treasures of Paris, "especially the Jewish property," until Hitler's representatives could examine the art and cart off the pick of the lot.

Met officials should have been better informed, because it was Francis Taylor, museum director, who in 1944 founded and led the MFA&A art recovery unit under an Executive Order signed by Roosevelt. Taylor's ranking field agents were assigned to the OSS (under Kronthal) and they became privy to intelligence on Nazis dealing in looted art on the black market.

Taylor's organization soon abandoned any aim of making restitution to victims of Nazi atrocities, however, and much of the art was spirited away to American vaults. The seizure of the art by the U.S. prompted Sumner Crosby, a French scholar serving with Taylor in the OSS art recovery operation, to resign from the unit in September 1945. "He learned," writes

Robin Winks in *Cloak & Dagger,* "that the United States Government was bringing from Germany art objects for storage and display.... Crosby and many others viewed this decision as a slap in the face to the various MFA&A officers in Germany, and they also suspected it was an effort to appropriate for American art galleries the very objects d'art that had just been rescued from Nazi hands."

The collected cultural spoils of Germany had piqued the interest of American politicians and military leaders. President Truman sent a representative from the National Gallery to the Army's art repository in Weisbaden (the former headquarters of Goering's Luftwaffe) to make arrangements to ship 202 of the collection's finest paintings to Washington. The officers at Weisbaden were appalled. They sent a protest to Gen. Lucius Clay, the high commissioner of Germany's American zone, decrying Truman's order as morally untenable.

Walter Farmer, an architect from Cincinnati and the ranking American officer at the Weisbaden collection point, wrote to his wife: "This is the first time that America has stolen the cultural heritage of another country. We are no less and no better than the Germans."

Taylor's "Art Commandos" retained as a consultant Ernst "Putzi" Hanfstangl, director of a Munich's Alte Pinakothek Museum, formerly one of a group of art experts who advised Hitler on Jewish-owned galleries and private collections worth plundering. "Putzi" was an American born, transatlantic socialite and Nazi spy. He'd attended Harvard with Roosevelt, resettled in Germany, and partially financed Hitler's early political career with funds from wealthy friends on Wall Street. Hitler's first printing press was purchased by Hanfstangl with American money.

"Putzi" returned to the U.S. in the mid 30s, covering as an art dealer, and established a network of Nazi cells in travel bureaus across the country. Among them was the New York branch of the Hamburg-American steamship line, directed by George Bush's maternal grandfather, George Herbert "Bert" Walker. Hamburg-American financed scores of Nazi propaganda efforts in 1930s America. The company was seized by the American government in 1942 under the Trading with the Enemy Act. Hanfstangl, threatened with deportation, was taken under wing by then Assistant Secretary of War John J. McCloy (a postwar CIA director), and quartered at Fort Myer, headquarters of the Washington garrison, comfortably housed as an honored guest of the government.

After the war, Hanfstangl resettled in Germany to assist the CIA/MFA&A art "restitution" program as director of Alte Pinakothek. In exchange, paintings taken from the museum by the U.S. were returned. The paintings had originally been given to Hanfstangl as Nazi plunder during 1943–44.

The Fine Arts unit was disbanded in 1951. Untold thousands of paintings were turned over to German officials, many of them Nazi Party veterans accused or convicted of wartime atrocities.

All of the Fine Art unit's records were stored at the National Gallery. Unfortunately, they disappeared during the presidency of Ronald Reagan. The files remain "lost" or "classified." The MFA&A has slipped into historical obscurity.

Revelations of postwar looting of priceless artifacts have also gradually surfaced in Great Britain as secret documents are declassified, and news of them trickles into the public print. England's monthly *Art Newspaper* reported in November 1994 that Anthony Blunt, the Soviet spy and an art historian, smuggled the Hanoverian crown jewels out of Germany at the close of the war, and hid them in Windsor Castle. Blunt's mission was graced with the blessing of King George VI to prevent "seizure by the Russians or Americans." At the time, Blunt was deputy director of the Courtauld Institute. He also cataloged old masters and drawings for the Royal Collection, and penned a number of articles on art history. He succeeded Kenneth Clark as surveyor of the King's collection of fine art.

He joined MI5, Britain's counter-intelligence service, in 1940. Blunt met with Ernst August, paternal head of the Hanovers, in December 1945, and departed with the crown jewels under the pretext of safeguarding them. The transfer of the precious jewels was met with alarm by the Intelligence Office, which had been trying to dissuade the Americans from looting art treasure, and feared setting a bad example. King George therefore returned some of the artifacts to Germany. Among the pieces not returned was the 12th-century *Gospel Book of King Henry the Lion,* which had disappeared from Austria in the 1930s. The book was put on sale at Sotheby's of London. Other pieces were returned to Germany.

A spokesman for the Royal collection explained that it had been necessary to take the valuables, because "there was a lot of looting in Germany at the end of the war."

In June of 1994 scores of "liberated" paintings were auctioned at Sotheby's, including a Corot landscape, a Rembrandt etching and assorted Impressionist paintings.

The Eastern Bloc has been nearly as callous in handling seized art as the U.S. In the 1950s the Russians returned many of the paintings looted from German museums when the Reich collapsed.

In Prague, tens of thousands of art objects confiscated by the Nazis still molder in a museum housed in a former synagogue. The makeshift museum stores row upon row of silver goblets, thousands of religious artifacts and textile art, taken from the 77,300 of 92,000 Czech Jews murdered in Nazi concentration camps. The Czech parliament is considering the transfer of the museum to local Jewish authorities.

But the U.S. government has not relinquished its share of the stolen art, and any information pertaining to the hidden collection remains a Company secret.

Sources

David G. Armstrong and Jack Calhoun, *The George Bush File* (unpublished galleys: Los Angeles), 1993.

Martin Bailey, "Blunt Smuggled Crown Jewels," *The Art Newspaper* (UK), November 1994, p. 1.

Anthony Cave Brown, *The Last Hero: Wild Bill Donovan* (Vintage: New York), 1982.

Sol Chaneles, "The Great Betrayal," *Art & Antiques,* December 1987, pp. 93–103.

William R. Corson, Susan B. Trento and Joseph J. Trento, *Widows* (Crown: New York), 1979.

Ladislas Farago, *Aftermath* (Avon: New York), 1976.

Peter Green, "Israel Lays Claim to Treasures of Nazi Museum," *London Times,* April 18, 1993, p. 20.

William Francis Hare, *The Brown Network: The Activities of the Nazis in Foreign Countries* (Knight: New York), 1936.

William H. Honan, "Stolen Medieval German Artwork Surface in Small Texas Farm Town," *Los Angeles Times,* June 14, 1990.

Glenn B. Infield, *Secrets of the SS* (Military Heritage: New York), 1981.

David Jones (writer and producer), "Spoils of War," *Time Machine* segment, Arts & Entertainment Network.

Douglas C. McGill, "Met Painting Traced to Nazis," *New York Times,* November 24, 1987, p. C-19.

Ian Sayer and Douglas Botting, *Nazi Gold: The Story of the World's Greatest Robbery and its Aftermath* (Gongdon & Weed, Inc.: New York), 1984.

John Shaw, "Art Treasures Seized by the Nazis Go on Sale," *London Times,* June 23, 1994, p. 20.

Christopher Simpson, *Blowback: America's Recruitment of Nazis and its Effects on the Cold War* (Weidenfeld & Nicolson: New York), 1988.

William Stevenson, *A Man Called Intrepid: The Secret War* (Ballantine: New York), 1976.

Antony Sutton, *Wall Street and the Rise of Hitler* ('76 Press: Seal Beach, Ca.).

Charles Whiting, *Patton's Last Battle* (Stein and Day: New York), 1987.

Robin W. Winks, *Cloak & Gown: Scholars in the Secret War* (William Morrow: New York), 1987.